Issues in Police Administration

by

Harold K. Becker

Associate Professor of Criminology
California State College, Long Beach, California

The Scarecrow Press, Inc.

Metuchen, N.J.   1970

To Donna, whose love, faith, and encouragement
shine more brightly than all the stars

The use of force alone is but <u>temporary</u>. It may subdue for a moment; but it does not remove the necessity of subduing again: and a nation is not governed, which is perpetually to be conquered.

Edmund Burke (1729-1797)
Second Speech on Conciliation with
America. The Thirteen Resolutions

Preface

Law enforcement, as a topic, has interested monarchies and democracies, conservatives and civil libertarians, private citizens and bureaucrats as issues of conflict in governmental policy, political philosophy, and practical application.

The search for the proper mix of civil direction and civil liberty is vital for a government's maturation, mental health, and survival. It is the purpose of this book to identify some of the areas of conflict that exist in many police organizations and communities.

Community policing is relatively new in man's attempt to govern macro and micro social interaction. With the advent of the London police system in 1829, the growth of police systems began to adapt to the needs of society. However, the needs perceived do not necessarily correspond to the needs anticipated.

The conflict areas identified in this book are certainly a limited selection of the manifold problems which confront man as protagonist or antagonist in the quest for justice.

The selection of these conflict areas in law enforcement has developed over a period of years in dialogue with students of criminology, practitioners of criminal justice and laymen. Criminal justice is a topic about which most persons have a deep interest.

Acknowledgement must be directed to the many students, past and present, in the Department of Criminology, California State College at Long Beach, who in effect create the intellectual arena in which substance and depth are given to the elusive phrase "the administration of criminal justice."

Harold K. Becker is Associate Professor of Criminology at California State College at Long Beach. Professor Becker is the author of <u>Law Enforcement: A Selected Bibliography</u> (with

George T. Felkenes,) and New Dimensions in Criminal Justice (with George T. Felkenes and Paul M. Whisenand). He is a former member of the Los Angeles Police Department and is experienced in patrol, in planning and in research. He has served as consultant to many private and public organizations dealing with areas in the administration of criminal justice.

Table of Contents

	Preface	v
I.	Contemporary Police	11
	Area of responsibility	13
	Training	14
	Recruitment	16
	The lack of logical approach to police-community relations	16
	Police professionalization	17
II.	Police Roles	25
	Refinement of the problem	25
	The social organization of police	26
	Organization	27
	Selection and training	28
	Department policy	31
	Enforcement practices and the law	32
	Public relations	33
	Police community relations	34
	Summary	34
III.	Historical-Philosophical Development of Administration	38
	Constitutional-legal approach	38
	Structural-descriptive approach	41
	Socio-psychological approach	43
	Rationality as a philosophical question	46
	Rationality and the decision-making process	51
	Attempts to formulate a theory of rationality in decision-making	54
	Values implicit in such theories	59
	Conclusions	62

IV. Police Bureaucratization 68
    The present status of municipal police agencies 71
    A new approach to police administration 73
    Physical and Psychological Attitudes 79
    Conclusion 80

V. Police Personnel 82
    Significance of the problem 82
    Advantages 83
    Definitions of terms used 84
    History of personnel administration 85
    The career system 86
    The civil service system 86
    Criticism of the career system 87
    Criticism of the civil service system 89
    The closed personnel system as opposed to
       the open system at the city level of
       government 91
    Lateral entry 94
    Turnover of personnel 96
    Police personnel administration 98
    Criticism of the specific agency 102
    Analysis of the Los Angeles Police Department 103
    Summary and conclusions 112
    Recommendations for further inquiry 113

VI. Community Relations and Change 117
    Training 119
    Summary and Conclusion 120

VII. A Review of Corrections: Analysis and Change 125
    Method of organizational analysis 125
    Corrections and organizational analysis 130
    Analytic applications 142
    Change factors relative to the correctional arena 147
    Methods for change 149
    Summary 150

VIII. Special Police Problems 155
    Problem #1- Professionalization 155

Problem #2-Abortion   158
Problem #3-Labor-Management Disputes   162
Problem #4-Homosexuality   171
Problem #5-Pornography   174
Problem #6-Riot Control   178
Problem #7-Integration of Police and Fire
  Services   185
Problem #8-Civil Defense and Disaster Planning   191
Problem #9-Licensing   196
Problem #10-Inspection   200
Problem #11-Subversives   201
Problem #12-Organized Crime   207
Problem #13-Departmental Reserve Officers   212
Problem #14-Mental Illness   217
Problem #15-Public Relations   229
Problem #16-Minority Group Relations   237
Problem #17-Personnel   246
IX   The Future of Policing   264
Appendices
         Appendix A: Law Enforcement Code of Ethics   269
         Appendix B: Role Interaction Example   270
         Appendix C: Sample Organization Charts   275
         Appendix D: Planning and Research Description   282
         Appendix E: Community Organizations   284
         Appendix F: Los Angeles Police Department
           Community Relations Program   304
         Index   325

I. Contemporary Police

Police agencies in America are anything but homogeneous. Agencies range in size from one full-time police department employee in Valdez, Alaska to more than twenty-seven thousand police officers in New York City. It has been estimated that, on the average, the thousands of municipal police agencies across America have approximately fifty police officers per agency.

American law enforcement is described by its own membership as being quasi-military. Ranks are identifiable by insignia and by verbal notation such as corporal, sergeant, lieutenant and captain. Strategy employed by law enforcement also follows a military pattern. Force is the ultimate weapon to be utilized on the side of police.

Police personnel are deployed within the confines of a given geographic area. Restricting factors are generally related to fixed city, county and state boundaries. In many cases agreements have worked out between two or more municipalities to form a Pact of Mutual Aid. Mutual aid provides that one agency will come to the aid of another. Mutual aid is seldom used for any activity short of a disaster, such as flood, fire, earthquake, tornado, riot, etc. In the past most disasters were considered acts of nature, uncontrollable by man. However, with the advent of social protest and demonstrations in this country, police have had to have assistance in dealing with these phenomena.

Under normal circumstances, police personnel are distributed within the confines of city boundaries. Within this main perimeter there is a further division or districting. These divisions frequently follow census tracts, which are clearly designated nationwide. Geographic divisions which correspond to census tracts are preferable for policing because the decennial Census as well as special censures provide invaluable information on many numerical aspects

11

of social economic conditions which are helpful to law enforcement.
They provide information as to age, sex, race, income, housing,
etc. The forward-looking agency can then compare its own crime
data to that of census information and develop an overall picture of
what is happening in particular areas.

Besides geographic distribution of personnel, police are also
divided according to their specific tasks. The majority of police officers, rather more than fifty percent of the personnel available,
are assigned to general patrol duty. These officers handle all
types of cases; serious crimes as well as crimes classified as
misdemeanors, and many times function in the role of specialists
when a specialist is not available. The patrol officer is a generalist. The patrol force of many municipalities operate under the
philosophy of prevention, suppression, and apprehension.

Prevention of crime and the suppression of criminal activity
is attempted under a further policy of Visibility contact. Law enforcement personnel feel that by being highly visible in uniform,
police car, etc., they will deter criminal activity. Apprehension
is, of course, seen as a complete elimination of crime by removal from society of the individual who perpetrates a crime.

The next major function of police personnel is that of traffic
enforcement. The second largest number of police manpower is
employed in this task. Most agencies consider this a specialty
function. Officers working this assignment are given additional
training and their primary responsibility is traffic regulation. These
officers will use a standard police patrol vehicle, a special motor-
ized pursuit vehicle or motorcylce and, in some cases, air vehicles.

The next major responsibility area is detective work.
Detective functions can include the following: investigations in
homicide, robbery, fraud, auto theft, juvenile crime, vice, and
criminality. A detective usually develops a specialty in depth in
only one of the above areas, thus creating specialization to a high
degree.

The patrol officer or generalist will be the first to arrive
at the scene of activity. If the activity is within the realm of his
responsibility, he will conduct the necessary investigation, write a

report and make an arrest, if necessary. On the other hand, if the activity requires a specialist, the patrol officer will act as a referral person; he will contact and obtain the necessary specialist, after which he may act as an aid to the specialist.

Area of Responsibility

The above three categories: patrol, traffic, and detective functions, constitute the major end activities or line activities of a policeman. An officer working any of the above assignments can be described as a line officer or field officer; i.e., one who actually performs the activity that the agency was designed for, "protection of life, property, and the maintaining of the peace."

In addition to line activities, police personnel are employed in staff functions. These include such necessary tasks as planning, research and budgeting. Planning, research, and budgeting (PRB) is often done in a haphazard way.

PRB is nothing more than preparing for the future in terms of present knowledge and anticipations. PRB is not an innovation in law enforcement. It has been done for many years by the majority of police agencies. However, informal PRB can best be defined as that approach which prepares for future needs by methods other than rational and objective means. Individual feelings or emotional impulses have not been eliminated from the development of PRB. To safeguard against bias and misguided direction, something more than informal methods of administration must be employed.

Formal PRB applies the methods which have been accepted by private as well as public business, and as postulated by the social sciences. Police administrators should have a thorough background in one or more disciplines of the behavioral sciences; the ability to understand, interpret, and use statistical data; and the capability to grasp proposed ideas in relationship to existing agency policy and procedures. Many have suggested the removal of administrators from day-to-day activities of law enforcement and development of a critical attitude in viewing and reviewing all activities of the agency.

This separation of line and staff is necessary in terms of
the types of personnel to be employed. Excellent line officers do
not make excellent staff officers if their training, selection, motivation, and levels of achievement are not in tune with their new responsibilities.

Line and staff present a conflict area in many municipal
agencies. Attitudes of those persons employed as line or staff
have a tendency to change because of the work situation. This
change which is noticeable within the agency work group commonly
is unnoticed by the public.

Another conflict area, to be added to line and staff, is
auxiliary. Auxiliary functions are concerned with those in-house
administrative problems such as jail, custodial services, maintaining supplies, etc. Such internal departmental services are
farther removed from line activities than from staff activities.
Many writers have suggested that it may be a waste of police manpower to use police for auxiliary services. Again conflict develops
outwardly from auxiliary to staff and line. Police personnel serving an auxiliary service, as well as staff officers, have been
criticized as "not being real policemen." Similarly, juvenile officers suffer from being considered "kiddie cops."

Training

Training of police personnel may range from on-the-job
training to an academy course in police science and administration.
In California as well as in many other states there is an abundance
of Junior Colleges and Colleges which offer courses leading to a
degree in law enforcement. Some police agencies have their own
police academies which provide several months of training in practical law enforcement. It is not mandatory that police agencies
participate in such programs and the trend is towards in-service
training.

The quality of training varies from community to community,
and from agency to agency. In general, training at the four-year
college, where there is opportunity for interdisciplinary approaches,
will develop broader and less parochial knowledge by combining

study of law enforcement with the more traditional discipline of
sociology, political science, and psychology. The Junior College
approach seems to take a less generalized direction and has a
tendency to stress the "how to" concept. The Junior College becomes more rigid in its presentation and less adaptable to related
disciplines. The police academy is the most rigid of the teaching
devices. Most police academies reflect the philosophy and credo
of only one agency, their own. Instructors are selected from their
own ranks and the teaching philosophy is "it was good enough for
me when I was a policeman and it's good enough for you."

In most law enforcement organizations promotion is made
from within. To be promoted from patrolman to sergeant, sergeant to lieutenant, etc., one will be judged, in large measure by
his success in the previous rank. Frequently, testing is not
directed toward filling the new position but toward retesting of the
old position. As an example: patromen seeking promotion to the
position of sergeant may not be tested on broad supervisory skills
but upon knowledge that is necessary to fill the position of patrolman.

Generally two tests are given. One, a written test, reflects
what the agency desires in the promotable personnel. The second
test, an oral interview, covers the general knowledge and personality characteristics of the candidates. The honesty and reliability
of these two tests are questionable. Many applicants have purchased
answers to the examination or have been given the answers by their
superiors. Also, the results of the oral interview may easily be
skewed by selecting the people for the oral interview board to
ensure that the candidate has an easy time and is given an automatic high score; or vice versa. When there are only one or two
positions available every year or two, competition becomes rather
severe. It has been the experience of some in the police field
that, even with civil service, irregularities in testing, hiring, and
advancement still take place at the municipal level of government.

Recruitment

Law enforcement personnel are attracted to policing for
many reasons. High on the list of motivations are economic
security and job stability. Contrary to popular opinion, law enforcement work is not exceedingly dangerous. From 1963 to
1966 there were, on the average, 55 police officers killed by
felons per year. Considering that there are more than 194,000
police personnel across the nation, one's chances of being killed
by a felon are approximately one in four thousand. Considering
the frequency of heart disease and cancer causing death in the
general populace, the odds of police longevity fit the notion of
security and job stability.

The need for improvement in law enforcement is not an
avant-garde notion. Arthur Woods, former Police Commissioner
of New York City, in his book Policeman and Public,[1] wrote that
a law enforcement agency must change to meet the needs of the
community, the public is entitled to be furnished with complete and
accurate police records and that a police force is very sensitive
and responsive to public opinion. Anyone who believes these statements were brought about because of current racial crises or other
ethnic group protest is wrong. Mr. Woods' book was published in
1919. Forty-eight years later the President's Commission on Law
Enforcement and Administration of Justice made the same points,
among others, in The Challenge of Crime in a Free Society.[2]

The Lack of a Logical Approach to Police Community Relations

Community relations within municipal police agencies may,
in general, be described by the following characteristics, just as
in 1919:

1.   a distinctive difference is seldom made between
      public relations and police community relations.

2.   municipal police personnel are not well trained
      in basic philosophical positions of police
      community relations.

3. necessary interdepartmental organizational
    changes have not been made to accommodate
    police community relations, and those that have
    been made are superficial.

4. there is great disparity between what is said and
    what is done in reference to police community
    relations.

5. there is a general distrust of police community
    relations by police personnel and a lack of under-
    standing, of definition and of agreement as to its
    purpose.

Understanding of behavioral sciences is mandatory in developing a sensitive police-community program. The behavioral sciences
are characterized by three major areas: anthropology, psychology,
and sociology. The behavioral sciences must satisfy two notions:
(1) to be involved with human behavior and (2) to develop understanding in a scientific manner.[3] If we follow human behavior per
se, we can include economics, history, and political science as
sources and reflections on human behavior. It must further be
emphasized that the behavioral approach tends to establish generalization about human behavior so one can better understand, explain,
and predict human conduct. Certainly we can relate all of the
above to what police community relations should be.

Police Professionalization

It must be stated as a foreword to the emotionally charged
topic of "professionalization" that many of the practitioners in law
enforcement seek the designation "professional" as a symbol under
which law enforcement can function more easily and gather increased respect from the community being served. As in other
issues which will be dealt with in this book, professionalization
has many overtones including public relations, image building,
recruitment, standardization of personnel within each department,
and the rather basic category of job security.

The attempt to professionalize, or the movement in the
direction of professionalization, is not unique to law enforcement.
Professionalization carries with it an aura, halo, or symbol of
status which the individual, regardless of his own capabilities,
can carry into his occupation. We think in terms of the professional boxer, professional football player or, in general, the professional athlete. We also think in terms of the professional criminal,
the professional executive, the professional theologian. But what
exactly is a professional?

Morris L. Cogan attempted to penetrate the problem of
professionalization by first attempting to define what a profession
is.[4] Cogan states that 300 years have failed to bring agreement
on a single definition of profession. In law enforcement there are
many views as to what, in effect, is a professional. One practitioner describes a professional in law enforcement as one who is
courteous, appears neat, has the ability to do his job well, and
is gifted by a sixth sense to detect or distinguish the criminal
from the noncriminal in our society. Municipal law enforcement
is constantly being compared and related to military organization.
Some professional law enforcement officers, when attempting to
explain their role, emphasize the maintaining of appearance in
terms of uniforms, personal grooming, personal social habits, and
building into law enforcement a picture of an individual who is
identified as someone far superior in intelligence, physical abilities
and training to the ordinary citizen in our society. Professionalization in law enforcement has also been assessed by the location
and type of training officers receive, such as on-the-job training
or training in nationally sponsored police schools. Training given
to law enforcement officers may include courses dealing with patrol
procedures, criminal investigation, self-defense, criminal code
administration, and the use of firearms. These and other courses
are viewed by the practitioner, in some degree, as the road to
professionalization.

However, the many articles and speeches about professionalization generally take one of two directions. The first is: "are we,

in fact, professionals? Can we be described as professional law
enforcement officers?" Others take the approach that law enforcement is moving in the direction of professionalization. In effect,
the second group is saying that we have not reached the ultimate
goal, we are not yet professional. The major fault with both of
these positions is the lack of a definition which can be accepted
by the thousands of local, municipal law enforcement agencies in
the United States. A more enlightened attitude towards police
professionalization comes from Radelet.[5] He indicates the criteria
by which a profession can be described:

1. A systematic body of knowledge and skills oriented
   by intellectual pursuit;

2. More or less well-established principles, methods,
   theories, etc.;

3. A clearly defined purpose;

4. Unesoteric terminology;

5. Profit not regarded as a primary objective;

6. Associations within the field are concerned with
   standards, accreditation, ethics or certain self-
   monitoring elements.

This attitude towards professionalization is certainly more
sophisticated than the emphasis upon personal appearance and image
which has been promulgated by many in law enforcement. If we
continue in this direction in attempting to define professionalism
some rather broad generalizations can be drawn. Webster's Dictionary indicates that a profession is a vocation or occupation requiring
advanced training in some liberal art or science and usually involving mental rather than manual work; examples might include:
teaching, engineering, writing, medicine, law and theology. The
concept of professionalization is thus an inclusive one, encompas-
sing many occupational areas.

Taking the three well-accepted occupations of medicine, law,
and theology as a basis, generic terms or processes may be developed by which any group of people might be considered in relation
to standards of professionalization. Harold Wilensky,[6] writing in the

American Journal of Sociology, portrays the process of professionalization as including:

1. full-time occupation;
2. the development of a training school;
3. university education;
4. the establishment of local professional associations;
5. development of national professional association;
6. State licensing;
7. a formal code of ethics.

Wilensky has indicated that the accepted or established professional
groups, including accounting (C.P.A.), architecture, civil engineering, dentistry, law, medicine and theology have all at different
times gone through these seven steps. Wilensky defines professionalization as including the following characteristics:

1. a technical foundation
2. an exclusive jurisdiction
3. standards of training
4. convincing the public that its services are uniquely
   trustworthy.[7]

He continues that there is a general tendency for occupations to
seek professional status in our society and that remarkably few
occupations attain it. Of his seven characteristics in the process
of professionalization, he begins with historical order in the development of a profession and the assertion that the obvious first step
to professionalization is to start doing, full-time, the thing that
needs doing.[8] We do have a dichotomy in the American law enforcement system. We not only have full-time officers employed
in police work; we also have categories of part-time law enforcement personnel. This part-time group may include police reserve,
auxiliaries, and honorary positions in law enforcement. Many
agencies and police administrators consider the reserve officer a
benefit to the department. Generally this benefit is in terms of
economics. Where it is not feasible for a particular law enforcement organization to maintain a full complement of personnel, reserve officers who can be called to duty, at little or no expense to

the agency, may be considered a desirable asset. However, such
use of part-time reserve officers is a departure from the first
of Wilensky's criteria for professionalization: doing full-time that
which needs doing.

Another dichotomy exists within the agencies, generally at
the local level, but also at State and Federal levels, concerning a
fully employed officer who also has a second job, what is popularly
called " moonlighting." There is no accepted administrative procedure within the 17,000 local agencies for controlling and regulating
secondary employment by law enforcement officers. One agency
may require its officers not to have any secondary source of income. This may even include employment of the officer's spouse
and possibly other members of his immediate family. At the other
end of the scale, an agency may allow great magnitude, possibly
allowing an officer to work as much as 20 hours per week at a
second job. Is it beneficial to the agency to have personnel hold
a second position, which may or may not have relationship to the
primary job of law enforcement? Many administrators in law
enforcement feel that outside employment has a degrading effect
upon the agency and may detract from the agency's professionalism.

As the second and third stages in the process of professionalization, Wilensky discusses the establishment of a training school
and the development of academic training. These are essential
in the attainment of professionalization. The training school or
the academy develops an academic area for further study, standardization, research, and a continuing need for expanding knowledge
within the particular occupational arena. The training school
criteria can be linked to the many police-oriented institutions, such
as Junior Colleges, which provide short courses for law enforcement personnel as well as two-year degree courses. However,
within the past ten years and in lesser degree in the 1930's, the
responsibility for law enforcement education has fallen to the
University. Law enforcement education has reached an all-time
pinnacle with the establishment of the Office of Law Enforcement
Assistance to aid Colleges' and universities' new emphasis on re-

search and development of new methods and concepts. With the
establishment of many new college and university programs
dedicated to teaching and research in law enforcement, many of
the requirements of training and academic achievement within law
enforcement have been fulfilled. There still exist in many geographic areas of the United States, however, municipal agencies
which require no special training for the position of law enforcement officer. The President's Commission on Law Enforcement
and Administration of Justice has noted that many law enforcement
agencies do not develop a standard training course for their law
enforcement personnel. If we can proudly point to many agencies,
training schools, colleges and universities which do an admirable
job in the teaching of law enforcement, we must also point to
many agencies which do not subscribe to the need for educational
standards.

In dealing with the local professional association and the
establishment of a national association we also may have some
difficulties. It is true that there are many local police groups.
They may take the form of police protective groups, fraternal
organizations, or possibly police benevolent associations. These
groups have, in the past, been rather parochial, demonstrative,
and have agitated for better police relationships. In terms of a
national professional association, there appears to be no particular
group which represents all of law enforcement in the United States.
This is a major vacuum in the process of law enforcement professionalization. There are, however, State agencies and top level
administrative officer agencies. But these are usually restricted
to top organizational personnel within law enforcement. Patrolmen,
Sergeants, and Lieutenants usually are not admitted as members
in these organizations.

The sixth category described by Wilensky discusses State
licensing of the particular group. At present, this is virtually
nonexistent within law enforcement. In California, there exists
the Peace Officers Standards and Training (P.O.S.T.) group which,

in effect, can function as an unofficial State licensing agency.
It is not mandatory for law enforcement agencies in the State of
California to prescribe to the P.O.S.T. requirements. Many
times it is to their benefit because of the availability of funds
from the State government for the local agency in the training of
personnel. But in essence, there does not exist a State licensing
group and many law enforcement agencies and associations would
apparently object to a licensing board which could recommend and
enforce standards and develop changes in terms of standardization
within law enforcement.

In regard to a code of ethics, law enforcement is again
deficient. A code of ethics does exist within each local agency
and is generally described in policy statements of each particular
agency. As an example, there are approximately 50 separate
agencies in Los Angeles County, California and some 22 separate
agencies within Orange County, California. Each agency develops
its own policy in terms of officer conduct independently; very few
requirements, if any, have consciously been agreed upon by all
agencies within these two counties. The same conditions, it is
believed, exist throughout the United States in terms of the lack
of a recognized, accepted, Code of Ethics for total law enforcement
(See Appendix A).

Notes

1.   Woods, Arthur Policeman and Public (New Haven: Yale
     University Press, 1919.) pp. 74-176.

2.   The President's Commission on Law Enforcement and
     Administration of Justice, The Challenge of Crime in a
     Free Society (Washington, D.C.: United States Government
     Printing Office, 1967).

3.   See Berelson, Bernard (Editor). The Behavioral Sciences
     Today (New York: Harper Torchbooks, 1964).

4.   The Annals of the American Academy of Political and Social
     Science, 297: January, 1955. "The Problem of Defining
     a Profession".

5.   Radelet, L. Police Chief, "Implications of Professionalization
       of Law Enforcement for Police Community Relations"
       July-August, p. 83, 1966.

6.   Wilensky, Harold "The Professionalization of Everyone?"
       American Journal of Sociology, LXX:137-158, September,
       1964.

7.   Ibid. 138

8.   Ibid. 142

II. Police Roles

The police role is complex if for no other reason than
the vast number of public law enforcement agencies in the United
States. It has been estimated that there are more than 40,000
separate, local, state, and Federal police agencies in the country,
all with limiting degrees of geographical jurisdiction and responsibilities.[1]

The complexity of the police role is further enforced by
the independence of each police agency. However, at the municipal
level there is strong dependency to local autonomy in terms of
individual state penal laws, municipal laws, local policy governing
the selection of laws to be enforced and the way in which they
shall be enforced, organizational policy developed by the policy
agency, and officer discretion ability.

The heterogenous police picture also includes nonconformity
in standards of personnel selection, training, and promotion. Although the Federal Bureau of Investigation has developed a system
of uniform crime reporting containing statistical information dealing
with crimes committed and persons committing crimes, little has
been done to coordinate efforts and requirements of municipal
agencies. Jealousy, anxieties, and distrust are not unknown in the
interactions between municipal police agencies.

The position of the police is further confused by the interpretation of role participation of the individual agency as a whole
and the expectation of community members in general (See Appendix
B).

Refinement of the problem

Within recent years there has been much action by law
enforcement agencies in the area of police-community relations.
Law enforcement, as a public office, has in many communities

taken the initiative in attempting to resolve community social
problems. With so many departments diverting police personnel
from the primary police functions to community leadership, some
rather basic questions need to be asked about this technique:

1. Should police agencies take the posture of
   social coordinator?
2. Are police agencies capable physically, psychologically,
   and philosophically to assume this role?
3. How do police agencies relate to the more
   orthodox socially-oriented organizations?
4. What is the proper mix in law enforcement
   orientation in regard to police-community
   relations?

Many police officials stress the importance of police-community relations in terms of: better communications between the
police and citizens, more training in human relations, and the
development of specialized units within police organizations responsible for community relations.

All of the above, it is felt by law enforcement, will establish better relations between citizen and police, reduce disorder
and violence, reduce crime, educate the public to combat crime,
reduce traffic accidents, increase recruitment and, overall, make
the job of law enforcement much easier. Police-community relations mean many things to many people.

The Social Organization of Police

Policemen in the American setting can best be described
as reactionists, for the simple reason that they react to criminal
activity. The "what" and "where" of law enforcement is regulated
by what type of criminal activity is predominant at a particular
time and where it is taking place. These factors are determined
through statistics maintained by the agency. Therefore, law enforcement is oriented primarily toward an action (the recording of
crime) and a reaction (the elimination of continuing criminal acts
based upon historical records). Thus the agency stresses the

importance of apprehension as part of the individual officer's
role.

Although enforcement seems to be the javelin point of
police responsibility, there are two other concepts which are
associated with police work: prevention and suppression. Prevention assumes that the visual-physical presence of a policeman
will deter criminal activity. This may be true when limited to
the confines of time and geographic area, but this notion may become microcosmic when related to the total concept of criminal
activity. However, much effort is made by law enforcement to
formalize and legitimize the preventive concept. Suppression
appears to be a resultant of both prevention and apprehension. It
is the dispersion of criminal activity either in time (present and
future) or from one geographic area into another (generally relative
to jurisdictional boundary).

Three characteristics[2] emerge as part of the role of law
enforcement: (1) the focus of police "...is chiefly upon the dis-
ruptions and aberrations of efficient human relationships"; (2) "...
the policeman is usually the initiator of his contacts with others.
He is the seeker rather than the sought ..."; and (3) "... while
the apprehension of a criminal or the arrest of a traffic violator
may be regarded as role fulfillment within the organization itself
...it tends to be unpalatable to those who are the direct recipients
of the policeman's action."

Organization

Most police organizations can be described physically as
closed systems. Recruitment is conducted at the lowest level in
the organization and promotions are made from within by members
competing for the next highest position. Most police agencies assume common bureaucratic characteristics of: hierarchy, specialization of task, specified sphere of competence, established norms
of conduct, and record keeping[3] (See Appendix C).

In terms of hierarchy the majority of police organizations
perceive their role as quasi-military in nature. J. Edgar Hoover

interprets municipal law enforcement as "the first line of defense, "
and former Chief Parker viewed the police as "the thin blue line."
In any event the military attitude is taken by most if not all municipal law enforcement agencies. The similarity of law enforcement
to a military organization may, however, create some difficulties:

> Although the similarity of the soldier and policeman
> seems obvious in terms of uniforms, armament, ex-
> posure to danger, discipline, etc., there are important
> differences. The primary one is that the soldier's
> object is the external enemy; he seldom takes punitive
> action against his own community. Thus his support is
> regarded as a matter of necessity, as a bulwark against
> alien threat. The investment in the soldier is regarded
> as insurance which may be expensive and little used but
> perilous to be without. The policeman, on the other
> hand, is the potential antagonist of every citizen, and,
> unlike the soldier, he is always at war. He is the public
> conscience, threatening the status and treasure of the
> wrongdoer. [4]

Most policemen show a sharp division between staff orientation and productivity orientation. Much criticism is generated
from the field officer toward the administrator. A feeling of
separation brings with it generally an apathetic approach in policy-
making or participation on the part of field personnel, regardless
of rank.

> Most policemen showed little sense of involvement in
> policy-making. Probably, this scarcity of constructive
> feedback can be attributed to the semimilitary structure
> of the department, which led to a fear that suggestions
> would be construed as criticisms and would result in
> punishment rather than approval.

> Thus there was fostered a tendency to take things as
> they came and not to waste energy in fruitless efforts
> to change the system ... reflecting a kind of apathy
> with respect to organizational routines in a manner
> quite characteristic of bureaucratic organizations. [5]

Selection and Training

Selection of policemen is initiated at the lowest level in
most police organizations. Selection is based upon intelligence,
physical ability, medical and mental tests, and personal appearance

and oral interview. Minimum levels of acceptance for these tests
are generally set by the agency. Prerequisites are often limited
to age and some attainment of elementary education.

In rank order physical prowess seems to be paramount,
followed by the officer's apparent capacity for ambition and initiative. However,

> The high ambition and high initiative which they
> sought in policemen could well be the qualities
> most conducive to internal friction, which, in
> turn, would probably intensify frustration and
> increase resignation rates. [6]

Most policemen do not seek the occupation for excitement
or adventure. The majority of policemen at the municipal level
are rather standard civil service types and might be found in any
department of municipal government.

> Among recruits there seemed to be a central interest
> in job stability and economic security. Such factors
> as seniority, automatic pay increments, well-ordered
> career lines, and routinized evaluations seemed to
> hold greater appeal for the recruit than the opportunities
> for personal glory or a life of excitement and adventure. [7]

During the training phase of policing there is little
standardization of subject matter or in depth of material covered
by municipal police agencies. Many police administrators feel
that a minimum of 400 hours, covering an array of subject matter,
should be offered to police recruits. It is estimated that less than
twenty-five percent of the nation's recruits receive the minimum
training. [8]

It is also apparent that physical ability is a more valued
trait for cadet officer survival than academic ability. However,

> . . . a strong aversion was expressed against so-
> called "killer" and "sadist" types. Good physical
> condition and outdoor interests thus constituted
> legitimate proof of masculinity, though masculinity
> was continually being tested. [9]

Complete conformity and loyalty to the particular agency
is demanded, and officers who show any deviance from this norm
are disciplined. The major agencies in Los Angeles County, which

conduct their own recruit training and in-service training, stress
conformity to rules (policy) and loyalty to the department. The
Los Angeles Police Department and the Los Angeles County Sheriff's
Department are examples of agencies which stress physical fitness
and unquestioned loyalty. Penalties for deviance may range from
days off (which means loss of pay) to forced resignation.

A conflict develops between selection and training in that
the desirable traits of initiative and ambition in an officer may
create individual frustration, aggression, psychological conflict,
and confusion in role expectations. The agency's viewpoint is
concerned with group norms and values, influence, and morale.

It has been suggested that attitudes toward the police agency
are most often characterized by "...some concept of loyalty, sometimes bordering on a demand for self-sacrificing and unquestioning
acceptance of orders from above." [10] Officers are expected to
develop the "right attitude." Failure to do so may bring about
adverse job assignments and increased employee hardships.

What the officer is taught and learns during the orientation
period of his employment, generally at a formally controlled police
academy or sponsored educational institution, is not needed for
actual field work. After completing the formal training the officer,
in most cases, will be assigned to an experienced policeman for
additional field training. The officer will be judged by the experienced policeman on his law enforcement knowledge and understanding. "Discussion with all ranks of personnel indicated that many
believed large discrepancies existed between school material and
field practice." [11]

> Many post pundits suggested that probationary policemen
> should 'forget everything they learned in recruit school,'
> the implication being that the rejection of school material
> was not merely convenient but often necessary if one were
> to gain the approval of field supervisors.
>
> School training was identified as a headquarters product,
> and thus, by definition, alien and unworkable in field
> situations.
>
> Therefore, at least by omission, training was often deemed

inadequate or unrealistic.

Many field supervisors seemed convinced that recruit school training was superficial and/or misleading and that the 'real' education of the new policeman began with the probationary phase.

For the recruit, the discrepancies outlined above posed immediate dilemmas for his own role behavior. In most cases where a choice of behavior was involved, the expectations of the field staff received priority. [12]

Department Policy

Most police agencies, in the manner of other bureaucratic organizations posit various types of "rules and regulations" and "special departmental orders," violation of which, it is announced, will bring departmental disciplinary action.

There is a general disparity between administrative interpretation and enforcement. This disparity is generally mediated by a system of supervisory sanctioning. "The general headquarters view was that a literal adherence to the rules was dysfunctional." [13] A tendency develops to overlook violations which are job-oriented and can be handled by the immediate supervisor. However, violations which are non-job- oriented or are social offenses which unmask the officer to the general public are strictly enforced.   The protection of law enforcement's image becomes paramount.   During a special study,

> ... trial board records revealed that more than two-thirds of all trials were for 'social' offenses, and contrasted with 'job content' offenses. The major social breaches were intoxication, sexual promiscuity, and financial negligence. The primary job-oriented offenses were negligence in handling complaints and absence without leave. [14]

The social offenses of intoxication and sexual promiscuity appear to relate to the general area of masculinity and physical prowess which seem to be continually tested and proven in law enforcement work.   It was also revealed that:

> ...veteran policemen were more inclined to risk breaking

rules than were younger ones. This undoubtedly
stemmed from a greater knowledge of the relative
importance of the regulations, the attitudes held by
post officers towards them, and the extent to which
violations could be safely made.[15]

Enforcement Practices and the Law

The police officer's job is related to other activities
beyond enforcement of the law.

The recruit soon discovered that the law itself provided
only a partial guide for carrying out his role. In the
first place, a considerable portion of his on-duty time
was devoted to preparatory and summarizing routines,
such as checking equipment .... reading logs and orders,
and writing reports.

Although his recruit school mentors had hinted that the
law was only the framework in which he was going to
function, the academic atmosphere of the classroom and
legal material which he had to memorize created a
sense of confidence in ' the book.' To the recruit, the
efficacy of his own judgment seemed puny indeed beside
the legal monolith he was trying to comprehend ...
One presumably judged acts, not people. This was the
safeguard of the policeman and it protected him from
misplaced sentiment and moral weakness. Armed with
this objective code, the recruit on probation was rather
unprepared for the attitudes of men in the field toward
the law.

Part of the debunking process was to reorient the recruit
to the law on the basis of local norms.[16]

Also, there appears to develop a dual standard for enforcement of the law. Law enforcement is not in practice a closed and
isolated system, as so many times prescribed. From personal
experience and involvement this dual standard does exist in establishing an ability to overlook violations and thus build goodwill and a
favorable image with the public.

Since post personnel and local citizens were generally
familiar to one another, it was deemed impolitic to
arrest traffic violators or other misdemeanants on the
same basis as the rest of the public, especially if the
citizen in question was prominent.

> Under the pressure of making proper distinctions,
> the policeman soon found himself rationalizing his
> conscious failures to enforce the law in terms of
> other needs of the department as it functioned in
> the community. Most veteran officers appeared as
> past masters....[17]

Public Relations

Arthur Woods, former police commissioner of New York
City, wrote of policing and the public in 1919. Much of what
Mr. Woods describes of the early twentieth century concerning
police relations is still being utilized today.[18]

The majority of police agencies are sensitive, "...some-
times bordering upon preoccupation with public relations."[19] Such
terms as sell, educate, and favorable reaction, all in relationship
to the public, are becoming common and acceptable in law enforcement.

Image making, in terms of public relations, becomes
a practice which must be protected and perpetuated. Preiss and
Ehrlich indicate that "There were few officers who were not
vitally interested in creating an image of policemen as courteous,
helpful public servants."[20]

The main effort in developing public relations usually
takes the following form:

> Selling the department to the 'local public' was
> construed as a general post responsibility. The
> policeman new to a post was frequently assigned
> first to learning the post area. Among other things,
> this meant distinguishing between the 'transient public'
> and the 'local public,' as well as learning who the
> local 'influentials' were. Policemen were expected
> to develop 'contacts' and potential informants, and on
> all routine patrols they were expected to spend some
> time in visiting and politicking in their patrol area.[21]

This selling or educating the public is generally, in Leavitt's
discussion, a one-way process, coming from the agency representative, and is protective, preplanned, fast and controlled.[22]

Public relations also is designed to obtain public support
to make the job of law enforcement easier. The feeling within law

enforcement is that with the advance of public support and opinion there also will develop a decrease in the frequency of law violations.

A twenty-nine page report entitled "Police Community Relations,"[23] submitted and released by the Los Angeles County Sheriff's office in 1961, lists in the table of contents such topics as: the image, creating a favorable press, how to influence groups, public opinion, what the police must do, all people are criminals, how to influence the public, and creation of the image.

Such how-to approaches concerning public relations are instilled in the new officer during his formal indoctrination into the police organization.

Police Community Relations

The topic of PCR in recent years has come to mean something different from police public relations. PCR is regarded as a two-way communication process intended to develop accuracy and generate feelings and positions. The purpose of this interaction is to effect change on the parties concerned.

The present focus of PCR is a mix between public relations and community relations. The Task Force Report on The Police, as prepared by the President's Commission on Law Enforcement and Administration of Justice, in dealing with "The Police and the Community," however, fails to distinguish adequately between public and community relations. Such areas as police salary, recruitment and image tend to be discussed in one-way, self-protective, defensive terms.

Summary

It can be seen from the foregoing that the social organization of law enforcement may produce disparities in such areas as the setting, organization, selection and training, rules and discipline, enforcement practices and the law, public relations, and police community relations. Role conflict may crystalize around actual role expectations, perceived role expectations, and role performance.

The agencies' philosophical position may set the tone for conflict by developing rigid, fixed role expectations which are not related to role performance. The very characteristics which the agency seeks in candidates for law enforcement organizations (motivation and initiative) may be the ingredients to produce conflict. A listing of law enforcement characteristics would include the following:

1. Law enforcement officers react to criminal activity.

2. Apprehension of social offenders becomes a yardstick for the officer in carrying out his role.

3. Police organizations can be described as closed bureaucratic subsystems which relate to other subsystems and to the whole system in pre-described ways.

4. In terms of hierarchy the majority of police organizations perceive their role as quasi-military.

5. A feeling of separation develops between staff oriented personnel and productivity oriented personnel.

6. Physical prowess seems to be paramount in the selection and training of police personnel.

7. Complete conformity and loyalty to the particular agency is demanded.

8. Discrepancies exist between taught police procedure and field application.

9. A disparity exists regarding departmental rules and discipline, and the enforcement of these organizational requirements.

10. Social offenses which are more prone to public view are more severely dealt with than job offenses which are internal and are viewed primarily by the agency.

11. Police agencies are very public relations conscious.

12. Little distinction is made between public and community relations.

Notes

1. Smith, Bruce Police Systems in the United States, 2nd. Rev. ed. (New York: Harper and Brothers, 1960), p. 22.

2. Preiss, Jack J. and Ehrlich, Howard J. An Examination of Role Theory: The Case of the State Police. Lincoln, Nebraska: University of Nebraska Press, 1966, p. 7.

3. Etzioni, Amitai Modern Organizations. Englewood Cliffs, Prentice-Hall, Inc., 1964.

4. Preiss and Ehrlich op. cit., p. 7.

5. Ibid., p. 11.

6. Ibid., p. 13.

7. Ibid., p. 13.

8. The President's Commission on Law Enforcement and Administration of Justice. Task Force on the Police, 1967.

9. Preiss and Ehrlich op. cit., p. 15.

10. Ibid., p. 15.

11. Ibid., p. 16.

12. Ibid., pp. 16-17.

13. Ibid., p. 17.

14. Ibid., pp. 18-19.

15. Ibid., p. 19.

16. Ibid., p. 20.

17. Ibid., p. 22.

18. Woods, Arthur Policeman and Public. New Haven: Yale University Press, 1919.

19. Preiss and Ehrlich, p. 23.

20. Ibid., p. 23.

21. Ibid., p. 23.

22. Leavitt, Harold H. Managerial Psychology. Chicago:
     The University of Chicago Press, 1964, pp. 138-152.

23. Police Community Relations: A Report of the Sheriff of
     Los Angeles County on Factors Involving Law Enforcement
     in Dealing with Community Problems, May, 1961.

III. Historical--Philosophical Development of Administration

Philosophy has been interpreted in many ways. It might
be understood as a love of wisdom; or a body of principles which
would appeal to the scientific managers of administration; or a set
of values involving the inquiries, debates, and verbiage of much
administrative literature concerning the dichotomy of "is" and
"ought"; or a view which could be related to the hue and cry for
universal principles; or a field of study. For the purposes of this
work and to develop topic parameters, philosophy is viewed as a
system of ideas. [1] In dealing with systems it is necessary to
categorize people, ideas, and issues. Three approaches are
utilized which have been modified from their original source: [2]

1. a constitutional-legal rational philosophy forged
    from a framework of legal rights and obligations
    of government;

2. a structural-descriptive philosophy with its primary
    impetus coming from the scientific management
    area; and

3. the socio-psychological philosophy which stresses
    the systematic study of human behavior (beginning
    with the Hawthorne studies) in an organizational
    environment.

The above three divisions are not necessarily sharply divided but
interact with, and react to, other systems and ideas as related to
public administration.

Constitutional-Legal Approach

In 1887 Woodrow Wilson set a precedent for his contemporaries (and those to follow) with his views on the nature of administration. Wilson's own philosophy, that man could remake
society, added substantially to the reform and progressive period

38

of the 1900's. The reform and progressive movement appeared
to blend naturally with the concept of scientific methods in public
administration. Science became all-important, facts became
"sovereign".[3] Wilson wrote that administration is an area of
business and that the object of administrative study is to obtain a
foundation laid deep in stable principle. He advocated the separation of politics and administration, asserting that administration
lies outside the proper sphere of politics and that administrative
questions are not political questions. Wilson, like Willoughby at
a later date, was legally oriented. Wilson emphasized that public
administration is the detailed and systematic execution of public
law. He was an early exponent of universal principles in dealing
with administration and a supporter of the concept of the "science
of administration".[4]

In writing Politics and Administration (1900), F. J. Goodnow was also caught in the stream of progressivism. He may have
been influenced by Wilson's essay since he continued the idea of
the separation of administration and politics. Goodnow stressed
the concept that politics were detrimental to administrative efficiency. The separation of politics and administration is more
complex than stated above, however, and Goodnow found both good
and bad in separation. He indicated that it is impossible to assign
these functions to separate authorities because governmental power
cannot be clearly divided.[5] Goodnow suggested a possible solution:
the assigning of a degree of control of administration by politics
dependent upon the type of administration. Administration could be
of a judicial or governmental type. Politics should not be involved
in justice. However, with regard to government (the executive
portion in particular), it must be subordinate to politics.[6]

W. F. Willoughby, who was legally oriented, discussed
weaknesses in government administration and advocated scientific
principles of public administration. Willoughby continued the Wilson-
Goodnow concept of administration as being "apolitical". Like Goodnow, who was dissatisfied with the trichotomy (executive, legislative,
and judicial) dictum of democratic government, Willoughby suggested

five divisions of governmental power: executive, legislative, judicial, administrative, and electoral. Willoughby was concerned both with the dichotomy between administration and politics and with the fact that administration is a separate function from the executive role of government. He restated the claim for scientific sophistication in his Principles of Public Administration (1927). He took the position that there are fundamental principles analogous to those characterizing any science which can be determined by the application of the scientific method. Willoughby's contributions were multi-philosophical. He presented a discussion of the administration-politics dichotomy and then emphasized the administrative process as a technical and management attitude which should be used as a foundation for the legal involvement.[7]

Summary of the constitutional-legal philosophy. This system was a continuation of Constitutional legal opinion and decision based on legal rights and obligations of government. It emphasized the normative and political aspects of government. Wilson has been credited with focussing attention on public administration as an area of study in his essay "The Study of Administration" (1887). He emphasized that public administration is the detailed and systematic execution of public law and the separation of politics and administration.

Goodnow and later Willoughby continued the idea of the separation of administration from politics. Goodnow does indicate that governmental power cannot be clearly divided and that it becomes impossible to divert these functions to other authorities. Willoughby suggested five divisions of governmental power with equal importance on the administrative role.

Wilson and Goodnow, in rejecting the rationalism of nineteenth century political ideology of a system of legal literary theory and the paper pictures of the Constitution, introduced the concept of administration as apolitical. Simon, at a later period, developed a similar theory focussing on the separation of facts and values.

The major criticism of the constitutional-legal philosophy

was its narrow approach to the study of administration.

Structural-Descriptive Approach

With the emphasis upon efficiency and scientific methodology the inquiry of administration retained the mantle of progressivism. Frederick W. Taylor represented the synthesization
of scientific management in his Shop Management (1903) and
Principles of Scientific Management (1910). Scientific management
was the vehicle for a positivist attitude concerning the universality
of management principles. Waldo has written that scientific
management has contributed techniques and philosophy to the study
and application of public administration.[8] Early contributors to
the development of scientific management as applicable to public
administration were: Henri Fayol, Industrial and General Administration (1930); V. A. Graicunas, "Relationship and Organization";
Gulick and Urwick, Papers on the Science of Administration (1937);
and F. A. Cleveland, W. E. Mosher, and Frank Gilbreth. With
the establishment of scientific management (efficiency and methodology) and the empirical investigation into principles, public
administration assumed a new sophistication and direction. Among
Taylor's contemporaries were persons interested in governmental
reform such as Morris L. Cooke, who was employed in government service, Henry P. Kendall, who advocated governmental
departmentalization according to functional management,[9] and Fayol,
who applied scientific concepts toward the managerial or executive
functions of administration. Waldo suggested that the philosophical
development from the negative and moral to the positive and
scientific attitude in personnel administration could be traced
directly to scientific management.[10]

Leonard D. White gave direction to the philosophy in his
definition of administration as organization and personnel management adjusted with financial and legal controls.[11] White, in his
Introduction to the Study of Public Administration (1926), emphasized
the structural and descriptive characteristics of administration.

He viewed administration as not apolitical in his administrative
history analyses: The Federalists (1948), The Jeffersonians (1951),
The Jacksonians (1954), and The Republican Era (1958). In writing
"The Meaning of Principles of Public Administration" [12] White
advocated the scientific approach to administration and suggested
that principles are tested universal hypotheses. Possibly White's
major force in relation to public administration is his role as
structural-descriptive historian and his emphasis and definition of
principles of administration.

Luther Gulick, together with Lyndall Urwick, continued
the movement of scientific management into public administration.
He carried the concept of work division of the "managers" into
theories of departmentalization. In his "Notes on the Theory of
Organization" he viewed governmental departments as being organized into divisions by purpose, with a further subdivision by
process (finance, personnel, etc.). Gulick stressed the concept
of efficiency as a basic good for public or private organizations.
The operationalization of public administration was identified by
Gulick (with its relationship to principles and universalism of
Taylor and Fayol) by the mnemonic word POSDCORB which syn-
thesized the scientific management approach. Urwick also presented the case for scientific management and dismissed the individual as being unimportant. Urwick's belief was in priority
of organization structure with the necessary ingredients of planning and design which are all highly related to various types of
principles. The organization came first, and man could be mold-
ed to fit the organization. In the Papers on the Science of Administration, Gulick and Urwick brought together a group of
articles which expressed the attitude that public administration
was nearing the position of a science in which values and ends
could be put to one side. However, the seeds of discontent were
also sown in the same publication, in two major essays: the first
dealing with the Hawthorne study by Anderson, Whitehead, and
Elton Mayo; and the second, an essay by Mary Parker Follett.

Herbert A. Simon has continued to a remarkable degree, though with some modifications, the application of science to public administration. Simon has stated the logical-positivist dictum that values can be removed from the science of public administration as they have been from the natural sciences. A true science is only concerned with fact. Simon has attacked the traditional concept of science, however, claiming that the so-called principles are only proverbs which have not been based on empirical research. This was not an attempt to eliminate principles but only a disagreement as to interpretation of fundamentals. Simon stressed decision-making, not the principles as indicated by the Papers, as the heart of administration. The concept of administration as apolitical came under attack since the separation of powers' position viewed administration as technical, and therefore based on the principles.

Another important movement within the structural-descriptive system was the President's Committee Report. This report, published in 1937, emphasized the Papers by agreeing that the foundations of effective management in public affairs are well known. This gave respectability to governments' efforts to develop efficiency by the use of certain well-established principles.

Summary of the structural-descriptive philosophy. This system emphasized the use of principles in describing public administration. Efficiency and scientific methodology were the framework for the approach. The belief that administrative study could disregard values was accepted. The more articulate members of this system were White, Gulick and Urwick. The major criticism of this system was its lack of interest in people. Organization and principles became paramount. Emphasis was placed on the science of administration and the development of facts.

Socio-Psychological Approach

This third dimension to "systems that have influenced thinking in public administration" was initiated by the classical

examples of the Hawthorne study by Mayo, Roethlisberger, and
Dickson; and by Mary Parker Follett's Dynamic Administration.
This particular system has been involved with man as the center
of inquiry in an administrative situation. As Pfiffner has indicated,
this system has "...a set of values which is highly humanitarian,
democratic, people-centered, and oriented in ideas of social
justice".[13] It was felt that the structural-descriptive system with
its lack of inquiry into values was cold and distant, and the
phrase "machine model" may be descriptively accurate.

As a result of the behavioral impetus in the area of
public administration, Simon, Smithburg, and Thompson have established their concept of administration as a social process. The
authors constructed, on a psychological and sociological frame of
reference, an explanation of public administration which was to be
non-normative, free from values, desires, and prejudices, "a
science in the sense of an objective understanding of the phenomena
without confusion between facts and values." [14]

The behavioral approach views organization as a social
group and work as a social activity. The individual brings to his
work organization his mental as well as his physical identity. As
well as the formal structure of the organization there exists an
informal social structure that is dynamic, responsive, and capable
of unknown power, which at times may be distinct from the formal
organization.

From this social-dynamic approach, which moves away
from the legalistic and mechanistic view of administration, inquiries
of administration can be made which have greater breadth and
depth. The following questions are indicative of this philosophical
system: [15]

1.   What is the social environment within which
      organizations, individuals, and varied combinations
      of individuals operate?

2.   What persons and group affiliations influence
      attitudes and decisions?

3.   How are human needs being met within the
organization?

4.   How will a proposed action be received by the
individuals who occupy centers of informal
authority?

The socio-psychological system brings together the elements of the behavioral sciences with their milieu of philosophy
and mythology, and views public administration from many directions. The primary approach of this system is to stress the
importance of empirical research and to find what is actually being
done in administrative areas before universals are developed to
describe public administration. Most of the principles have come
under attack by a newer group of writers on public administration.[16]

Summary of the socio-psychological philosophy. The study
of public administration under this system adopted the proposition
that administration is a social process, rather than simply an
exercise of authority and command, in terms of formal responsibilities and functions. The focus is now on relationships of people,
processes, and patterns of communication. This system has moved
away from the concept of formal organization, principles, and the
legal foundation of administration. This system has taken an anti-
management position, and has attacked the traditionalists' parochial
orientation based on POSDCORB and the machine model. The overview is that some kind of millennium has developed in the name of
socio-psychological philosophy where there is a meeting of the
legal, scientific manager, and socio-groups. The basic concepts
of the past are coming into conflict with the empirical studies which
are being directed into all areas of public administration. This
shift in administrative thinking is not new. Dahl and Sayre stated
in the Public Administrative Review (1950) that interest in public
administration has moved from an emphasis upon science of administration to one of placing administration in its larger social
bureaucratic setting.

Rationality as a Philosophical Question

Barrett, in the Irrational Man, expressed the view that
human beings are irrational much if not all of the time. His
primary thesis is that man has no alternative but to be irrational,
since the situation in which human beings find themselves is
essentially meaningless and absurd. To be rational presupposes
that one can find some sense and meaning in things.

However, Veatch's view, in Rational Man, is that rationality is a defensible end or goal of man. It becomes an end
which is not automatic and without criticism but nevertheless one
based upon reason, and desired as a proper position.

Rationality is not a new concept to administrative students.
In the constitutional-legal approach, which stressed the concepts
of legal rights and obligations of government and the beginnings
of a science, rationality took two forms: (1) rationality emphasized
the power of human reason to understand the facts of human relationships and to manipulate relationships in logically determined
ways to achieve predetermined goals, and (2) the role of the administrator was burdened with the use of techniques and principles
in dealing with organization and especially in the concept of
manipulation of organization.

The present approach to rationality in administration has
changed in philosophy and has extended its parameters. The present position encompasses the rational and irrational factors in
human envolvement. Rationality also considers inquiry concerning
social factors which may influence reasoning. The newer rationality
philosophy has subordinated the position of techniques and principles
on the part of the administrator and his monocratic behavior, suggesting that "there are even beginnings of what might be called
democratic administrative theory, in contrast to theory that has
been authority-oriented. "[17]

The Standard College Dictionary defined rationality as: (1)
the quality or condition of being rational; reasonableness; (2) the
cause of reason; rationale; and (3) something rational, as an act,

belief, practice, etc.   In attempting to be more specific and provide a firmer foundation for administrative relationships Pfiffner
defined rationality to mean "...the capacity of man to make
choices based upon conscious deliberation about the means selected
to achieve specified ends". [18]

Simon, in Administrative Behavior, defined rationality as
"concerned with the selection of preferred behavior alternatives in
terms of some system of values" [19] where the results of the
behavior can be evaluated.   Unlike Pfiffner's definition, which
indicated the phenomenon of "conscious deliberation," Simon
indicated that the selection of alternatives can be of a conscious
or subconscious nature.   Simon then redefined rationality to be
related to specific situations: [20]

1.   Objectively rational, if in fact it is the correct
     behavior, for maximizing given values in a given
     situation.

2.   Subjectively rational, if it maximizes attainment
     relative to the actual knowledge of the subject.

3.   Consciously rational, if it has made the adjustment
     of means to ends as in a conscious process.

4.   Deliberately rational, if the adjustment of means
     to ends has been deliberately brought about by the
     individual or by the organization.

5.   Organizationally rational, if it is oriented to the
     organization's goals.

6.   Personally rational, if it is oriented to the individual's
     goals.

Pfiffner's definition may be weak in that it deals with a
conscious state of mind and neglects subconscious interactions in
selecting the proper means to develop specific ends.   Simon's
multi-definition is also weak in that there is no universality of
the concept of rationality but a fragmented approach depending on
situation.

Pfiffner's definition will be modified to indicate selection
of alternatives based upon conscious and subconscious deliberations

about the means selected to achieve specific ends.

Having operationalized a definition of rationality it is now
necessary to view the limits to which rationality can proceed. The
crux of the problem of limitation lies within the means-ends
phenomenon.

The ends to be obtained by the development of certain
means will have the following relationships: (1) means available
for selection will be limited; (2) means cannot be completely separated from ends; and (3) ends may be formally defined in terms
of policy statements of an organization whereas means are generally
more flexible although limited. The analogy can be drawn between
economic man and administrative man in that both these concepts
of rational behavior are held constant in dealing with means and
ends. Rational behavior would find axiomatic the following three
conditions: [21] (1) to view all the alternatives prior to making the
decision; (2) to consider all the alternatives to choice with their
many complex systems; and (3) to select a system of values as
criteria, singling out one from a complete set of alternatives.

Simon agrees with the above description of real behavior
being dominated by irrational sequences. He did indicate that
behavior reveals segment of rationality but that there is little
interaction between these bits and pieces of rational indulgences.
Simon has described limits of rationality to be functional in three
areas: knowledge, value, and behavior. [22]

1. Rationality requires complete knowledge and
   anticipation of end results which will follow each
   choice. Knowledge of end results, however, is not
   always complete. Rationality implies a complete
   knowledge of end results and consequences for each
   choice. In actual practice ability to know the
   maximum data concerning a particular end result
   might be analogous to geometric progression. As
   pieces of information, related to the original
   phenomenon, are brought together, new decisions
   might be made with the necessity of making new

choices and obtaining additional knowledge. In
actuality, complete knowledge concerning a
phenomenon is seldom obtained. Knowledge is
generally related to time, effort, and funds. The
longer the time period a phenomenon can be
investigated, the greater the effort made by
personnel; and adequate funds available will relate
directly to the obtainable knowledge.

2. Since consequences lie in the future, imagination
must supplement the lack of experience of similar
situations. Anticipation can only partially be
imagined since related values are attached to
nonexistent situations. Simon indicates that an
experience which is anticipated may be very
different from the realization of the situation.
This relates not only to the failure to anticipate
end results but also to a lack of mental ability
to focus on a particular end result in its entirety.
Attention will drift from sets of values or subunits
of values relating to one end result to other sets
of values relating to different end results. There
are limiting factors in imagining end results and
assigning values to them.

3. Rationality requires a choice among all possible
alternative behaviors. Only a small number of
possible behaviors will be reviewed for selection.
In actuality an array of possible patterns of behavior
exist, consciously as well as unconsciously, which
will have three stages of involvement: mental processes which accept, store, and relate to patterns of
behavior; physical processes which might be related
to reflex actions and unconscious physical manip-
ulations; and biological processes which are occurrences of tissue reproduction and cell division which
receive no formal direction from the mental processes.

Of all these pattern processes only a few appear
to be possible behavior alternatives which can be
placed in a position of choice.

Simon has indicated that the primary concern of administrative theory is "with the boundary between the rational and
the nonrational aspects of human social behavior." [23] The limits
of rationality are concerned with human activity which satisfies
rather than maximizes.   Economic man attempts to maximize his
ends based on rational choice while administrative man accepts
solutions which are lesser in degree than the concept of maximization.   Simon also makes the comparison between economic man
who deals with the world and administrative man who he says
deals with something less than the real world.   Administrative
man considers the real world as "empty and that facts of the real
world have no great relevance to any particular situation he is
facing." [24] Administrative man develops simplified models which
take into account just a few of the factors that are felt to be most
relevant.   The major characteristics of administrative man according to Simon, are: [25]

1. A tendency to satisfy, rather than maximize, by
     making choices without examining all possible
     behavior alternatives.

2. Ignores the interrelatedness of behavior and means-
     ends.

3. Makes decision with relatively simple rules of thumb
     that do not make impossible demands upon capacity
     for thought.

Summary concerning limits of rationality as a philosophical
question. Rationality as a man-goal is expressed in this paper as
reflecting an end result which is based upon reason and is desired
as a proper position. A modified definition of rationality was
derived from Pfiffner's and Simon's approach to rationality and is
expressed as the selection of alternatives based on conscious and
subconscious deliberations about the means selected to achieve
specific ends. There is general agreement among writers on public

administration as to the limitations of rationality. Limitations
have been grouped into three primary areas: knowledge, which is
not always complete because of the sheer magnitude of information
which may relate directly and indirectly to a particular end result;
value distribution, which will alternate between end results and
expectations which correspond to values attached to nonexistent
situations; and behavior, which will be limited because of the
magnitude of patterns of behavior which would theoretically be
considered. Therefore, the limits of rationality are directly related to the inability of the human mind to focus on a single
situation with all the possible alternatives of knowledge, value, and
behavior that would be necessary to make a choice from available
alternatives.

Rationality and the Decision-Making Process

Nicolaidis, in his Policy-Decision and Organization Theory,[26]
interpreted decision-making as something different from the traditional concepts of rationality. He related orthodox concepts of
rationality to economic man, engineering man, and the scientific
method where all relevant facts are obtained and a selection is
made from an array of end results. This system excluded human
prejudice and bias which might influence the decision. Nicolaidis
attempted to go beyond the orthodox concept and attempted to
operationalize social factors which interact with, and influence the
facts, and in turn present facts of their own. Nicolaidis appears
to travel farther than Simon in the direction of making social data
accountable in the decision-making process.

Banfield's description of a decision-making process can
be used as an example of the orthodox approach to rational
decision-making:[27]

1. The decision maker lists the opportunities for action
open to him.

2. He identifies the consequences that would follow
from the adoption of each of the possible actions.

52   Police Administration

3. He selects the action that would lead to the
    preferred set of consequences.

Banfield further suggests that "for practical purposes, a
rational decision is one in which alternatives and consequences are
considered as fully as the decision ...given the time and other
resources available...."[28] The contrast between Nicolaidis and
Banfield is apparent. The former is influenced by a myriad of
social factors which influence decisions and the latter takes as
a premise a mechanical, automated approach.

In describing the decision-process Nicolaidis suggested
that there was a continuum of decision-making models varying
from classical rationality at one extreme to intuition at the other.
Within this continuum there exists a plurality of values:[29]

1. A decision must have some degree of conformity
    with the personal interests, values, and benefits
    of the decision-maker.

2. It should meet the value yardsticks of superiors.

3. It should be acceptable to those who are affected
    as well as those charged with its implementation.

4. It should be reasonable within its context.

5. It should contain built-in justification which will
    furnish an excuse, and possibly an avenue of
    retreat, in case results are not as anticipated.

In moving away from orthodoxy in administrative rationality an array of social phenomena becomes suspect. Concepts such
as emotions, politics, power, group dynamics, personality, and
mental health become worthy of inquiry or, at least, of recognition
that they exist if nothing more than as unknowns. Behavioral
science information assumes a relative position among the data in
developing a solution to a particular problem. A broader base is
used to develop solutions to particular problems.

The decision-making processes have been found as entities
in five approaches or views in categorizing decision-making. The
five approaches would be: a mental process, a social process, an
organizational process, a general problem-solving process, and a

specific problem process.[30]

1. A mental process utilizes the choice of alternative
    possibilities and the mental characteristics which
    bring about a choice. Simon's trichotomy of
    knowledge, value, and behavior would be character-
    istic of the mental process.

2. In the social process decisions are made in a social
    setting by individual thinking which is related to
    social influence, or by interaction within a group
    process. The primary characteristic of this process
    is that decisions are recognized as being made in
    a social setting interacting with individual values
    and goals.

3. An organizational process is in part a subdivision
    of a social process. However, since it is such a
    large division of the social process, it has been
    set aside and is dealt with as a specific function
    of the social process.

4. A general problem-solving process gives emphasis
    to techniques of selecting alternative solutions. It
    is also an attempt to develop a general theory which
    is applicable in selecting alternative end results
    regardless of knowledge, value, and behavior
    involved.

5. A specific problem-solving process emphasizes the
    process of developing specific categories of decisions
    such as personnel decisions, economic decisions,
    etc.; and the development of a general theory which
    is applicable to the specific category.

In Simon's approach decision-making is the heart of administration. A decision is defined as a conclusion drawn from
a set of premises. Premises are of two kinds: (1) facts, and (2)
values. The validity of facts can be determined by empirical
propositions. Values are imperatives; they have to do with oughts
and they cannot be empirically validated. They are neither true nor

untrue in any empirical sense.

Summary of rationality and the decision-making process.

Traditional concepts of rational decision-making accept man as an individual who maximizes his position by making a determined valuation of all possible factors which relate to a particular problem and then selects the best choice from an array of end results. Examples of this phenomenon would be administrative man, engineering man, and economic man. Economic theory has reinforced the image of man as a rational creature. Economic theory is concerned with a rational man who would save his money, spend wisely, and generally exhibit predictable behavior in the area of economic choice.[31]

The traditional concept excludes social factors of an unconscious as well as a conscious nature. Human bias which might influence the decision is not considered. This type of decision-making is mechanical and appeals to the scientific management concept of efficiency, economy, and selection of a one best way.

In contrast to the traditional rational concept in dealing with decisions is a move toward the consideration of an array of social factors which might influence a decision. Simon and, to a greater degree, Nicolaidis have directed much attention to this approach. Nicolaidis indicates that decision-making is not a single process but can be attributed to several independent processes: social, mental, and organizational.

In the practical application of decision-making, fact and value are organically related and incapable of separation. Simon's purpose was to view decision-making by isolating characteristics of the process for purposes of analysis and to develop an ideal type.

Attempts to Formulate a Theory of Rationality in Decision-Making

Attempts to formulate theories relative to rationality are not new or confined to writers on public administration. John Dewey (1859-1952) is one of the significant writers who examined rationality outside the fortress of public administration. His philosophy held that the characteristics of human activity are instruments for solving psychological and social problems. He postulated that value propositions can be arrived at by the power of human reason. He recognized unconscious motivation and related this to the concept of habit. The concept of unconscious motivation dates back to Spinoza (1632-1677), Leibniz (1646-1716), and Freud (1856-1939). The evolution of ethical thought is characterized by the fact that value judgments concerning human conduct were made in reference to the motivations underlying the act rather than to the act itself.[32] The main emphasis in Dewey's position is one the relationship between means and ends as the empirical basis for the validity of norm. The end, to Dewey, is merely a series of acts viewed at a remote stage, and means merely represent the series viewed at an earlier one. The end is the last act thought of, the means are the acts to be performed prior to it in time. Means and ends are two names for the same reality.[33]

Simon pursued the concept of means-end as being merely a continuum in which ends have a hierarchical arrangement. The means-end hierarchy has three primary limitations:[34]

1. The ends to be attained by the choice of a particular behavior alternative are often incomplete or incorrectly stated through failure to consider the alternative ends that could be reached by selection of another behavior.

2. In actual situations a complete separation of means from ends is usually impossible, for the alternative means are not usually valuationally neutral.

3. The means-end terminology tends to obscure the role of the time element in decision-making.

The concept of means-ends is to maximize satisfaction of needs with a minimum disposal of means. As Nicolaidis has indicated, this is the concept of the economic principle "...which is identical with the concept of rationality. Rationality has been

considered as the administrative version of the economic principle."[35] The economic principle is formulated around two
concepts: (1) unlimited ends, and (2) limited means.

Dewey's concept of means-ends as a validity of norms
has been expanded to include Simon's limitations and modified to
be a phenomenon of administrative rationality as analogous to
economic concepts. Therefore, in developing a theory of rationality, it is necessary to view the relationship of means-end to the
total view of rationality.

In an attempt to move away from rationality based on
economic principles of ends and means, consideration should be
given to two ideal types:[36] (1) the fourfold model of the real social
man; and (2) the model of the rationalized organizational man.

The fourfold model can be divided into the area of expected rational behavior which considers the facts which the decision-
maker knows and can evaluate himself, and the area dealing with
anticipated nonrational behavior which considers value judgments
and factors which are either unknown or which the decision-maker
cannot evaluate by himself. The emphasis of the fourfold model
is the acceptance of man's being irrational. Realizing this, man
can adjust himself to a systematic approach to decision-making
and therefore become rational. The shift is away from man and
toward the system into which man must fit in order to be rational
in solving problems.

The second model, which deals with the rationalized
organization man, can be divided into three primary areas: (1)
the area of expected natural rationality which deals with known
facts which the decision-maker can evaluate by his own computation-
al capacities and a consideration of factual judgments expected to
be naturally rational; (2) an area of improved rationality which
considers unknown factors that the decision-maker can evaluate
by using staff work, computers, statistics, probabilities, etc.; and
(3) an area of controlled rationality which deals with value judgments
controlled and predetermined by given policies. This approach has
been criticized by Melman[37] as being an extension of the "one best

way" and as mythology from the traditionalist concept of
industrial engineering. He also indicated that from a mathematical point of view the one best way is not justifiable.

Rationality theory has been attacked by Simon as developing a notion of a man who never existed since "the capacity of
the human mind for formulating and solving complex problems
is very small compared with the size of problems whose solution
is required for objectively rational behavior in the real world."[38]
An argument in favor of rationality theory is the view that theoretical models are necessary as ideal types which describe rational
behavior. It is not the purpose here to recommend an ideal model
as a working entity but only to suggest that it represent certain
characteristics which relate to the concept of administrative rationality. Weber's formulation of bureaucracy consists of such an
ideal type. In Weber's attempts to develop his concept of bureaucracy there also develops an aura of rationality and, as indicated
by Pfiffner, "Perhaps the major characteristic of the ideal type
of bureaucracy is its effort to achieve rationality."[39]

In attempting to formulate theories of rationality as related
to decision-making it is necessary to further describe: (1) the
classical model; (2) the normative model; and (3) the behavioral
model.

The classical model of rationality has been described
by March and Simon as the machine model. This assumption is
derived from the mechanical attitude toward human motivation and
behavior which, according to this view, is primarily related to
self-interest. The machine model stressed the means-end relationship as one in which the decision-maker analyzes the ends and
then selects the means which are necessary to obtain the end goal.
This Machiavellian view ignores the necessity of values except those
of self-interest in that decisions are "completely independent of
ethics, that a ruler serving the ends of his state can do no wrong."[40]
The emphasis in the classical model is the maximization of self-
interest. This approach is characteristic of formal logic, pure

reasoning, and the application of scientific methodology. Classical
decision-making attempted to solve problems by looking for the one
best way of rational man. In contrast, the behaviorist selected
ideal types which emphasized major characteristics of decision-
making.

The normative model moves away from the mechanistic
model in that it suggests "oughts," or what should be. A normative model is one that accepts a principle or action which is
binding upon the members of a group and serves to guide, control,
or regulate proper and acceptable behavior. The normative model
of rationality is not necessarily based upon any scientific inquiry
or hypothesis. The normative model may be of a minority view
which is in conflict with the total group view relating to ought and
should concepts. A normative view is also related to some agreement of what is good and what is bad. When principles of good
and bad have been resolved, the normativist can deal with oughts
in normative terms. However, it is felt by some that the questions of good-bad, right-wrong, are concepts which defy definitive
agreement.

The behavioral model of rationality attempts in a systematic way to describe, measure, and predict human behavior. The
decision-maker is still dealing in part with self-interest realities
but is willing to compromise to obtain the end result. However,
in compromising, there may be a shift to a less desirable end
result. The administrative decision-maker who assumes the
behavioral model approach of give-and-take by dealing with and
anticipating human behavior is involved in the area of administrative politics, according to Pfiffner.[41] Behavioral models deal
with areas of intuition, objective analysis, indecisiveness, administrative leadership and authoritarian leadership, while the
classical models were concerned with factual decision-making,
charismatic leadership, and decisiveness.

Summary of attempts to formulate a theory of rationality
in decision-making. Spinoza, Leibniz, and Freud were among the
first to inquire into the unconscious acts of man. Dewey continued

inquiry into unconscious motivation of man in making decisions.
His main emphasis was on the relationship between means and
ends. He felt the end was a minor factor in a series of means.
Simon also pursued the concept of means-end as being a continuum
in which ends were at the top level of a hierarchy. The means-
end phenomenon is faulty because it is based on incomplete information; a complete separation of means-end is impossible, and the
time element is often not considered in ideal types of decision-
making. The basic concept of means-end is to maximize satisfaction of needs with a minimum disposal of means: (1) unlimited ends,
and (2) limited means.

Theories of rationality were related to three descriptive
models: the classical model, the normative model, and the behavioral model. The classical model attempted to solve problems
by looking for the one best way of rational man. In contrast, the
behavioralist selected ideal types which emphasized major characteristics of decision-making. The behavioral model dealt with areas
of intuition and objective analysis. The normative model was one
that accepts a principle or action which is binding on the members
of a group and serves to guide and control.

Values Implicit In Such Theories

Rationality of decision-making suggests that thinking about
what is desirable and right can be systematic and directed into
action.

Philosophies of other generations have declared various
concepts relating to rationality and the universality of standards.
Philosophers have developed a value framework in dealing with
standards.

The nineteenth century philosophers were skeptical about
universal values and the impracticability of the concept "that every
person already knew in his heart what was right, and that the
conscience, moral sense, or reason of all humanity was identical.[42]"
The trend was away from universal standards, and criticism by
Hegel and Marx in dealing with nationalism and class-struggle theory

gave emphasis to this skepticism.

However, in the early years of the twentieth century
Nietzsche called for a "...re-valuation of all values and the
pragmatists were insisting that there are no problems in general,
hence, there could be no principles that solved all problems."[43]

In an attempt to move away from a universal approach
philosophers developed a logical positivism concept which made a
distinction between facts and values. The assertion is made that
values can be removed from facts by decision-makers in solving
problems. The comparison is generally made between the natural
scientist and his ability to eliminate value in the laboratory, and
the approach of the social scientist in the field with his efforts
to eliminate value in his studies.

Mailick, in Concepts and Issues in Administrative Behavior,
has identified six standards which, if viewed independently, have
the characteristics of a universal. These values are listed below
with the names of individuals who believed each standard represented a complete universal system:

1. Happiness; which can also be described in terms of
    desirable results, maximized satisfactions, and
    efficiency. Writers who believed in happiness as a
    universal were Epicurus (341-27C B.C.) who develop-
    ed a theory of life, defined philosophy as the art of
    making life happy, with intellectual pleasure or
    serenity the only good; Jeremy Bentham (1748-1832)
    who advocated the greatest happiness for the greatest
    number; and John Stuart Mill (1806-1873) who deter-
    mined that universals were related to inductive reason-
    ing.

2. Lawfulness; which would include precedents, customs,
    contracts, and authorizations. A writer who believed
    in lawfulness was Thomas Aquinas (1225-1274) who
    felt that reasoning starts with sense data.

3. Harmony; which might include logical consistency,
    platonic justice, order, plan, and common good.

Writers who believed in harmony as a universal
were Plato (428/427-348/347 B.C.) who investigated
the development of a rational moral personality;
and Immanuel Kant (1724-1804) whose Critique of
Pure Reason opposed the concept that human intelligence has powers to arrive by pure thought at
truths about entities which in their nature can never
be objects of experience.

4. Survival; political power, and effect on friend-foe
   relations. A writer who believed in survival as a
   universal was Thomas Hobbes (1588-1679) who felt
   it was necessary to give everyone a guarantee of the
   good behavior of his fellows by creating a power
   sufficient to keep them in awe.

5. Integrity; which could be described as self-respect,
   the rationality of the individual, and peace of mind.
   Writers who believed in integrity as a universal were
   Epictetus who viewed the world as a whole; Baruch
   Spinoza (1632-1677) who, regarding the world as a
   whole which would render it completely intelligible,
   attempted to build a mathematical philosophy filled
   with geometric axioms, postulates, and theories; and
   George Santayana (1863-1952) who, in The Life of
   Reason, advocated that reason is based on instinct
   which has become reflective and enlightened.

6. Loyalty; institutional trends and social causes. Writers
   who believed in loyalty as a universal were Georg
   Wilhelm Hegel (1770-1831) who, in The Encyclopaedia
   of the Philosophical Science, stated that reason can
   be related to logic, nature, and the mind; Karl
   Marx (1818-1883) who, besides his more renowned
   work, wrote The Poverty of Philosophy (1847) as an
   interpretation of economic history; and Josiah Royce
   (1855-1916) who stated that scientific laws can be
   used as statistical formulas for behavior.

Mailick suggests that there is no universal value but many values which relate to the decision-making process. He further denies the universalist approach in this statement: "No one rule, no one goal, no one system sums up human wisdom."[44] He goes further to indicate that a decision-maker

> ...may make a very different evaluation of the contemplated action, if he asks himself how the action looks from another point of view, particularly from the standpoint that is diametrically opposite his present view (harmony as opposed to survival, lawfulness as opposed to happiness, and integrity as opposed to loyalty).[45]

Generally, decision-making has been performed as a one-sided, partial, incomplete operation; it has not involved criticism of some values which are important and permanent parts of the decision-maker's personality and culture.

Nicolaidis has also suggested that decisions are not based on a single standard or value but rather must meet many values, and has outlined five areas in which values become apparent in decision-making.[46]

Summary of values implicit in such theories. The topic of values in making rational decisions has been a source of discussion from Plato and Epicurus to the present writers of public administration. There has been little agreement as to the role of values in decision-making. An outstanding discourse on this conflict is that presented by Simon and Waldo, the former suggesting a value-free approach, the latter negating the separation of facts and values. Simon has modified the concept of earlier philosophers to move away from a universalist position and develop a logical positivist attitude which makes a distinction between facts and values. Nicolaidis has also suggested that decisions are not independent from values but suggests that there are many values which influence facts and the eventual decision.

Conclusions

Three approaches were utilized in this chapter which have been modified from their original source: (1) a constitutional-legal

rational philosophy forged from a framework of legal rights and
obligations of government, emphasizing the normative and political
aspects and the detailed and systematic execution of public law
and the separation of politics and administration. The major
criticism of the constitutional-legal philosophy was its narrow
approach to the study of administration. (2) A structural-descriptive philosophy, with its primary impetus coming from the scientific
management era which emphasized the use of principles in describing public administration in a framework of efficiency and
scientific methodology. This system is also narrow with its
singular direction concerning principles, facts and efficiency. (3)
The socio-psychological philosophy which stresses the systematic
study of human behavior and which views organization as a social
group and work as a social activity. This system has taken an
anti-management position, and has attacked the traditionalists and
their parochial orientation based on POSDCORB and the machine
model.

Rationality is not a new concept in administrative students.
In the constitutional-legal approach rationality took two forms: (1)
rationality emphasized the power of human reason to understand
the facts of human relationships and to manipulate relationships in
logically determined ways to achieve predetermined goals; and (2)
the role of the administration was burdened with the use of techniques and principles in dealing with organization and especially
in the concept of manipulation of organization. A definition of
rationality would indicate selection of alternatives based upon
conscious and subconscious deliberations about the means selected
to achieve specific ends. The problem of limitation lies within
the means-ends phenomenon.

The ends to be obtained by the development of certain
means will have the following relationships: (1) means available
for selection will be limited; (2) means cannot be completely
separated from ends; and (3) ends may be formally defined in
terms of policy statements of an organization whereas means are
generally more flexible although limited. Rational behavior would

find axiomatic the following conditions: (1) to view all the alternatives prior to making the decision, (2) consider all the alternatives to choice with their many complex systems, and (3) select
a system of values as criterion singling out one from a complete
set of alternatives. Simon has described limits of rationality to
be functional in three areas: knowledge, value, and behavior.

The limits of rationality are concerned with human activity
which satisfies rather than maximizes. Economic man attempts
to maximize his ends based on rational choice while administrative
man satisfies and accepts solutions which are lesser in degree than
the concept of maximization. Administrative man in satisfying
develops simplified models which take into account just a few of
the factors that are felt to be most relevant.

In describing rationality and the decision-process there
was a continuum of decision-making models varying from classical
rationality at one extreme to intuition at the other. Within this
continuum there exists a plurality of values.

In Simon's approach decision-making is the heart of administration. A decision is defined as a conclusion drawn from a
set of premises. Premises are of two kinds: (1) facts and (2)
values. The validity of facts can be determined by empirical propositions. Values are imperatives; they have to do with oughts
and they cannot be empirically validated. They are neither true
nor untrue in any empirical sense.

In attempts to formulate a theory of rationality the end
has been considered as merely a series of acts viewed at a remote
stage, and means merely represent the series viewed at an earlier
one. The end is the last act thought of, the means are the acts
to be performed prior to it in time. The concept of means-ends
is to maximize satisfaction of needs with a minimum disposal of
means. In developing a theory of rationality, it is necessary to
view the relationship of means-end to the total view of rationality.
Examples of two ideal types of rationality are: the fourfold model
of the real social man, and the model of the rationalized organization man. Rationality theory has been attacked by Simon in that

it develops a concept of a man who never existed.
Values in rationality of decision-making suggest that
thinking about what is desirable and right can be systematic and
directed into action. In an attempt to move away from a universalist approach philosophers developed a logical positivist concept
which made a distinction between facts and values. Six values
have been identified and have been viewed independently as
universal: happiness, lawfulness, harmony, survival, integrity,
and loyalty. Nicolaidis has suggested that decisions are not based
on a single standard or value but rather must meet many values.
He suggests five areas in which values become apparent in decision-
making.

Notes

1. Stover, Carl F. "Changing Patterns in the Philosophy of
    Management", Public Administration Review, Winter,
    1958, p. 21.

2. Pfiffner, John M. and Presthus, Robert V. Public
    Administration (New York: The Ronald Press, 1960),
    p. 7.

3. The Administrative State (New York: The Ronald Press, 1948).

4. Wilson, Woodrow "The Study of Administration",
    Political Science Quarterly, December, 1941, pp. 493-504.

5. Op. cit., Waldo, p. 16.

6. Ibid., p. 79.

7. Willoughby wrote The Government of Modern States (1919),
    Principles of Judicial Administration (1929), Principles of
    Legislative Organization and Administration (1934).

8. Op. cit., Waldo, p. 47.

9. Op. cit., Pfiffner, p. 191.

10. Op. cit., Waldo, p. 59.

11. Op. cit., Pfiffner, p. 90.

12. Gaus, John M., White, Leonard D., and Dimock,
    Marshall E. The Frontiers of Public Administration
    (Chicago: University of Chicago Press, 1936).

66   Police Administration

13. Op. cit., Pfiffner.

14. Simon, Herbert A., Smithburg, Donald W., and Thompson,
    Victor A., Public Administration (New York: Alfred A.
    Knopf, Inc., 1950).

15. Stover, Carl F., "Changing Patterns in the Philosophy
    of Management," Public Administration Review, Winter
    1950, Vol. 18, Num. 1., pp. 21-27.

16. A few of the names which have become associated with
    the "new" group would include but not be restricted to:
    Robert K. Merton, Reader in Bureaucracy; Daniel Lerner
    and Harold D. Lasswell, The Policy Sciences; Rensis
    Likert, Developing Patterns of Management; Sam A.
    Stouffer, et at., The American Soldier; Chester I.
    Barnard, The Functions of the Executive; Talcott Parsons
    and Edward A. Shills, Toward a General Theory of Action;
    and Peter M. Blau, The Dynamics of Bureaucracy, to name
    a few.

17. Waldo, Dwight Ideas and Issues in Public Administration
    (New York: McGraw-Hill, 1953), p. 104.

18. Op. cit., Pfiffner, p. 116.

19. Simon, Herbert A. Administrative Behavior (New York:
    The Macmillan, 1945), p. 75.

20. Ibid., pp. 76-77.

21. Ibid., p. 80.

22. Ibid., p. 81.

23. Ibid., p. xxiv.

24. Ibid., p. xxv.

25. Ibid., p. xxvi.

26. Nicolaidis, Nicholas G. Policy-Decision and Organization
    Theory (University of Southern California Bookstore,
    John W. Donner Memorial Fund, Publication No. 11, 1960).

27. Banfield, Edward C. "Ends and Means in Planning,"
    Concepts and Issues in Administrative Behavior
    (Englewood Cliffs, N.J.: Prentice Hall Inc., 1962),
    edited by Sidney Mailick and Edward H. Van Ness, p. 71.

28.   Ibid., p. 71.

29.   Op. cit., Nicolaidis

30.   Op. cit., Nicolaidis, pp. 36-42.

31.   Simon, Herbert A. "Recent Advances in Organization
      Theory," Research Frontiers in Politics and Government,
      S. Bailey, editor (Washington, D.C.: Brookings
      Institution, 1955), pp. 32-35.

32.   Mullahy, Patrick "Values, Scientific Method and
      Psychoanalysis," Psychiatry, May, 1943.

33.   Dewey, John Human Nature and Conduct (New York:
      The Modern Library, Random House, 1930), p. 34.

34.   Ibid., Administrative Behavior, pp. 62-66.

35.   Op. cit., Nicolaidis, pp. 99-102.

36.   Ibid., pp. 103-7.

37.   Melman, Seymour Decision-Making and Productivity
      (New York: John Wiley and Sons, 1958), p. v.

38.   Simon, Herbert A. Models of Man-Social and Rational
      (New York: John Wiley and Sons, 1957), p. 198.

39.   Op. cit., Pfiffner, p. 44.

40.   March, James G., and Simon, Herbert A. Organizations.
      (New York: John Wiley and Sons, 1958).

41.   Op. cit., Administrative Rationality, p. 131.

42.   Mailick, Sidney and Van Ness, E.H., Concepts and Issues
      in Administrative Behavior (Englewood Cliffs, N.J.:
      Prentice-Hall Inc., 1962), p. 82.

43.   Ibid., p. 82.

44.   Ibid., p. 89.

45.   Ibid., p. 88.

46.   Pfiffner, John M. "Administrative Rationality," Public
      Administration Review, Spring 1960, Vol. 10, no. 2,
      p. 129.

IV. Police Bureaucratization

Eisenstadt has indicated that analyses of bureaucratic
organizations as an instrument for efficient implementation of
goals on the one hand, and for gaining, maintaining, and exercising
power on the other, are usually separated in the literature and
have employed different sets of concepts and assumptions. He
further suggests that the analysis of organizations as composite
social systems that are in continuous interaction with their environment, and the analysis of the forces in this environment impinge
on these organizations.[1]

The main problem facing any inquiry into bureaucracy
appears to be the relationship between bureaucracy and bureaucratization. The development of organizations aiming at implementing and providing goals on one hand, and the growing acquisition
of power on the other, place within the bureaucracy vast potential
for regimentation and the domination of social life.[2]

There are two points of view in the literature about bureaucracy. It is seen: (1) as a tool for successful and efficient implementation of a certain goal or goals. Bureaucracy in this view,
is the epitome of rationality and of efficient implementation of goals
and provision of services; and (2) as an instrument of power, control
over people and spheres of life, and continuous expansion of such
power either in the interests of bureaucracy itself or in the interests of others. This two-fold attitude may be observed in varying
degree in classical writers such as Weber, Mosca, and Michels,
and in contemporary writers on sociology, political science and
public administration. These points indicate various possibilities
for inquiry which are inherent in bureaucracy.[3]

Historically, the general view of bureaucracies is that
they have been created by elites (rulers, economic entrepreneurs,
etc.) to develop a service or a strategic power position. The
literature also suggests that bureaucratic organizations are related

68

to social conditions, based upon resources, necessity, and power
in terms of competition for position. A bureaucracy is in constant
interaction with its environment and must develop a position of
dynamic equilibrium. The bureaucratic organization is a social
world in the development of subgroups.[4]

One of the links connecting the organization to the total
social structure is the organization goal. The most important
goal of the organization is usually interpreted by society as the
function of the organization.[5]

A question of rationality: concern has been generated by
some, such as Reissman with his study of role conception in
bureaucracy and Couldner's analysis of organization, over the
dysfunctional aspects of bureaucracy's rationality. It has been
found that rules, order, and maintenance of structure have a
tendency to become ends in themselves. Blau has also taken the
position that rational bureaucratic action may produce irrational
results.

This position of rational bureaucratic action producing
irrational characteristics has been a central criticism of Weber's
model. Michels, in 1912, stated that democratic social action is
possible only through bureaucratic organization; and that in turn
bureaucratic organization is destructive of democratic values.

Merton has criticized bureaucratic action in that it
produces secondary consequences that run counter to its initial
objectives and "principles." In effect, Merton suggested that
standardized behavior which is required in a bureaucratic organization would bring about a displacement of goals in terms of the
individual, the immediate work group, and the organization. He
attempted to show that the bureaucracy ideal included inefficiencies
which help explain discrepancies between Weber's model and
reality.

Udy found that bureaucratic structure was not always
associated with rationality. He indicated bureaucratic characteristics such as hierarchical authority structure, administrative staff
units, and income graduations according to office that were in

conflict with such "rational" claims as limited objectives, participation based upon mutual limited agreement among members,
and compensatory rewards whereby those in authority allocated
rewards to members in return for participation.[6]

Presthus has indicated that in some societies with highly
bureaucratized governmental organizations, often the product of
French or British influence, their behavioral consequences and
goals are mainly a function of the particular social context in
which the bureaucratic apparatus exists. He further indicates
that the underlying social values and class structure bend the
organization in ways that document their own major assumptions.[7]
The bureaucratic model, with its structural and behavioral elements
of efficiency, rationality, and control, rests upon certain normative assumptions about time, man, and motivation. Where social
values do not assign a high priority to objectivity, productivity,
and economic gain, the structure of bureaucracy is of little relevance as a guide either to its performance or its goals.[8] Traditional ideology and institutions have provided subtle, deep seated,
and pervasive resistance to change.[9]

In a study conducted by McNulty, of thirty companies, he
indicated that rational attempts to introduce change produced irrational results. His results indicate a high degree of "paper"
changes in administrative arrangements, but of greater interest
is the suggestion that adaptation was not clearly better in the case
of companies which explicitly introduced organization changes than
it was in companies which did not.[10]

The status of bureaucracy in terms of Weber's ideal type
is changing. Writers from the behavioral sciences are critical
of Weber's stereotyped ideal. Bureaucracy is declining into
splinter factions which have outdistanced innovations at the municipal police level. Areas in which the military as well as the
social scientists have directed special attention within the framework of administrative responsibility include: development of research and planning along the lines of natural and social science
methodology; administrative leadership; and delegation of decision-

making responsibility.

The Present Status of Municipal Police Agencies

Much criticism of municipal police has been generated by various individuals, groups, and institutions, and much of this criticism has been emotional and biased. From the police comes an almost equal deluge of emotional and prejudiced verbiage attacking the critics of municipal policing.

To understand this social drama we must resort to generalizations and oversimplifications which will describe contributing characteristics of the participants. The three main groups are: (1) the average citizen, (2) interested pressure groups, and (3) the police. The common link between these divisions is Attitude.

The attitude of the average citizen toward municipal police is generally one of apathy. The feeling of not wanting to be involved, of not being concerned with facts relating to issues, of observation from a distance, and of no direct participation in our democratic society contribute to mass neglect and lack of interest on the part of the average citizen.

However, the average citizen becomes a participant when he receives a traffic citation, or when he has to issue a complaint as the victim of a misdemeanor or felonious crime. The average citizen's contact with his local police will be agreeable or disagreeable, depending on the situation. Apathy may be changed to a positive or negative feeling by the relationship. However, contacts between the average citizen and police are few in number. A generalization can be drawn that the average citizen is functioning in a sea of apathy.

At the other extreme is the pressure group led by articulate individuals, or institutions that are responsible for review, criticism, and suggesting changes of police policy and procedures.

These pressure groups stage a direct ideological battle with the municipal police. It is felt that all areas of our government are subject to review and criticism, and certainly policing falls within this concept. Criticism is direct and often highly emotional.

Areas of criticism cover all aspects of municipal policing. To
name only a few, questions are raised concerning search and
seizure of evidence, methods of interrogation, constitutional rights,
and police brutality. In many of these areas changes have been
brought about in police practices by this discontent.

The police respond to this direct, blunt, and sometimes
enraged criticism with verbosity and emotion. Municipal policing
is often organizationally static. The basic police philosophy and
management have not changed in the past twenty-five years. While
most other organizations, private and public, have made changes--
some rather dynamic--of their organization's philosophies, goals,
and administrative methods to obtain these goals, police administrators have not. The municipal police is often not in step with
the community in which it functions in terms of service, attitudes,
and social norms. As a result, municipal police becomes defensive,
emotional and self-protective.

These are the primary positions taken by these three
interests. At the present time these positions are three atolls of
emotional self-interest which somehow must be united and directed
toward cooperative, objective and mutual understanding.

The nation has seen in recent times a greater awareness
of our municipal police on the part of the community. Civil unrest has brought the municipal police into conflict with many
individuals and groups. Riots have shaken the equilibrium of many
major cities, including New York, Los Angeles, Detroit, and
Chicago, to name only a few. All this conflict has left the police
visibly shaken in morale, poor recruitment, and increased employee
turnover.

To counteract this phenomenon municipal police have be-
gun in many cities a planned program to rebuild their public
image. However, in attempting to produce better community and
police relations and reopen lines of communication with the community most agencies are directly or indirectly resorting to propaganda techniques. Emphasis is placed on changing the attitudes
of the community, with little or no change in attitudes of the police.

Municipal police often ignore the social norms and mores
of the society they are serving. As governmental organs municipal
police agencies are governed by laws and regulations, but they are
also equally governed by the moral dictates of society. The
present philosophy of federal and state government is recognition
that laws and regulatory procedures are only a part of our social
involvement.

Possibly a better precept for police to follow would be
that we are first a nation of men and secondly a nation of laws.
Laws are meaningless without men to debate, legislate, judge,
interpret, and change if necessary. The common denominator is
man. Law is the end result of man's wants, vision, and destiny.
There are no bad laws, only bad lawmakers and enforcers.

Municipal police agencies are attempting to rebuild the
police image on a faulty foundation. Police administrators are
not properly evaluating the problem. The solution to this problem
is not one of police salesmanship and persuasion, but of proper
Social Evaluation. Contemporary police evaluation and definition
is urgently needed in areas of: the police role, philosophy of
policing, complete social representation by police, and the moral
obligation of police.

Without proper attention to these and similar questions
our cities may be rocked by greater and more devasting conflict
between police and community.

The charge of responsibility must be with the municipal
police. A fusion of community and police attitudes and positions
is paramount. A truly objective evaluation, understanding and
unity must be developed.

A New Approach to Police Administration

Municipal police administrators have made significant
advances in material and procedural techniques. Many administrators have developed expertise in deployment of personnel, radio
communication, and criminal investigation. If it were possible
to develop a statistical average of all municipal policing agencies,

we would find a very high rating for practical know-how.
Nevertheless, since there is relatively little research,
we can only formalize opinions and suggestions based upon experience and observation. At present we face the dilemma of not
being able to prove or disprove such basic inquiries as optimum
physical standards for policeman, one-man versus two-men automobile patrol, and promotional procedures. We are, in most
instances, making decisions based upon inadequate research or
trial and error methods.

It is my feeling that most policing agencies lack a dynamic
attitude towards such nonmaterial areas as administrative concepts,
organizational innovation, and a rational philosophy of law enforcement. Most police administrators can be described as archaic in
their philosophy and knowledge of the management of men and
institutions. Therefore, a "new" approach to police administration
will be discussed by borrowing from the social sciences attitudes
which are more closely related to our present complex society.

Stress must be placed on real administrative abilities and
not on a combination of primary law enforcement techniques and
secondary pseudo-managerial ability. The modern police administrator must understand concepts of executive leadership which are
being applied in private industrial organizations and many areas of
the federal government. It is no longer practical to use nineteenth
century concepts in dealing with municipal police organization any
more than it is practical to use nineteenth century expertise in
solving crimes. Many of the administrative concepts being used
today in policing organizations have been adopted and adapted from
philosophies of Adam Smith and his concern with specialization of
function; Max Weber's ideal concept of bureaucracy; and Frederich
Winslow Taylor's development of scientific management. Many
of the accepted authorities in law enforcement literature hitch their
wagons to organization structure and administrative procedure in
this traditional view of management. Traditional ideology reflects
formal organization as something to be graphically represented on
an organization chart; it proposes that authority comes from the top

down, demanding a narrow span of control, a centralization of
decision-making, and an impersonality of the organization and
members of the organization, and describes the organization
completely.

   We might continue to develop a listing of traditional concepts but these few will suffice for the present. It is now suggested that we literally unhitch this over-used and abused wagon of
administration and look for a more up-to-date vehicle. This is
not a denunciation of traditional concepts per se; to the contrary,
many of these concepts are very applicable today, but in a limited
way.

   New research in administration and organization have
questioned, negated, and neutralized many of the concepts which
are at present being verbalized by writers in law enforcement. A
possible reason why no attempt has been made to utilize newer
developments in administration and organization is the areas from
which the new research is coming. Research is developing from
disciplines which have been critical of law enforcement, and in
turn, law enforcement has been critical of these disciplines, which
include but are not limited to: sociology, psychology, anthropology,
political science and demography.

   Conflict, real or imagined, between law enforcement and
the behavioral sciences must be put aside. We face too many real
and imposing problems to let ecological attitudes turn us from the
problems of efficiently, economically, and socially-oriented municipal policing.

   Administrators must be selected on the basis of universal
administrative know-how. The problem many agencies now face
is that entrance promotional examinations are directed toward law
enforcement expertise and not administrative expertise. Most
agencies which are aware of the need for administrative ability
make the mistake of testing only on the basis of regurgitation of
managerial procedures found in their own departmental manuals.
The agency which tests for knowledge of this sort has developed
a closed-circuit technique for management inbreeding. This may be

another reason for the continuation of traditional concepts in law enforcement organization. The question might be raised at this point whether the number of municipal police officers continuing their education at two-year and four-year college and university law enforcement programs will introduce the newer concepts of administration and organization.

No, and for two reasons. Many law enforcement programs, and this is especially true at the two-year college level, do not introduce the newer administrative concepts; and the officers who have received an exposure to the new concepts are generally bound by present organizational pressures not to rock the boat. Thus, there is a built-in blockage of modern administrative techniques which might be introduced to law enforcement. It is interesting to note that this blockage does not apply to the introduction of the natural sciences into municipal policing. The introduction of criminalistics into policing has met resistance by some police organizations but only to a negligible degree. A possible reason for this acceptance may be the ability of present administrators to understand that not everyone in the agency can perform as a criminalist, that a person who is a "criminalist" must be educated in a very special way. Police administration must now be viewed in the same manner. The police administrator must be academically educated to perform his administrative function. Personnel can no longer be promoted from within police organizations to administrative positions exclusively on their talents as intelligent working field policemen with a knowledge of law and police techniques. Are we, in fact, now getting the best man to perform the administrative tasks? To answer this question we can look individually at our own related policing agencies.

In choosing a spark mechanism which would set into motion the engine of police organization, no better starting point could be selected than research and planning within the agency. (See Appendix D). Restrictions must be placed upon research and planning which will emphasize the objective and scientific methodology, and also preserve this function for bona fide fact-finding and rational decision making.

Research must not be prostituted in order to develop only conclusions which are favorable to the agency. Only academically educated personnel should be employed in such research. Familiarity with research methodology is equally as important as knowledge of past, present, and possibly future police trends.

With adequate research and planning, implementation and experimentation concerning police administrative leadership can be conducted. After testing administrative leadership attitudes from other governmental and private organizations, we may be in a better position to accept, alter, or totally reject these concepts as related to police work.

Innovation, of necessity, must follow research. Once we start looking inward we may become aware of more than a few inefficient, uneconomical, and socially disoriented patterns operating within the agency.

Policemen by training and work association, have developed characteristics of suspicion and skepticism. These characteristics are the ones most needed to initiate research and produce innovation. Innovation, in terms of change and alteration, has lagged badly in the areas of police administration and organization.

One area of possible change is in recruitment. Such basic questions as: what is a policeman? are present physical standards too restrictive? what are the functions of a policeman? what deployment methods are most effective? and many others relating to municipal policing might be resolved.

Innovations, or changes, are needed concerning level of entrance into the organization. Possibly the present method of recruitment only to the lowest level should be reconsidered in terms of present-day administrative knowledge. Some adaptations can be made in the light of recruitment practices being utilized by the military services. Also, the closed system for promotion can be reviewed. By selecting candidates for promotion from a closed system, are we getting the best man for the job to be filled?

Innovation is needed in terms of competition for personnel.
The present trend is toward college education of policemen and
prepolicemen. This is not a trend that is particularly descriptive
of law enforcement today but is a general trend of our American
society. If this trend continues, can police agencies compete
with private industry and other sections of local, state, and federal
government for personnel? In terms of our present unchanged administrative ideology we may be losing in the recruitment program.
Very seldom do municipal police agencies venture onto the college
campuses to recruit openly. The agency must change its organization structure to attract the talent which it most seriously needs,
i.e., administrative personnel. Salary increases and security
consciousness have too long been used to attract and hold employees.
Under newer concepts of administration the importance of these
factors has been questioned.

Now, after we have methodically questioned and criticized
most of the accepted planks of police administration and organization, we stand on the threshold of the most important development of policing in the twentieth century: the development of a
rational philosophy of municipal law enforcement which reflects
present social needs.

Within the development of such a philosophy a position
should be taken to state publicly an intelligent strategy for law
enforcement which is acceptable on a national scale. In creating
such a philosophy, or bill of responsibility for law enforcement,
within the parameters of social desires and acceptance, will be
found the embryo-mutation of professional policing. We may think
of policing today as being professional, but in terms of the medical
profession, theology, and law, it falls well short of the mark.
However, with a philosophical unification we may truly become
professional in every sense of the word.

Planning is nothing more than preparing for the future in
terms of present knowledge and anticipations. Planning is not a
new innovation in law enforcement. Planning according to needs

and desires of the department have been performed in the past in
a multitude of ways which can best be categorized as "informal"
in character.

Formal methods of planning have been accepted by private
as well as public business and postulated by the social sciences.
The first step necessary to institute a "formal" approach to planning is to develop the physical and psychological attitudes necessary
for such a venture.

Physical

The development of a staff for conducting planning is
needed. This staff may be either ad hoc, made up of members
of the police agency as part-time planners; or an on-going staff
consisting of members of the department assigned full-time to
the responsibility of planning. Other physical paraphernalia
consist of adequate office space, furniture, typewriters and cal-
culators, and secreterial personnel. The planning office and
personnel should be removed, in terms of accessibility, from
other units in the police department. Influence, pressure, and
ridicule directed toward the planning staff must carefully be avoided. By developing a notion of hierarchical status and by reducing
the opportunity for contact and accessibility with other members
of the agency, many initial problems can be eliminated.

Psychological

A proper psychological position would be the development
of an awareness or need on the part of the department for "formal"
planning. The psychological position would also relate to the type
and characteristics of the personnel who will function in this activity. It is highly desirable that they possess skills beyond those
required of law enforcement. Examples of such skills are: a
thorough background in one or several disciplines of the behavioral
sciences; the ability to understand, interpret, and use statistical
data; and the capability to grasp proposed ideas in relationship to
existing agency policy and procedures. What is being suggested is

that formal planning personnel be able to remove themselves from
day-to-day activities of law enforcement and develop a critical
attitude in viewing and reviewing all activities of the agency.

Conclusion

The administrative qualities of municipal police agencies
must be reviewed in terms of: executive leadership, delegation of
decision-making responsibility, and the position of research and
planning in the fashion of the natural and behavioral science methodology. Organizational innovation must be assayed in such practical
applications as recruitment, lines of promotion, and entrance requirements. It is paramount that a rational philosophy of law
enforcement be developed which reflects the present social needs
on a broad scale, not a localized one. And lastly, municipal law
enforcement must develop a position of intellectual strategy for
police administration which is efficient, economical, and socially
oriented.

Notes

1. Eisentadt, S. N. "Bureaucracy, Bureaucratization, and
    Debureaucratization" Administrative Science Quarterly,
    Dec. 1959, pp. 302-320.

2. Eisenstadt, S. N. "Bureaucracy and Bureaucratization,"
    Current Sociology, 1958.

3. Ibid.

4. Ibid.

5. Ibid.

6. Udy, Stanley H. "Bureaucracy and Rationality in Weber's
    Organization Theory; and Empirical Study," American
    Sociological Review, 1959.

7. Presthus, Robert V. "The Social Basis of Bureaucratic
    Organization," Social Forces, Dec. 1959, pp. 103-109.

8. Ibid.

9. Presthus, Robert V. "Weberian vs. Welfare Bureaucracy
    in Traditional Society," Administrative Science Quarterly,
    June 1961, pp. 1-24.

10. McNulty, James E. "Organizational Change in Growing
    Enterprises," Administrative Science Quarterly,
    June 1962, pp. 1-21.

V. Police Personnel

The major dilemma in selecting personnel for a government agency is whether to fill positions or occupational categories from one area or many areas. As Stahl indicates "...attention should be turned to all practical sources of candidates whether inside or outside the service." [1]

Significance of the Problem

In its initial recruitment an agency is not concerned to a great degree with the morale of the recruitment universe. However, for promotional purposes, morale becomes a dramatic personnel problem. Selection of personnel has characteristically been from outside the government service at the lower levels of various occupational areas, leaving the higher positions to be filled generally from within the service. A major trend indicates a basic attitude that recruitment outside the particular service is undesirable except at the beginning levels of the employment structure.

Some highly inbred agencies have taken great pains to maintain the closed promotion-from-within policy. It is significant that many of these agencies are far from the best-run and productive agencies in their respective jurisdictions. [2]

This is not to refute the importance of selection by promotion. Rather, it demands careful analysis of methods and goals and the avoidance of an oversimplified concept of promotion which results in little more than the progressive advancement of mediocrity. [3]

For centuries, the closed personnel system has been a chronic area of difficulty in the military service. Closed systems have often been advocated on the concept that the most effective recruiting at lower levels could only be achieved if the upper positions were reserved for those who can be promoted from below. The service would become unattractive to younger recruits if it were known to discriminate against its own people in making promotions at

82

Personnel

the higher levels. Recruitment from outside at higher levels
might also arouse suspicions of influence or corruption, whether
such existed or not. It has to be pointed out that those already
on the inside would have many advantages in obtaining promotions
to advanced positions in any fair competition. Protection against
all competition from the recruitment universe in the intermediate
and higher positions might lead to mediocrity and sterility unless
the closed type of system is managed with care.[4]

A negative factor limiting the span of personnel selection
for promotion in many law enforcement agencies has been the
propensity to view personnel only in terms of original entrance
job classifications. The emphasis is placed upon existing skills
needed for the particular original work assignment rather than for
future needs and abilities. Traditionally, the philosophy has been
to fill positions which are often highly specialized without much
regard to promotional advancement. Qualifications are established
and a testing instrument devised which is related to requirements
of the particular position to be filled. This procedure limits the
possibility of obtaining desirable personnel from within for administrative positions. Another negative factor related to promotion is
the restriction of competition for an advanced area within the
agency.[5]

Advantages

Advantages of a closed personnel system might include:
the ability to maintain a particular image, which is more easily
perpetuated by selection from within; high morale; low personnel
turnover; and greater control within the agency by top administrators (tradition, philosophy, and goals).

Unlike the closed personnel system, an open system is
said to offer a larger universe for selection, on the theory that
competition produces a better ultimate choice. However, an
apparent disadvantage of an open system might be low personnel
morale and high turnover.

84   Police Administration

Definitions of Terms Used

Open selective system. Entry can be achieved at almost
any level of rank or job classification, resulting in an infusion
of new personnel and ideas at levels where they are likely to count
and with as much opportunity for advancement as any other member
of the agency.[6]

Closed selective system. The system of low entrance age
and the filling of higher positions almost entirely from within the
agency. An example of such a selective system would be the
officer corps of each of the military services, except in time of
war. They are almost totally replenished by new junior officers
at the second lieutenant or ensign rank, with little insertion at
middle or senior levels.[7]

Personnel system. A personnel system is one which is
established by statute or ordinance, by constitution or charter
provision, and which implies that there is a clearly defined
responsibility for personnel management. Also, it implies that,
when justified by the size of the agency, one or more persons
devote substantially full time to these activities, whatever their
job title.[8]

Executive. The term will be defined, as used in the sociology of formal organizations of any sort, to designate the functions
of deliberate control, management, supervision, and administration,
the people who perform such functions, the positions they occupy,
and the sector of the large organization in which they are found.[9]

Career executive. A series of adjustments made by an
individual who functions as an executive in formal organizations,
institutions, or informal social relationships involved in the occupation, or sequence of occupations, which make up the work
history of a person.[10]

Career Service. The term career service in its strict
sense refers to a system of employment of young people at beginning level jobs and planned progression to positions of greater
responsibility and higher pay until their retirement.[11]

History of Personnel Administration

Specifically, very little attention has been directed toward the peculiar problems of selecting, promoting, and training higher level managers and to the effect these personnel have upon the agency.

> There is a negligible amount of study of the special problems of personnel management in government. Even though the federal government is the principle supporter of social science research throughout the country, there is virtually no in-house personnel research except that conducted by the military departments on military personnel. The in-house research conducted by the U.S. Civil Service Commission and also by the Canadian Civil Service Commission is on a very small scale, and mostly on testing and rating for selection.[12]

Some investigators feel that some organizations have been constituted a forbidden territory because of the reluctance of administrators to endorse research which might be unflattering to their agencies or to themselves.[13]

The Civil Service Commission sets general standards and boundaries for guidance, but in actuality, agencies have been left free to conduct personnel operations. Compliance to legal requirements, rules, and regulations are examined by periodic personnel inspections.[14]

The Commission has assumed the additional responsibility in recent years of giving renewed importance to career development and training at the federal government level.

> A statement of federal training policy developed by the Commission was issued by direction of the President in 1955, and the Commission's continuing efforts in this area culminated in the enactment of the new Government Employees Training Act in 1958.[15]

However, as pointed out by Mosher,[16] the civil service system was only one of three systems for selecting personnel utilized by the government. First is the system of political appointments. The contemporary meaning of "political appointment" is generally related to a top policy position rather than to party politics. Usually there is a lack of job security and high turnover. The

remaining two personnel systems are career systems and civil
service systems. Traditionally and philosophically these two systems are separated. An increasing refinement of the career system, as exemplified by the military services, clearly portrays
the differences of the two systems.

The Career System

In the career service, emphasis has been placed upon
recruitment of personnel immediately following the candidates'
education and at a young entrance age. The entrance examination
tests for requirements of the position being applied for and also
for potential of the examinee. Once admitted to the service,
through testing procedures and final personnel selection, the individual can expect a gradual and progressive movement through job
assignments. This upward trend within the agency has not meant
total job security. If the individual has failed to perform in
accordance with the limits set by the agency, his career can be
blocked or possibly terminated. Competition between personnel
holding the same rank within the agency has been fairly severe.
Career service personnel are insulated from outside competition,
but if they have failed to meet the requirements in some way, they
may be removed from the service by a process that is called
"selection out." In a closed system this "selection out" is in
effect a forced premature resignation from the service. As in
the military service and the Foreign Service, officers, upon
reaching a moderately high rank, must have either met certain
standards of the service to permit further promotion or be retired
from the service.

The successful rank is not determined by the position,
but the rank may control or at least influence position assignments.

The Civil Service System

The traditional civil service system is quite the opposite
of the career system. Recruitment of personnel is usually at any
educational or age level, and is directed toward a specific job clas-

Personnel   87

sification or work assignment. There is no assurance of steady
advancement within the agency. Some personnel have progressed
from one job to another, leading to higher responsibility. Transfer
between agencies may or may not be allowed. Civil servants may
have obtained experience in several agencies in their climb to higher positions. Rank, status, or pay level is usually determined
by the difficulty of the job and not the ability of the individual.

A study conducted by the U.S. Civil Service Commission showed
that federal executives in most instances start in the service at
the beginning job classification at grade GS-6 or lower and spend
most of their employable life in one agency.[17] In direct conflict
with this Civil Service study was a statement made by Warner
that "...two-thirds of the career executives have been associated
with two or more government departments, public agencies, or
private organizations."[18]

A study conducted by Warner[19] investigated 7,640 Federal
career civil servant executives at the GS-14 level and above.
The study indicated that education is a basic requirement for career
executives in that 78% of these personnel are college graduates, with
approximately one in ten attaining the doctorate degree. Warner
further pointed out that government at the higher levels is an
environment dominated by professionally trained men.

Criticism of the Career System

Ginzberg[20] indicated that changes in the rules are needed
if levels of qualified personnel are to be maintained in the public
service.

The modern career system has attempted to combine the
principles of belonging, status, advancement, and planning of
personnel needs. The American Assembly study indicated that the
concept of belonging, in many ways the most necessary of the four,
is undermined to the degree that status distinctions and planned
progression are stressed. Belonging, then, has become "belonging
with a difference," and is comparable to second class citizenship
for those who are not in the mainstream of career advancement.[21]

An illustrative example is that of the Foreign Service.
In the Foreign Service there are two major divisions. Separate
positions of Foreign Service staff officer (FSS) and Foreign Service
officer (FSO) exist. Many of the FSS's have responsibilities, experience, and achievements which are equal to the FSO's. Both areas
are equally exposed to risk and hardship. However, the FSO's
have superior social and diplomatic status, and a recognized claim
to promotion to the higher levels of the service. Clearly, the
staff officers do not belong in any sense of the word, and problems
of coordination and poor working relations result.

A similar situation exists in the military with the distinction between the military regulars (officers graduated from a military
academy) and reserve officers.

This typically closed system has been described as being
unsatisfactory when recruiting and selecting for advanced positions
within the agency begins at the lower levels. David and Pollock[22]
stressed that this emphasized the need for more effective selection
at junior levels, and possibly top levels, and a refinement of the
promotional system. The American Assembly in 1954 stated:

> The Federal career system should be cut to the
> pattern of American customs and institutions. A
> closed, self-contained system is not in the American
> tradition. The Federal service should provide both
> for promotion from within and for the lateral entry
> of personnel, particularly in the middle and higher
> grades. It should be open to interchange with the
> other fields of American life: business, trade unions,
> universities, the professions, state and local govern-
> ments. Such exchanges benefit both the Federal service
> and these groups, and our society is the richer. Efforts
> to close the door on such interchange should be vigorously
> resisted.[23]

There appears to be a need for change in personnel selection within well-established career-oriented agencies. A policy
that combines promotion from within with an open type career system seems to be the only policy that can be followed consistently
and effectively under changing conditions of public goals, philosophy,
and political transition. Open career systems that are deliberately
planned with ample opportunity for entry at intermediate levels could

absorb substantial numbers of personnel with little change in
agency operations.   They are much more amenable than closed
career systems to the readjustments that might become necessary
in any time of political transitions, as well as adjustments that
become necessary when temporary activities are either liquidated
or made permanent.[24]

    This attitude of change in the selection process permeates
personnel literature. Litchfield[25] wrote that recruitment methods
should be revised, that selection practices of personnel were too
rigid, and that the old doctrines needed substantial change in
recruitment at the middle or later years of career life.

    There has been growing sentiment among writers in
personnel areas that the career system should draw upon university
trained recruits, with lateral entry to provide a constantly re-
invigorated fresh outlook on the part of the agency.[26]

Criticism of the Civil Service System

    In viewing the civil service system it is necessary to
explore the importance of "openness" of competition. Once an
examination is given and a list of names developed, it usually
continues in force until it is exhausted. The list may be effective
for months or possibly years. Person who might become qualified
and interested after the examination has been given cannot compete
again until the current listing has expired. The list might stand
until the most minimally acceptable candidate is selected, while
higher qualified individuals are waiting to take the qualification
tests. Possibly better qualified persons would thus not be employed.

    The American Assembly[27] reported that "a major reason
why the Federal Service fails to attract the talent which its work
requires is that it recruits for jobs rather than for careers. Selection which emphasizes immediate job position has several disadvantages. First, it offers much less to the person applying, in that
it presents only a few tasks to be performed which are related to
the specific job. Secondly, the emphasis being placed upon specific

knowledge and ability neglects the need for future growth, motivation, and agency utilization of administrative talents.

In 1959 the Federal Merit Promotion Program was initiated. Prior to the program the Civil Service Commission conducted a survey which showed that there was definitely a need for revision in the selection process in the federal service. It also showed that successful progress was dependent upon flexibility and adaptability to varying personnel needs in the government service. The Commission's attack on this problem emphasized principles rather than procedures.[28]

Change has been taking place in the civil service. One area of change has been in the interchange of personnel between established agencies. Acting under a provision added to the Civil Service Rules in 1955, the Commission has approved standards for identifying equivalent independent merit systems in the executive branch of government that were not part of the competitive service. These standards emphasized basic principles rather than processes, so that systems which differed in operating procedures might be recognized providing they achieved basic merit-system objectives.[29] In 1957, the Commission reached interchange agreements with the Atomic Energy Commission and the Tennessee Valley Authority providing for free movement of qualified employees between these two agencies and the competitive service.

Another change was a significant departure from the traditional civil service system concept made in 1957. The Commission authorized the establishment of the Air Reserve Technician Plan. This plan was unique in that civilians were employed in jobs that they would fill in a military capacity should they be called to active duty. One result of the plan was that jobs that would otherwise be filled by active duty military personnel were made available to civilians, which allowed Air Force personnel to be released for assignment to active duty organizations. The selection of personnel for these positions followed normal civil service procedures, including open competitive examinations.

The Commission has tried to increase the prestige of the service. Prestige as an accepted attribute of government service was important to the morale of the employee.

The first Hoover Commission suggested that procedures to facilitate the promotion of career employees be worked out within the individual departments, that administrative positions be more clearly identified for career possibilities, and that the Civil Service Commission facilitate transfer of competent career personnel from one agency to another.[30]

The Closed Personnel System as Opposed to
The Open System at the City Level of Government

The International City Managers' Association indicated that selection of personnel at the city level of government, using civil service rules and procedures, would utilize practical open competitive examinations with appointment on the basis of grade rank.[31]

The following is based on the Model State Civil Service Law prepared by the Public Administration Services and the League of California Cities. Personnel rules and regulations for a closed system at the municipal level would exhibit the following selection characteristics in the areas of entrance, promotions, and appointments:

1. Competitive examination. All applicants for positions in the classified service are to be subject to competitive examination. All such tests are either assembled or unassembled as provided for in these rules.

2. Rating examinations. Sound measurement techniques and procedures are used in rating the results of tests and determining the relative ranking of the candidates. The final earned rating of a competitor is determined by averaging the earned rating on each part of the examination in accordance with the weights established for each part prior to the date of the examination and announced in the public notice of the examination.

3. <u>Promotion policy.</u> Vacancies in positions above the lowest rank in any category are filled as far as practical by the lowest rank in any category and as far as practical by the promotion of employees in the service. The personnel officer in each case determines whether an open competitive examination or a promotional examination would best serve the interests of the service in attracting well-qualified candidates.

4. <u>Promotional examinations.</u> The term "promotional examination" signifies a fitness test to determine the relative standing of applicants for positions in the specific class. Promotional examinations are open only to employees in the classified service who are serving in other specified classes for such a period as is prescribed by the personnel officer. A promotional examination might include employees in specific classes in all departments or only in the department for which the eligible list is being established.

5. <u>Notification.</u> Notice of promotional examinations is published and posted in departments in which eligibles are employed.

6. <u>Types of promotional examinations.</u> Promotional examinations will consist of the same type of tests as are prescribed for entrance examinations. Credit for seniority is given by adding a percentage to the final score of a contestant.

7. <u>Promotion without examination.</u> Promotion of an eligible employee is made without competition upon presentation by the department head of a written statement showing that the duties performed by the employee nominated are natural preparation for the higher position, that such employee is entitled to promotion by reason of service and effective performance, and that no other employee of the department

meets the foregoing conditions.

8. <u>Types of appointments.</u> The following types of appointments might be made to the service in conformity with the rules established.

a. <u>Permanent employees.</u> A permanent employee who works full-time and on a continuing basis. He is subject to all rules and regulations and receives all benefits and rights as provided by the personnel ordinance and rules and regulations.

b. <u>Seasonal employees.</u> These employees are appointed in the same manner and are subject to the same procedures as permanent employees except that they are laid off at the close of the season for which they have been appointed.

c. <u>Student appointments.</u> Student appointments afford students an opportunity to gain actual work experience. Such appointments are for a definite period of time, not to exceed 12 months.

d. <u>Emergency appointments.</u> In order to prevent stoppage of public business or serious inconvenience to the public, appointment of employees on a temporary basis may be authorized.

e. <u>Provisional appointments.</u> When no eligible list exists for the vacancy, a person may be appointed to the position on a provisional basis.

f. <u>Part-time employees.</u> Part-time employees are employees who work less than the normal work week, but on a regular basis.

g. <u>Limited-term appointments.</u> Limited-term appointments are made when a special project requires the addition of employees for a specific time, or to fill a position of an employee on a leave of absence.[32]

Kingsley[33] indicated that in a career service system it is
necessary to select personnel with "a view to promotion and to the
level they may be expected ultimately to reach." He also took the
position that it was not enough to relate educational requirements
only to the requirements of the entrance level. Nigro[34] critisized
the "closed examination" as being an antiquated device which has
been a disadvantage to recruiting of personnel. He made reference
to examinations with fixed closing dates for filing, after which no
further applications were to be accepted. The result was that the
list of eligibles would be used to fill current vacancies as well as
future vacancies which might occur during the life of the list.

Lateral Entry

Lateral entry has been introduced throughout the literature
as a means to obtain a better selection of personnel at all levels
of governmental positions. Warner[35] conducted an investigation
of 10,851 executives in top administrative positions in government
and produced the following findings:

1. Lateral entry above the lowest levels was more
    characteristic than not among those who rise to the
    highest levels in the civilian services of our national
    government.

2. Interorganizational movement has been much more
    characteristic of civilian federal executives than of
    business executives and the military. Contrary to
    some assumptions, this was true of executives as
    well as at lower levels.

3. Experience in private enterprise has been a positive
    asset to civilian federal executives in their rise to
    high position.

4. Similarly, interorganizational movement within govern-
    ment itself has been an asset to a career as a
    civilian federal executive.

5. The effects of this kind of movement to some extent

varied with the type of organization entered during
a civilian federal executive's career.

6. The movement from one government agency to
    another was not felt by civilians to be of as much
    consequence as movement from one business firm
    or military service to another.

At the military level officers showed the least tendency
toward more than single organization mobility. These personnel
were, in overwhelming proportions, educated in military science
at the various academies, entered the service young, and tended
to stay within the first organization they entered.

In comparison to military personnel, civilian personnel
at the federal level moved from one organization to another four
or five times in their career. However, the movement by civilian
personnel from one government agency to another was not of as
much consequence as movement from one military service to
another.

It was indicated by the Warner study that interorganizational
mobility was not the same for all personnel groups. Within the
civilian and military federal services, the effect of lateral entry
was somewhat complicated.

The study indicated that some organizational mobility was
good for career development but that seven or more moves had a
retarding effect upon the individual's career. Four to six moves
were advantageous to career civil servants and to those in the
foreign service.

Lateral entry into the various governmental organizations
appeared to reduce considerably the number of years personnel
had to serve in order to achieve advanced positions. Where lateral
entry had been preceded by experience in a relative employment
area, movement was accelerated. Many of the civilian personnel
moved into the government service after achieving some degree
of professional or occupational status in other organizations.[36]

Jones also indicated a need for lateral entry and the
ability to move from one organization to another:

Furthermore, we need to develop a system which
will permit entry into the career service in the
middle and higher grades; by selective and competitive recruitment, but not necessarily by nationwide
open competition. The best of companies does not
train all its top people within its own organization.
It can't foresee every need. Neither can government.[37]

The American Assembly directed some of its attention
toward the concept of lateral entry. It was felt that government
service would be improved if the practice were more frequent.
This paper also favored the transfer of top personnel within the
government on a systematic and planned basis.[38]

Turnover of Personnel

The concept of personnel turnover is an adaptation from
the field of merchandising. It is discussed in terms of the gross
movement of people into and out of active employment status. The
index of this movement is the measurement of labor turnover known
as the turnover rate. Turnover is one of the few readily measura-
ble indicators of personnel instability. It has been described by
Scheer[39] as one of the best tests of relative value of personnel
relations, policies, and practices within an agency.

From Boyd's[40] article concerning personnel turnover the
following generalizations were made:

1. In understanding the cause of turnover it was
    evident that there are some little known problems
    of compatibility between organizations and individuals.

2. In addition to its recognized effect on costs and
    efficiency, turnover might have an unrecognized
    effect on the character of the stream of manpower
    replacements. This could eventually alter the com-
    position of the organization or, alternatively, re-
    quire relatively costly and unsatisfactory compensa-
    ting action by way of recruiting a large proportion
    of personnel.

3. More knowledge is required about the causes and

effects of turnover in general and also in particular organizations. Still more important is an
understanding of the composition of members
which an organization needed to accomplish its
objectives effectively. This by no means implies
conforming to a single "type" of employee. It
is more likely that a scientifically built organization would incorporate a wide variety of
abilities, interests and points of view.

4. An organization might find that it must adapt itself
to the needs of the kind of members it requires.
We have been accustomed to organizations offering
inducements such as high salaries and generous
benefits in order to attract and maintain membership. In most other respects, however, we think
of individuals adapting themselves to the life of
the organization rather than the reverse. But it
is evident that the adaptation should be genuinely
a two-way affair. An organization's management
climate, the boundaries of its jobs, etc., determined whether the people who could best do its
work were going to be willing to live within it.

5. Research methods provide ways of identifying
critical factors ralated to living and working
effectively in organizations.

The three standard methods of computing turnover are
based on accessions, replacements or separations. In any com-
putation, the rate is generally described as the number of accessions, replacements, or terminations per month per one hundred
of the personnel force. Terms used could be defined as: (1) ac-
cessions--the hiring of new personnel or the rehiring of former
organization personnel; (2) replacements--persons hired to fill
vacancies caused by terminations; and (2) separations--including all
quits, layoffs, and discharges. The formula for computing turn-

over is the average number of personnel during the month or year.

This gives the turnover rate for the month or year. The formula
is expressed as follows:[41]

$$\text{personnel turnover rate} = \frac{\text{number of separations (month or year)}}{\text{average number of personnel on payroll}}$$

Brenneman indicated that there is good turnover control
when the annual total resignations and dismissals are less than
12 percent of the average total employees, including supervisory
and administrative personnel.[42]

Police Personnel Administration

Vollmer indicated that the purpose of a policing organization for the most part deals with the actions and behavior of
human beings. He further indicated that there are at least four
different types of criminal behavior: (1) major crimes--felonious
homicide, rape, etc.; (2) offenses against public morals--vice,
gambling, etc.; (3) offenses which have to do with the maintenance
of peace--disorderly conduct, etc.; and (4) violations of traffic and
other regulations, licensing, inspections, etc.[43]

According to the International City Managers' Association,[44]
in addition to being a law enforcing agency the modern police
department, especially in California, has taken on a broader responsibility and has become involved in the following activities:

1. The prevention of criminality. This is one of the
     newer responsibilities of the police. It is more
     and more clearly realized that a constructive
     approach to the crime problem must go to its very
     roots, to the factors in community life which created
     criminal tendencies and led the criminal to indulge
     in antisocial behavior. There has been a need for
     studies of actual cases to determine the causes that
     led to delinquency, and on the basis of the facts,
     for efforts to eradicate the causes.

2. <u>Repression of Crime.</u> This is a function more firm-
   ly embedded in police practice. Adequate patrol
   plus continuous effort toward eliminating or reducing
   hazards is stressed as a means of reducing the
   opportunities for criminal activity.

3. <u>Apprehension of offenders.</u> Quick apprehension and
   certain punishment discourage the would-be offender
   by making the consequence of crime seem less
   pleasant. In addition to its repressive influence,
   apprehension enables society to punish offenders, to
   prevent a repetition of their offenses by restraining
   their movements, and to provide an opportunity for
   their rehabilitation.

4. <u>Recovery of property.</u> This is an activity intended
   to reduce the money cost of crime, as well as to
   restrain those who, though not active criminals,
   might benefit from the gains of crime.

5. <u>Regulation of noncriminal conduct.</u> Many police
   activities are concerned only incidentally with
   criminal behavior. Their main purpose is regulation,
   apprehension, and punishment of offenders. Other
   methods used to obtain compliance are education of
   the public to the dangers inherent in the disobedience
   of regulations, and the use of warnings.

Qualifications for police agency personnel are the responsibility of the policing agency and the central personnel agency.
The central personnel agency will work closely with the police administrator and the department personnel officer in determining
desirable qualifications for police work. The knowledge of the
police department is combined with the specialized ability of the
central personnel agency regarding personnel aptitudes and abilities,
and testing techniques, to select employees who have a high
probability of success on the job.[45]

Indicators of job success are:[46]

1. <u>Intelligence.</u> Some type of intelligence testing should be utilized.

2. <u>Education.</u> At present, many cities require applicants for police work to have a high school education. Additional cities would adopt this requirement were it not for charter provisions which prohibit a formal educational standard. There is every reason to believe that the educational requirements will gradually be raised.

3. <u>Experience.</u> Only under exceptional circumstances is there justification for requiring experience of applicants for entrance level police positions.

4. <u>Personality.</u> No single personality type, or more properly no single pattern of personality traits, is singled out as most desirable for police work. What is wanted is a well-adjusted personality, free of extreme or marked traits.

5. <u>Physical attributes.</u> To have a high probability of success a police candidate should have met the following standards:

   a. Physical condition must be excellent.

   b. Physical agility and strength equal at least to the average possessed by high school seniors is required.

   c. Height requirements for police candidates have a psychological rather than a medical basis.

6. <u>Character and reputation.</u> A policeman's character and reputation must be of the highest order.

The International City Managers' Association indicates that promotion has been one of the strong career attractions of the police service for the young man, with the opportunity to rise through the ranks. The chances for promotion are, however, only about one in five in the smaller cities and as low as one in ten in large cities.[47]

The characteristics of promotion for municipal police
personnel were indicated as follows:[48]

1. Promotion is limited to about 8 to 20 percent of
    all employees who entered at the bottom of the
    scale. A few will have been promoted from within
    the service, but the majority will have remained at
    the bottom grade with their advancement being
    limited to within-the-range salary increases.

2. In filling the higher posts in the department there
    are differences of opinion and practice concerning
    the relative value of making promotions entirely
    from within the department or opening the top
    positions to competition by qualified nonresidents.
    Strong opposition often developed from within the
    police force and from the groups advocating a
    closed system, but the trend is definitely in the
    direction of the broader base.

3. As a prerequisite for promotion, some departments
    require a minimum number of years of police exper-
    ience, or a minimum number of years of experience
    in the next lower class, or a combination of both.

4. In contrast to written tests used in original selection,
    the promotional written tests emphasize measurement
    of the candidates' factual knowledge regarding police
    work rather than aptitudes for learning police work.
    The importance of written tests in promotional
    examinations is somewhat less than in the original
    selection of patrolmen.

In a study by Marsh[49] which investigated the selection
process of deputy sheriffs, the attempt was made to determine the
extent to which predictors of job success could be identified. His
data were obtained by studying 619 men who were appointed deputy
sheriffs as a result of civil service examinations conducted between
1947 and 1950. It was found that the success ratio of employees
whose written scores were at the very top of the scale was striking-

ly high. However, it was also discovered that there was a higher
turnover for the personnel at this level.

Criticism of the Specific Agency

At the municipal level of government Stanley[50] indicates
that there are three main areas for concern: (1) recruitment--
the need for more funds, more expert staff, more advanced
programing of the city government's recruiting efforts, and the
need to set up more jobs that can be filled by young college
graduates without work experience; (2) selection--the slowness
of the regular civil service examining process, the lack of
flexibility in the certification process, the narrowness and
rigidity of promotion methods, and the barriers to interagency
transfers; and (3) training--the need to move so much farther
and faster in the training of personnel to keep up professionally,
the development of the leaders of the future in professional, technical, and managerial fields.

Pfiffner has described the police function as:

...ages old and has undergone modification to meet
changing social needs. The full-time paid police
operation as we know it today is essentially a product
of the industrial revolution, prior to which folk policing
was the rule... The point to be made here is that the
police subculture still possesses a set of values,
standards and job goals more appropriate to the days
of public hangings than to a society which is making
some progress toward ameliorating the lot of those
who for one reason or another have not adjusted to
the demands of society.[51]

Pfiffner notes also a distrust on the part of police toward
those who might be in a more professional position to view the
police function.

There can sometimes be detected a mutual suspicion
and antagonism between the police and social scientists.
The police have for the most part been pragmatic and
empirical in their approach to problem solving, being
more interested in what works now than in long range
theoretical answers. They are typically defensive toward those who would investigate their operations and
practices, as are all bureaucracies.[52]

Turnover: The concept of the police service is that recruiting
should be directed toward young men before they have established
themselves in another vocation. The turnover rate, therefore,
will probably be lower, since younger men without training in
other fields are less likely to be enticed into other areas of
employment.[53]

Analysis of the Los Angeles Police Department

It was found that the State constitution authorizes a charter
for the City of Los Angeles which provides for the regulation of
a municipal police force. The charter described is in the following legal provisions:

1. Article XI, Section 8 1/2, of the Constitution of
   the State of California, authorizes the City of Los
   Angeles to provide for a board of police commissioners and municipal police force.

2. The Police Commission is declared to be the
   "Head of the Department."

   a. Police Commission executive power.

      1) The general executive powers and duties of
         Police Commission are to: supervise, control,
         regulate, and manage the department and to
         make and enforce all necessary rules and
         regulations thereof and for the exercise of
         the powers conferred upon the department by
         this charter.

   b. The chief administrative officer.

      1) The chief administrative officer of the Police
         Department shall be known as the Chief of
         Police of the Police Department, who shall
         be appointed by, and may be removed by,
         the Board of Police Commissioners.

   c. Administrative powers and duties of the Chief
      of Police.

      1) Subject to the provisions of charter, the
         rules of the Department and the instructions
         of his board, the chief shall:

         a) Administer the affairs of the department as
            its chief administrative officer

b) Appoint, discharge, suspend, or transfer
   employees of the department, all subject
   to the Civil Service provisions of the
   charter.

c) To expend the funds of the department,
   recommend a budget, and certify all
   expenditures.

Rules and standards regarding leaves of absence policy
under the City Charter of Los Angeles indicated that it would be
the policy of the City to disapprove requests for leaves of absence
in the following areas:

1. Upon transfer from one department, bureau or
   major division to a position in another department,
   bureau or major division.

2. To engage in private employment.

3. To accept a position with another government
   agency.

4. To engage in political activity.

A survey of the Los Angeles Police Department Manual
indicated the following organizations and functions of the Personnel
and Training Bureau:

1. The Personnel and Training Bureau has
   responsibility for the induction, training, and
   placement of Department employees, and for the
   handling of those personnel services necessary to
   regulate and to guide an employee throughout his
   period of service with the Department.

2. Administration of all Department personnel services.

   a. Recruitment and induction of Department
      employees.

   b. Employment investigation.

   c. Personnel distribution and assignment.

   d. Personnel counseling.

3. Bureau commander acts in an advisory capacity
   to the Chief of Police, and exercises staff
   responsibility over all personnel and training

matters within the Department.

4. Administrative duties:

    a. Administration and interpretation of intelligence and temperament scale tests.

    b. Issuance of permits for outside employment to employees.

    c. Collection of moneys received by officers as rewards, contributions, or as witness fees, and arranging for the proper transmittal of the moneys to the appropriate City or Fire and Police Pension Funds.

    d. Maintenance of files of the following information:

        1) Department personnel rating reports.

        2) Permits for outside employment.

        3) Intelligence and temperament scale tests given to employees.

5. Compilation and issuance of assignment and transfer lists, deploying employees throughout the department, as designated by the Department's table of organization.

6. Interviewing and processing of new candidates.

    a. Determination of the availability of a candidate for employment.

    b. Pre-employment medical examination.

    c. Background investigations.

7. Coordinate activities pertaining to the recruitment, employment, and processing of Department employees.

8. Processing and screening of applicants for civilian employment, and maintenance of a civilian position control system.

    a. Interviewing of applicants certified from Civil Service lists, recommending appointment or rejections.

9. A supervisory and specialized training section responsible for the following:

   a. Courses designed to improve performance at all supervisory levels.

   b. Courses designed to increase the technical skill and efficiency of officers assigned to or preparing for specialized duties.

   c. Courses designed to increase the technical skill and efficiency of civilian personnel.

   d. Research in the development of law enforcement techniques.

10. The order of rank in the Department, as established by the Civil Service Commission, shall be as follows:

   a. Chief of Police

   b. Deputy chief of police

   c. Inspector of police

   d. Captain

   e. Lieutenant

   f. Sergeant

   g. Policeman

Table I

Requirements for Promotion, Duties, and Qualifications
For Los Angeles Police Personnel, 1964

Rank	Requirements	Duties
Sergeant	1. Four years of experience as policeman in the Los Angeles Police Department 2. Valid Class D drivers License	1. Immediate charge of policemen or civilian employees 2. Supervises and instructs subordinates as to their assigned duties 3. Initial and follow-up investigation of crimes 4. Surveillance work to detect or prevent crime
Lieutenant	1. Two years of experience as sergeant in the L.A.P.D.	1. Has charge of activities of a tour of duty in a division or investigation unit 2. Interprets orders, directives, and exercises supervision
Captain	1. Two years of experience as lieutenant in the L.A.P.D.	1. Commands a geographical or specialized division 2. Uses own discretion in application of department policy and procedure 3. Develops new practices and procedures
Inspector	1. Two years of experience as captain in the L.A.P.D.	1. Commands an area 2. Assistant commander of a bureau 3. Conducts studies and surveys 4. Recommends change
Deputy Chief	1. Four years of experience as captain or inspector of police in the L.A.P.D.	1. Directs the activities of a bureau 2. Member of the Chief's general staff

Table II

Requirements for Promotion, Duties, and Qualifications
For Los Angeles Police Personnel, 1964

Rank	Qualifications (examination)	Seniority Credit
Sergeant	1. Knowledge of criminal law 2. A working knowledge of the organization, functions, responsibilities, and procedures of Los Angeles Police Department 3. Crime information	1. 0.25 of a point for each year of continuous service as a policeman in L.A.P.D.
Lieutenant	1. Thorough knowledge of criminal law 2. A good knowledge of the organization, responsibilities, functions, procedures, and limitations on authority of L.A.P.D. 3. A working knowledge of police science and administration	1. 0.25 of a point for each year of continuous service as a sergeant in L.A.P.D.
Captain	1. A thorough knowledge of the organization, responsibilities, functions procedures, and limitations on authority of L.A.P.D. 2. A thorough knowledge of police science and administration 3. A thorough knowledge of criminal law	1. 0.25 of a point for each year of continuous service as a lieutenant in L.A.P.D.
Inspector	1. A thorough knowledge of police science and administration 2. A thorough knowledge of organization & procedures of L.A.P.D. 3. A thorough knowledge of criminal law	1. 0.25 of a point each year of continuous service as a captain in L.A.P.D.
Deputy Chief	1. A thorough knowledge of police science and administration 2. A thorough knowledge of criminal law	1. 0.25 of a point for each year of continuous service as a captain or inspector in L.A.P.D.

Requirements for advancement for each pay grade of the Los Angeles Police Department are characterized in Tables I and II. This Department is traditionally a closed personnel system. Advancements are made from the lower ranks based upon minimum requirements. Educational requirements are not mentioned as being necessary for advancement, other than a high school education which is a basic entrance level requirement. Emphasis is placed upon previous experience in the rank below from which the person is seeking promotion. An example of this would be a sergeant seeking promotion to lieutenant, the only requirement for which is two years of experience as a sergeant in the Los Angeles Police Department. The candidate would be tested upon three basic areas for advancement to lieutenant: (1) a knowledge of criminal law, (2) a working knowledge of police science and administration, and (3) a working knowledge of the organization, functions, responsibilities, and procedures of the Department. One of the major functions of a lieutenant is to interpret orders, directives, and exercise supervisory abilities.

In Table III, the number of personnel holding degrees by rank are recorded for 1963. Of the 993 sergeants in the Department, only 12 percent of the personnel held the A.B. degree or higher, and only 20 percent of the 174 lieutenants held an A.B. degree or higher. In no instance where there were two or more personnel per rank did there exist 50 percent or more of the personnel having an A.B. degree or higher.

If the first administrative position could be classified at the Lieutenant's level or above, then only 30 percent of the Department's administrators had an A.B. degree or higher. Relating the educational proficiency to the entire Department, approximately 6 percent of the entire personnel had an A.B. degree or higher.

Table III [a]

Los Angeles Police Personnel Holding Degrees 1963

Positions Available	Rank	A.A.	A.B. & LL.B	Masters	Doctorate	% with A.B. or Higher
(1)	Chief		1			100
(7)	Deputy Chief		2			30
(14)	Inspector		5	1		45
(48)	Captain	3	14	1		33
(174)	Lieutenant	11	33	8	1	24
(993)	Sergeant	62	107	4		12
(29)	Sgt. Police-woman	3	6			20
(3,278)	Policeman	209	124	2		4
(81)	Policewoman	6	7			9
		294	299	16	1	

[a] Data obtained from Los Angeles Police Department, Planning and Research Division, 1963

From observation it was found that possession of a degree might produce a negative influence upon advancement. Top administrators, at the Inspector and deputy chief level, have often indicated to other police-oriented persons that degree holders (especially at the lower levels) are a burden to the Department because "many policies and procedures must be proven to these people." Blind acceptance was not one of the attributes of the degree holder at the lower levels of police work.

Another interesting characteristic, found in Table II, is that of seniority credit for each year of continuous service in the previous rank, an additional .25 of a point being added to the final score of the candidate. This continuous service must have been with the Los Angeles Police Department.

A comparison of police personnel salaries, Table IV, with those of federal employees indicated that a sergeant's pay compared to GS-11 and a lieutenant's pay compared to GS-12. However, requirements, duties, and education were quite different. In contrast, minimum requirements for the United States Treasury Department enforcement officers include an A.B. or LL.B. degree and the entrance level started at GS-5 or GS-7.

Table IV[a]

Los Angeles Police Personnel Compared to Federal Employees By Salary 1964

Police Pay			General Schedule Pay		
Position			Position		
	Low	High		Low	High
Chief		$24,210	GS-18		$24,500
Deputy Chief	$19,524	21,792	GS-15	$16,460	21,590
Inspector	15,672	17,496	GS-14	14,470	18,580
Captain	12,576	14,040	GS-13	12,075	15,855
Lieutenant	10,668	11,904	GS-12	10,250	13,445
Sergeant	9,060	10,104	GS-11	8,650	11,305

[a]Los Angeles Policeman Salary Schedule 1964-65
General Schedule Salary, August 14, 1964

Summary and Conclusions

  The selection of personnel for a government agency must
be a process of filling positions or occupational categories with
the best personnel available. The rigidity of one method over
another based upon traditional concepts should be abandoned.
Growth of the organization must depend upon planned growth and
development of personnel.

  The following characteristics are descriptive of a closed
personnel system as opposed to an open personnel system:

1. Selection of personnel has characteristically been
from outside the government service at the lower
levels of various occupational areas.

2. Higher positions are to be filled generally from
within the service.

3. A closed personnel system has a tendency to
develop inbreeding within the agency.

4. Closed systems advocate the concept that the most
effective recruiting at lower levels can only be
achieved if the upper positions are reserved for
those who can be promoted from below.

5. Recruitment from outside at higher levels may
involve the risk of lowered morale within the agency.

6. In a closed system emphasis is placed upon existing
skills needed for the particular entrance level job
and not for advancement.

7. Top-level administrators have a tendency to restrict
research concerning personnel selection at most
levels of government service.

8. Transfers between agencies at municipal levels are
restricted or nonexistent.

9. Municipal police agencies have virtually total control
over requirements and selection of their personnel.

10. Transfer from one municipal agency to another is
restricted or nonexistent.

11. Leaves of absence are strongly regulated.

12. Police requirements for employment stress physical rather than educational ability.

13. Not enough emphasis is placed upon administrative ability in a police agency.

The Los Angeles Police Department is considered by those in the field of police administration as one of the advanced departments and a leader in the field of police personnel selection. This agency has the following characteristics:

1. Maintains a closed personnel system to perpetuate a planned image.

2. Relies upon traditional concepts of policing, personnel selection, and promotion.

3. Has inbred to the extreme.

4. Does not utilize administrative abilities of personnel effectively.

5. Does little or no research to redirect personnel selection. What research is conducted is directed by top administrators with a fixed conclusion in mind.

Recommendations for Further Inquiry

1. Greater experimentation and research should be conducted in policing organizations by various disciplines.

2. Emphasis should be placed upon education when listing requirements for advancement.

3. The city government should adopt a system for transfer of administrative personnel from one department to another within the city.

4. An open system should be developed for the police department, with a means for lateral entry of top administrators.

Notes

1. Stahl, Glenn O. Public Personnel Administration (New York: Harper and Brothers, 1956), p. 119.

2. Ibid., p. 144.

3. Ibid., p. 145.

4. Meriam, Lewis Public Personnel Problems: From Standpoint of the Operating Officer (Washington, D. C.: The Brookings Institution, 1938), pp. 57-63.

5. Stahl, op. cit. pp. 147-50.

6. Ibid., p. 174.

7. Ibid., p. 173.

8. Municipal Personnel Administration, Sixth Edition (Chicago: The International City Managers' Association, 1960), p. 3.

9. Gould, Julius and Kolb, William L., A Dictionary of the Social Sciences (New York: The Free Press of Glenco, 1964), p. 249.

10. Ibid., p. 73.

11. Ibid., p. 3.

12. Goode, Cecil E. Personnel Research Frontiers (Chicago: Public Personnel Association, 1958), p. 94.

13. Ibid., pp. 59-60.

14. Jones, Roger W. "The Federal Civil Service Today," Public Personnel Review, 22:114-20, April, 1960.

15. Ibid., p. 115.

16. Mosher, Frederick C. "Careers and Career Services in the Public Service," Public Personnel Review, 24:46-51, January, 1963.

17. Memorandum, "Data About Federal Career Executives."

18. Warner, W. Lloyd and others, "A New Look at the Career Civil Service Executive," Public Administration Review, 22: 188-94, December 1962.

19. Ibid., pp. 190-94.

20. Ginzberg, Eli and Anderson, James K. Manpower for Government: A Decade's Forecast (Chicago: Public Personnel Association, 1958), p. 29.

21. The American Assembly, The Federal Government Service: Its Character, Prestige, and Problems (New York: Columbia University, 1955), pp. 162-169.

22. David, Paul T. and Pollock, Ross Executives for Government: Central Issues of Federal Personnel Administration (New York: The Brookings Institution, 1957) p. 65.

23. The American Assembly, op. cit., p. 184.

24. David and Pollock, op. cit., p. 65.

25. Lichfield, Edward H. "Apostasy of a Merit Man," Public Personnel Review, 22:85-89, April, 1961.

26. Nigro, op. cit., p. 144.

27. The American Assembly, op. cit., pp. 168-69.

28. Jones, op. cit., pp. 118-19.

29. Ibid., p. 115.

30. Stahl, op. cit., p. 146.

31. Municipal Personnel Administration (Chicago: International City Managers' Associations, 1960), p. 8.

32. Ibid., pp. 357-60.

33. Kingsley, J. Donald "Recruiting Applicants for the Public Service: The Problem and Its Setting," Ideas and Issues in Public Administration edited by Dwight Waldo (New York, McGraw-Hill, 1953), p. 521.

34. Nigro, op. cit., p. 165.

35. Warner, W. Lloyd and others, "New Light on Lateral Entry," Personnel Administration, 26:17-23, May-June, 1963.

36. Ibid., pp. 20-23.

37. Jones, op. cit., p. 119.

116   Police Administration

38. The American Assembly, op. cit., p. 170.

39. Scheer, W. E., "Reduce Turnover, Increase Profits,"
    Personnel Journal, 41:559-61, December, 1962.

40. Boyd, J. B. "Hidden Factors in Employee Turnover:
    Implications Regarding Manpower Composition,"
    Personnel Administration, 26:4-10 November-December,
    1963.

41. Scheer, op. cit., pp. 559-60.

42. Brenneman, Leroy J. "Attacking the Employee Turnover
    Problem," Personnel Review, 21:129-32, April, 1960.

43. Vollmer, August The Police and Modern Society
    (Berkeley: University of California Press, 1936).

44. The International City Managers' Association,
    Municipal Police Administration (Chicago: The
    International City Managers' Association, 1961),
    pp. 7-8.

45. Ibid., p. 131.

46. Ibid., pp. 131-32.

47. Ibid., p. 150.

48. Ibid., pp. 150-51.

49. Marsh, Stewart H. "Validating the Selection of Deputy
    Sheriffs," Public Personnel Review, 23:41-44,
    January, 1962.

50. Stanley, David T. Modernizing Manhattan's Manpower
    Methods: Some Problems," Public Administration Review,
    23:155-60, Sept., 1963.

51. Pfiffner, John M. The Function of the Police in A
    Democratic Society, unpublished paper, Youth Studies
    Center, University of Southern California, 1963, pp. 9-10.

52. Ibid., p. 14.

53. City Managers' Association, op. cit., p. 133.

VI. Community Relations and Change

With social tensions mounting throughout the nation police agencies cannot preserve the public peace without the public participating in a positive way more fully than it now does. Poor community feeling does more than create social distance, it produces irrational responses to rational problems.[1]

A community relations program is not a public-relations program to "sell the police image" to the community. It is not a panacea which will tranquilize an angry neighborhood by, for example, suddenly promoting a few Negro officers in the wake of a racial disturbance. It is a long-range, full-scale effort to acquaint the police and the community with each other's problems, and to stimulate action aimed at solving those problems.

Community relations are not the exclusive business of specialized units, but the business of the entire department from the chief to the patrolman. Community relations are not a matter of special programs but encompass all aspects of police work. They must be considered in the selection, training, deployment and promotion of personnel; in the execution of field procedures; in staff policy making and planning; in the enforcement of departmental discipline; and in the handling of citizen's complaints. A community's attitude toward the police is influenced by the actions of individual officers on the street. No community relations or recruiting or training program will succeed if courteous and compassionate behavior by policemen in their contacts with citizens is not encouraged.

This is a time when traditional ideas and institutions are increasingly being challenged. The poor want an equal opportunity to earn a share of America's wealth. Minority groups want a final end to discrimination. Young people, the fastest growing segment of the population, desire a greater share in decision making. The police must be willing and able to deal understandingly and constructively with these often unsettling, even threatening,

117

changes.

Police-community relations is the total participative involvement of the whole community in the process of establishing
order and social control in our society.

Formal methods to achieve citizen involvement have been
established, such as the ballot, the initiative, and referendum.
However, other methods must be developed to make possible continuous communication between institutional government and its
constituents. Very little is known about the ways in which the
members of a complex society can indeed become so involved.
Nevertheless, it is evident that the ingredients of this process
include effective two-way communication, [2] a mutual development
of insights, and the nurturing of trust and confidence.

Los Angeles, like many cities, has developed very
extensive programs (See Appendix F) designed to improve police-
community relations. Programs include: youth, schools (students
and administrators), colleges and universities, minority communities, militant communities, religious groups and the news media--
and the interaction of each with the police department.

Improving community relations involves not only institutional programs and changes in procedures and practices, but a
re-examination of fundamental attitudes. The police must learn
to communicate with and understand people who are openly critical
or hostile to them, since those people are precisely the ones with
whom relations have deteriorated the most. Police and citizen
relationships on the streets must become person-to-person en-
counters rather than the black-versus-white, oppressed-versus-
oppressor confrontations they have been.

With the responsibility for change being a two-way matter,
one necessary element in creating such change is compromise, as
practiced in international affairs.

Training in community relations, although of contemporary
interest, is not new in law enforcement. Cincinnati and Cleveland,
Ohio started race relations programs in 1945 and Richmond,
California developed a program jointly with the State Department of

Justice and the American Council on Race Relations in the
forties.[3]

Training

Community relations must be identified with training and
change. Training is a device by which change is fostered by the
trainee, the trainer, the organization, or the community.
In effecting change, patterns of behavior, more than just
information, skill, attitudes and feelings of the individual, must
be considered. Training requires an environment that will
encourage and sustain appropriate changes in behavior. In reviewing the problems of organizational change, Katz and Kahn note that:

It is common practice to pull officials out of their
organizational roles and give them training in human
relations. Then they return to their customary positions
with the same role expectations from their subordinates,
the same pressures from their superiors, and the same
functions to perform as before their special training.[4]

The concept of environmental influence in changing individuals is certainly not new. Some professional "change agents"
manipulate the environment to develop change. Psychiatrists use
special institutions for programs in environmental therapy. The
assumption is made that the environment provides opportunities to
learn, and the improvements come from an accumulation of learning experiences. Social workers who utilize settlement houses
and recreation areas for young people use the environment to
provide new learning experiences. The educational system itself
exemplifies this notion by using the physical and psychological
surroundings of the school to provide the atmosphere for learning
that is stimulated through books and instruction. "This means not
that the environment itself produces learning or a change in the
student but only that the environment and the stimulus to change
...are all of a piece and should not be separated."[5]

Numerous studies have been conducted to determine the
best ways to train and develop individuals within organizations.[6]
Administrators and managers have often followed the results of

these studies in implementing change. Further problems have arisen from failure to recognize the individual, the group, the organization and its external environment as all part of a system. Systems and subsystems, acting and reacting, each influence the other.

Katz and Kahn indicate that, in order to overcome this, behavior determined largely by structured roles within organizations must be distinguished from behavior that is determined more directly by personality needs and values. When this division is made, programs for implementing change can deal not only with the methods to be used but also with the target at which that change is directed. Some of the targets to be considered are:

> ...the individual as an individual personality, the interpersonal relationships between members of peer groups, the norms of peer groups, the interpersonal relationships between members of an organizational family, the structure of a role, the role relationships of some segment of organizational space, or the structure of the organization as a whole. [7]

Lippitt and others offer a process by which methods of change are implemented. Their system, developed at least in part from the studies of Kurt Lewin, [8] embodies the concept of a change agent and the client system. The change agent is the catalyst who attempts to bring about change, and the client system is the entity which is to undergo planned change. The client system exists on four levels: 1) the individual, 2) the face-to-face group, 3) the organization, 4) and the community. Each of these levels exists as a dynamic open system. As each of these systems is confronted with new internal or external forces, the system is challenged to alter its structure or ways of functioning. [9]

Summary and Conclusions

Needless to say, the manifold causative factors of our social problems are often beyond the realm of understanding or correction by law enforcement agencies. The police training officer alone can no longer supply the sophisticated material and learning environments necessary to develop positive community and police

relations. Communities, composed of sub-communities which in
turn are made up of individuals of varying capacities, represent
a complex society in need of complex problem solving.[10]

The defensiveness of police, when viewed against the historical patterns of our society, is understandable although it is
not acceptable today. It arises from much destructive criticism
and misunderstanding of the role of law enforcement, and from
an unwillingness, on the part of some, to devote the necessary
time and energy to evaluation in depth as against superficial study
and quick and prejudiced judgment from within as well as outside
law enforcement.

Change and training must be considered as inseparable
entities in the achievement of improved police and community relations. Community relations is a total effort to acquaint the
police and the community with each other's problems, and to
stimulate positive action aimed at solving these problems. Attempts
must be made to change individuals within law enforcement and, at
the same time, the entire system of criminal justice must be reviewed in the light of organizational change. A better adjustment
to reality must be developed between policemen, the organization,
and the community. Training has often been inadequate and un-
enlightened within many areas of law enforcement, and many of
the deficiencies in training are the result of police isolation from
the community.

One of the most sensitive areas, demanding understanding
and compassion, is today's youth. Emphasis must be placed on
bridging the youth-authority gap. Programs have been developed
to communicate with youth from preschoolers to high-schoolers,
but very little is being done to develop a dialogue with school
dropouts and the very anti-establishment youth.

Sensitivity training may be suggested as one program to
help develop insight into one's self and one's personal relations
with others.

The advantages of higher formal education, especially for
police personnel, are a factor of importance. With increasing levels

of education there appears to develop greater tolerance and
rationality on the part of the individual.

If training programs, however, are merely exercises in
self-image building, little or no modification will result, and mis-
trust, separation, and negative attitudes will continue.

Based upon past experience with attempts to make community improvements, the future does not look optimistic. With
American cities becoming areas of physical and social conflict,
involving such factors as transportation, water and sewage, pol-
lution, slum dwellings, lack of open space, crime, poverty and
segregation, to name just a few,[11] do we have the men to meet
the challenge?

In California, as in other communities, we have had
warnings that poor community relations, if not corrected, cause
greater separation and possible violence.[12] To what extent were
these warnings headed?

Toynbee[13] has indicated that the history of civilization
may be seen as a succession of changes. When problems are
presented and solutions found, communities move on to new and
higher levels of achievement. However, when solutions are not
found, communities stagnate and decline.

Rationality of decision making is paramount in dealing with
community problems. Change and training must be of the highest
calibre. Change is inevitable.

It is not likely that we will be successful in controlling
crime without seriously changing the organization and
administration of criminal justice.[14]

Notes

1.   For an adequate presentation of this problem see: Rights in
      Conflict, the Walker Report to the National Commission
      on the cause and prevention of violence (New York:
      Bantam Books, 1968); Report of the National Advisory
      Commission on Civil Disorders (New York: Bantam Books,
      1968); and David Stahl et. al. (Editors). The Community
      and Racial Crises (New York: Practising Law Institute,
      1966).

2. Methodology for improving communications between alien
    cultures and between sub-groups within one culture has
    been suggested by John W. Adams, General Research
    Corporation, in a speech delivered to the Western College
    Placement Association, January 18, 1968. His thesis was
    that peer communications led to misunderstanding of
    meanings, motives, and morals.

3. A monograph presented by Milton A. Senn, "A Study of
    Police Training Programs in Minority Relations," to
    the Law Enforcement Committee of the Los Angeles
    County Conference on Community Relations, Circa 1949,
    pp. 20-29.

4. Katz, Daniel and Kahn, Robert L. The Social Psychology
    of Organizations (New York: John Wiley & Sons, Inc.
    1966), p. 390. Also see John M. Pfiffner and Marshall
    Fels, The Supervision of Personnel (Englewood Cliffs:
    Prentice Hall, Inc. 1964); Edgar H. Schein, Organizational
    Psychology (Englewood Cliffs: Prentice-Hall, Inc. 1965);
    and Philip Selznick, Leadership in Administration (White
    Plains: Row, Peterson, 1957).

5. Lippitt, Ronald; Watson, Jeanne; and Westly, Bruce,
    The Dynamics of Planned Change (New York: Harcourt,
    Brace & World, Inc., 1958), pp. 110-111.

6. See for example: Etzioni, Amitai and Etzioni, Eva (editors).
    Social Change: Sources, Patterns, and Consequences (New
    York: Basic Books, Inc., 1964); Golembiewski, Robert T.
    and Gibson, Frank (editors), Managerial Behavior and
    Organization Demands (Chicago: Rand McNally, 1967);
    Leavitt, Harold J. Managerial Psychology (Chicago:
    University of Chicago Press, McGraw-Hill, 1961).

7. Katz and Kahn, op. cit., p. 392.

8. See the following works by Kurt Lewis: "Frontiers in Group
    Dynamics," Human Relations, 1, pp. 5-14, 1947: and
    Field Theory in Social Science, Cartwright, D. (ed.),
    (New York: Harper, 1951).

9. Lippitt (et al.), op. cit. pp. 110-111.

10. Reisman, Leonard E. "Relating the Police Community to
    the Academic Community," The Police Chief, August
    1966, p. 16.

11. Cities in Crisis, prepared by the U. S. Department of
    Health, Education and Welfare (Washington D. C.: U. S.
    Government Printing Office, 1967), Welfare Administration
    Publication No. 20.

12. A very good example is: the Report on California: Police-
    Minority Group Relations, by the California Advisory
    Committee to the United States Commission on Civil
    Rights, 1963, describing conditions in Los Angeles and
    the San Francisco Bay Area and the probability of racial
    or ethnic group violence in Los Angeles and possible
    solutions. Two years later the Watts Riot more drama-
    tically presented the same problem.

13. Toynbee, Arnold J. A Study of History (New York: Oxford
    University Press, 1946).

14. Lohman, Joseph D. "Crises of a Society in Ferment, "
    Crime and Delinquency, January 1968, p. 31.

VII. A Review of Corrections: Analysis and Change

Tappan has said that "The great need in modern correctional practice is to avoid a static dogmatism and to move experimentally toward methods that are practical and effective in retraining individuals to achieve adequate adjustment in the community."[1] It is the purpose here to bypass the experimental melange by developing a conceptual scheme by which the total correctional arena, i.e., penal institutions, probation, and parole, can be portrayed in terms of: (1) a method of organizational analysis; (2) corrections and organizational analysis; (3) analytic application; and (4) change factors relative to the correctional arena.

The general focus of this chapter is concerned with organization structure and people reacting in the parameters of organizational influence, i.e., employees, clients, and interested nonparticipants.

It is apparent that many analytical techniques may be adapted to the study of corrections. A survey of the literature dealing with organization analysis yields a harvest of descriptive tools.

Depending on one's preference an array of disciplinary approaches is available, for example, economic, sociological, psychological, anthropological, plus multi-disciplinary combinations.

The criterion for selection of an analytic tool here, therefore, has not been restricted to a particular disciplinary approach, but the universality and adaptability of the methodology. Homans model[2] of a social system meets this criterion and provides the additional advantage of a multi-disciplinary view of organization and people.

Method of Organizational Analysis

Regardless of organizational structure and goals there are underlying assumptions[3] which contribute to a position of universalism in describing organizations. Organization is relative to size, complexity, conscious rationality, and presence of purpose, as summed up in the following definition:

> Organization is the pattern of ways in which large
> numbers of people, too many to have intimate face-
> to-face contact with all others, and engaged in a
> complexity of tasks, relate themselves to each other
> in the conscious, systematic establishment and
> accomplishment of mutually agreed purposes.[4]

The elements of correction--penal institutions, probation,
and parole--are characteristics of organizational phenomena. Each
element of correction can further be divided into more finite organizational phenomena. Therefore, analysis can take place on a
general systems approach to investigate relationship, goal(s) and
direction of the "whole" as well as developing inquiry into the
parts and sub-parts to the total system.

Homans model describes organization as a social system.
Much like Pfiffner and Sherwood, Katz and Kahn, Likert, Leavitt,
Argyris, and other administrative behaviorists, Homans views
organization in terms of social behavior. This behavior can broadly be separated into two distinct categories: internal and external
systems.

The internal system is characteristic of emergent behavior
which develops as a non-prescribed additive to the activity, function, or organization, such as the interaction of people in the work
group, employee-employee, and employee-non-employee relations.

In each work situation there emerge behavior patterns that
are suited to the needs of the individual and the needs of the interacting group members. Some of these internal phenomena will be
carried into the organization by the individual in his internalization
of role expectation(s) and perception(s). Such things are horseplay
and joking, [5] and group pressure to establish work standards[6] can
be described as internal phenomena.

The second concept, external system, describes the required behavior. The external system is that which is demanded
by the formal organization, such as rules and regulations, job
classification and description, work methods, and the standardization of personnel selection. Management molds or forms the
external system.[7] Understanding of the internal (emergent informal

behavior) system is the first step in developing Homans model
for organization analysis.

Homans then considers three universalisms which are
characteristic of all organizations: activities, interactions, and
sentiments. Regardless of the type of organization (penal institution, probation office, or parole office), the three measurements
of organization develop a common framework for analysis.

Activities: Activities are the things people do which are
related to the work situation. The activities which can be prescribed are external acts which follow the requirements and direction of the organization. Other acts emerge from the work environment and become internal-oriented.

Interactions: Interaction develops when two or more people
are brought together in relation to their internal or external activities. Interaction occurs when activity boundaries coincide.
Interactions can be a required part, or part, of the external system, or emerge informally as part of the internal system. An
observer can differentiate interactions in several ways: duration,
frequency, and order or direction.[8]

Sentiments: Internal sentiments "...include a person's
emotions or feelings, his beliefs or values, aspirations or objectives...in short, all the factors within a person which motivate
his activities...."[9] Sentiments in the external system are of two
types. The first consists of those things a person brings with
him to the work environment, such as prejudice, expectations, and
frustrations. The second type of external sentiments are those
which are demanded by the organization. Required organizational
sentiments might be loyalty and high morale. Organizational
norms in terms of behavior, attitude, and beliefs which employees
are required to meet are also external sentiments.

Homans model has now developed a framework of six
characteristics; activities, interactions, and sentiments in an internal system and external system. An underlying relationship exists
between these six characteristics. As in physics, there is an

128   Police Administration

assumption that for every action there is a reaction regardless
of the initial magnitude. Homans model suggests the same relationship (see Figure I): that any alteration in one of the six characteristics will produce a corresponding alteration in one or all of the
remaining characteristics. The primary example would be an
external elimination of an activity which would eliminate the external interactions associated with the activity and might produce a
change in internal as well as external sentiment (for every action
there is a reaction). Therefore, there are a number of problems
". . .that can occur when a person's job is changed (activity),
which may influence his acquired status (sentiment) or lead to
strong feelings of pleasure or disappointment with his new position
(emergent sentiment), and possibly to subsequent actions such as
complaining to the boss, filing a grievance, etc."[10] Homans model
can be useful in analyzing historical development of organization,
contemporary organization, and as a predictive device to measure
what will happen if proposed changes were made in the organization.

Homans model, however, is not a panacea for organizational analysis. It is nothing more than a tool which can be used well
or poorly. It is also apparent that the resultant of analysis is
determined by the sophisticated parameters for inquiry and analytical expertise of the researcher.

Figure I

Homans Model for Organizational Analysis

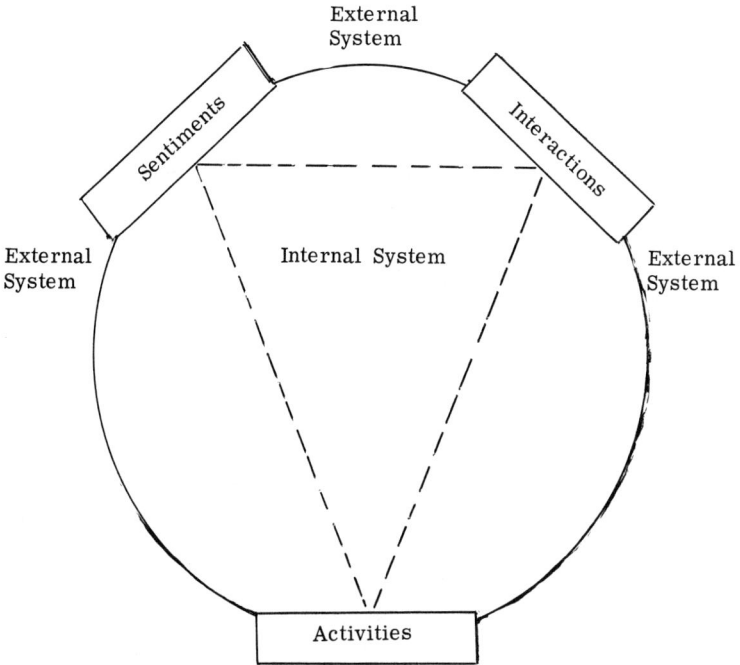

Corrections and Organizational Analysis

The arena of corrections is only one part of the formal criminal justice system (see Figure 2). In varying degree the police, prosecution, courts, and corrections are all involved in establishing societal conformity. Each major element of the criminal justice system attempts to correct the individual as an internal or external requisite of the situation in terms of activity, interaction, or sentiment.

The four parts of the criminal justice system, possibly because of the need to develop organizational expertise and the demand, in terms of efficiency, effectiveness, and economy, to increase in size, have developed individual philosophical positions and an attitude of independence, and have become isolated from each other within the system.

Therefore, in establishing areas for organizational analysis within the corrections scheme, it is necessary to relate to the other components: police, prosecution, and courts. To paraphrase John Donne, corrections is not an island.

Figure 2

The formal Criminal Justice System

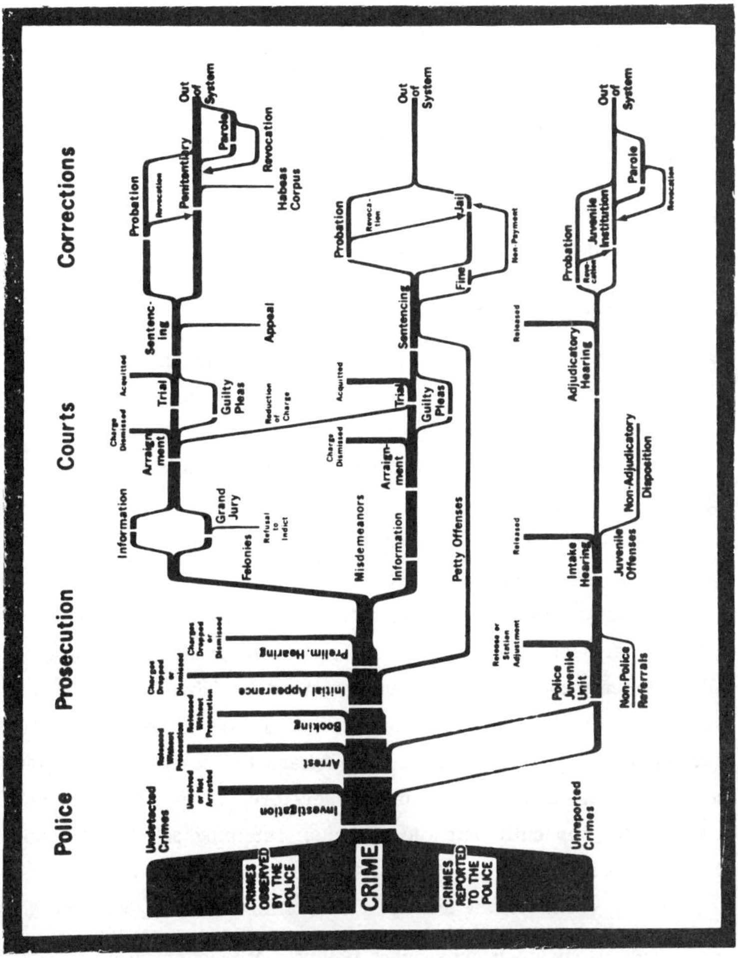

Source: Adapted from The President's Commission on Law
Enforcement and the Administration of Justice: The Challenge of
Crime in a Free Society (Washington: Government Printing Office,
1967), pp. 8-9.

The history and objectives of correction[11] are difficult
to separate, for each is part of the other. Tappan has outlined
the objectives[12] of correction to include the following:

1. The protection of society;

2. Retribution (vindictive response to the criminal's
   victim and potential victim);

3. Deterrence (Bentham's hedonistic calculus--the
   threat of punishment and later refined to meet the
   condition that punishment should fit the crime);

4. Incapacitation (custody, as well as "preventive
   detention" as in European countries);

5. Rehabilitation (psychiatry, psychology, and case
   work);

6. Social reconstruction (following Hermann Mannheim,
   viewing the total criminal justice system);

7. Diagnosis and classification;

8. Orientation of the offender (orientation of offender
   toward treatment);

9. Program planning (proper mix of plan to offender);

10. Community attitudes.

Content analysis of Tappan's objectives serves the purpose
of historical development, from retribution to program planning
and community attitudes, all interwoven in the fabric of societal
protection. As each development became a part of the correctional
scheme, a fusion process took place where the new did not replace
the old but was added to the old. Therefore, in molecular fashion,
new process was built onto old process, retaining all the ideologies
of corrections.

> . . .each, as it has been crystallized in law, custom,
> and correctional practice, has impressed a persisting
> influence upon subsequent policy. Moreover, each
> objective has become encrusted with layers of ration-
> alization to justify and perpetuate the established treat-
> ment methods. The ultimate consequence is a mélange
> of purposes, some deeply bedded in the channels of
> history.[13]

The juvenile corrections model (see Figure 3) portrays the major interacting parts of corrections, police, prosecution, and courts.

Juvenile corrections, dealing with youths from 8 to 21 years of age, can further be subdivided into four parts: juvenile detention, juvenile probation, juvenile institutions and juvenile aftercare.

Juvenile detention. Juvenile detention is the holding of minors in custody for court disposition. Under the California Welfare and Institution Code detention would include delinquent and pre-delinquent cases.

Detention facilities have existed in the United States since 1899, when Chicago established physical quarters for juveniles separate from the adult jail. Juveniles then were housed together regardless of age differentials or delinquent and pre-delinquent participation.

In the late 1940's, the city of Cleveland developed the unit concept which separated juveniles according to age distribution and degree of delinquency. In 1965, there were approximately 242 detention homes in the nation, handling an estimated number of 13,000 juveniles per day, with an average stay of 12 days and an average cost of $130 per juvenile.

Detention facilities, in practice, are being used for other purposes than holding for court disposition. Police and probation use detention as a disposition. The courts use it for punishment, protection, storage, and placement based upon lack of other available institutionalism and care. Detention, in many cases, serves as a substitution for cure, without proper juvenile selection, classification, and referral.

It has been suggested that

if the evils of detention are to be corrected, it is necessary first to strengthen probation and other correctional treatment services; second, to develop community resources for shelter care; third, to use detention only for its proper functions.[14]

134

Figure 3

JUVENILE CORRECTIONS MODEL

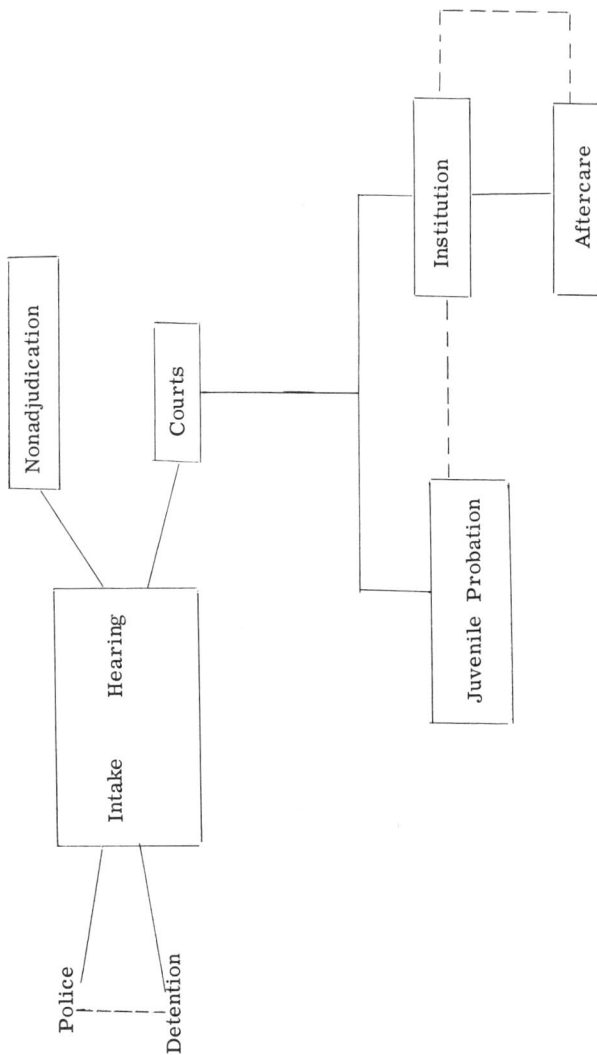

Juvenile probation. Juvenile probation is the activity that allows the juvenile to remain in the community under the supervision of a probation officer, within the legal framework as prescribed by the court. Probation implies that the juvenile has been introduced to the criminal justice system, involving one or more of the areas of police, detention, intake hearing, prosecution, court, and probation. Rather than being placed in a formal institution, the juvenile is placed in a community under specified conditions. These supervised conditions or restrictions of the juvenile's behavior are part of the correcting process.

In 1869, Massachusetts developed one of the earliest juvenile probation organizations.[15] Since the late 1800's, juvenile probation has become a major part of the local court structure.[16] The increasing numbers of juveniles serviced by probation adds to the complexity of the organization. It has been estimated that about 11 percent of all juveniles will be referred to the court and probation during their adolescent years, and 18 percent of all boys will be processed.[17]

The system of juvenile probation is further complicated by its organization and administration. Juvenile probation systems are organized in one of several ways: a centralized system with state authority; a decentralized system with individual county or city authority; or a combination of state and local autonomous programs. The responsibility for administration of probation programs is delegated to the court; to the probation department; to other agencies, such as state or local public welfare departments; or to a combination of the above. There appears to be no standard juvenile probation organization in terms of activity, interaction, or sentiment.

The total structure of juvenile probation rests on a foundation of humanitarian instincts, rather than empirical data.

Juvenile institutions. The juvenile institution is, in practice, a penal institution with the goal of training. The institution's involvement with the juvenile is custodial, educational, and remedial.

In the mid 1800's, the juvenile institution appeared in the
United States in Massachusetts, New York, and Maine. Although
from its inception the institution was directed toward training of
the juvenile for return to the community, other purposes have
sometimes been substituted, [18] such as:

1. Use as a detention or holding facility for youngsters
   awaiting completion of other plans for placement.

2. Providing basic housing for youngsters whose primary
   need is a foster home or residential housing.

3. Housing large numbers of youngsters whose involvement in trouble is primarily situational rather than
   deep-seated and who could be handled more efficiently
   under community supervision.

4. Caring for mentally retarded youngsters committed
   to the training school because there is no room in
   a mental retardation facility or because no such
   institution exists.

5. Providing care for youngsters with severe psychiatric
   problems who are committed to the training school
   because no juvenile residential treatment program
   exists.

6. Use of girls' facilities to provide maternity services.

The juvenile institutional program can best be summed up as a
panoramic system of demands receiving a unilateral correction
". . .wherein no one is best served and most are served in de-
fault." [19]

Juvenile aftercare. Juvenile aftercare is the condition
that follows institutionalism, and the juvenile remains under supervision in the community. In essence, the juvenile is on parole.
Like probation, aftercare takes place in the framework of a set
of conditions and supervision.

In the early 1800's, Pennsylvania and New York began a
system of aftercare of juveniles returned to the community from
formal institutions. The present position of aftercare is one of
state organization and administration. Of 40 states which offer a

state operated program, the organization and administration may
be the responsibility of the state department of public welfare,
state youth correction agency, state department of correction,
institution board, state training school board, or the state department of health.[20]

There appears to be no national standardization of juvenile
aftercare. The service performed varies from one extreme of
superficial supervision to the other extreme of innovative supervision.

Adult Corrections Model. The adult corrections model
(see Figure 4) has the following subsystems: misdemeanant probation, local adult institutions and jails, adult felony probation, and
state institutions for adults.

It is interesting to note the differences between the juvenile
model and the adult model. There is an underlying philosophy in
the correctional arena that presupposes the juvenile is a better
target for correction than the adult. In actual practice, however,
the delinquent adult may have had a delinquent juvenile background.
In discussing the distribution of age to arrest, Neumeyer has indicated that "a detailed analysis by age groups reveals that arrests
fluctuate somewhat but remain relatively high from age 15 to over
age 25 . . ."[21] thereby transgressing the boundary line separating
juvenile from adult.

Under the adult model there is, at times, fusion between
the juvenile model and the adult model in the following areas:
probation, parole (aftercare), and local jails.

Misdemeanant probation. Probation, misdemeanant and
felony can be defined as:

> . . . a sentence, as an organization, or as a process.
> As a sentence, probation represents a judicial disposition
> which establishes the defendant's legal status under which
> his freedom in the community is continued, subject to
> supervision by a probation organization and subject to
> conditions imposed by the court. As an organization,
> probation is a service agency designed to assist the court
> and to execute certain services in the administration of
> criminal justice. As a process, probation involves the
> pre-sentence investigation for the court and the supervision
> of persons in the community.[22]

138

Figure 4

ADULT CORRECTIONS MODEL

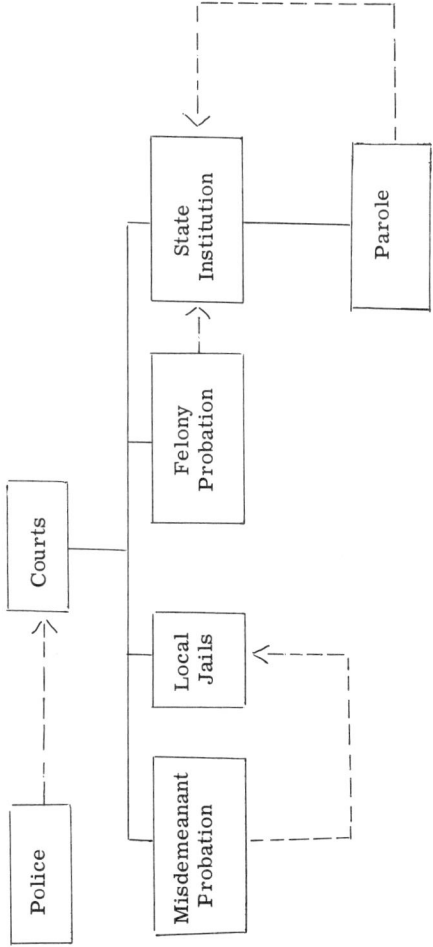

Corrections   139

Misdemeanant probation started in Boston in the mid 1800's with John Augustus, as did many aspects of corrections, delaing with lower court case loads of drunkards and vagrants.

The most outstanding fact about misdemeanant probation is its paucity of application. A national survey[23] in 1964, of selected misdemeanants (prostitution, liquor laws, driving while intoxicated, disorderly conduct, drunkenness, vagrancy, and gambling), accounted for approximately 2 1/2 million arrests. Drunkenness alone constituted approximately 1 1/2 million arrests. In the majority of cases of those convicted, probation was not used in place of incarceration or fine.

The organization of misdemeanant probation is normally one of the following: a state system, with emphasis of direction coming from a correctional agency, court agency, or department of public welfare; or separate local autonomous agencies at the county or city level of government; or combined state and local systems.

In practice there are three types of probation: (1) conviction of a crime and placement on probation; (2) summary probation, which is probation without pre-sentence investigation and without supervision; and (3) probation without verdict--deferred conviction or a nullification of conviction if no other offense is committed within a specific period. There is little empirical data available to substantiate the efficiency, effectiveness, and economy of the above varieties of probation.

Limitations placed upon probation arise from: heavy volume in the lower courts, inadequate diagnostic aid, a limited range of treatment alternatives and limited quality of treatment, and inadequate statistical data for evaluation of programs.

Adult jails. "In the vast majority of city and county jails and local short-term institutions, no significant progress has been made in the past 50 years."[24]

The Manual of Correctional Standards describes the jail facility:

In most instances this institution houses both offenders
awaiting court action and those serving short sentences,
usually up to one year. Frequently, it is the only
facility available for the detention of the juvenile offender
and for the care of the non-criminally insane pending
commitment to a state hospital. It may be administered
by the city police department, the county sheriff or
(as in Kentucky) the county jailer, or by a city or county
governing board with an appointed warden. [25]

The jail may be used for the non-criminal as a detention

facility or for those awaiting pretrial or whose trial is in progress,

as well as for sentenced persons. Generally, major emphasis

is placed on custody, with very little emphasis on education and

treatment.

The condition of jail facilities is best summed up in the

following statement:

Every criminology textbook written within the past 40
years includes a graphic description of the physical and
moral decay that grips the majority of jails across the
Nation. The indiscriminate mixing of all types of
prisoners--the sick and the well, the old and the young,
hardened criminals and petty offenders, the mentally
defective, the psychotic, the vagrants and alcoholics,
the habitual recidivists serving life sentences in short
installments--has been recognized for years but, with
few exceptions, has remained unchanged. [26]

Felony probation. Probation, as described under mis-

demeanant probation, can be defined as the release of persons

back to the community under certain conditions and supervisions.

Two primary functions emerge: (1) investigation and presentence

reports which assist in court decision-making during the pre-ar-

raignment, prepleading, and pretrial; and (2) supervision, which

attempts to aid the person in his adjustment to the non-criminal

community.

The organization of adult probation, throughout the nation,

is administered either at the county or state level of government.

There are 14 states that have county directed programs, and 37

states that have a state directed program. [27]

Felony institutions. Adult felony institutions are those

facilities which receive felons sentenced by the criminal courts.

The major effort of the felony institution is directed toward custodial care, followed in lesser degree by education and treatment.
In 1966, 201,220 persons were confined in felony institutions, with
an average custodial staff of 31,000 employees, an additional 1,500
employees responsible for education, and another 1,500 personnel
responsible for treatment.[28]   Of the total correctional institutions
available (398) in the United States, "170 may be classified as
prisons, penitentiaries, or major correctional institutions..."[29]
From these data, there derive the following ratios: one guard per
7 inmates, one education-oriented employee per 133 inmates, and
one treatment-oriented employee per 133 inmates.

Adult parole.   Parole can be described as:

. . .a procedure by which prisoners are selected
for release and a service by which they are provided
with necessary controls, assistance, and guidance as
they serve the remainder of their sentences within the
free community.[30]

The objectives[31] of parole can be listed as follows:

1.   Release of each person from confinement at the
     most favorable time.

2.   The largest possible number of successful parole
     completions.

3.   The smallest possible number of new crimes
     committed by released offenders.

4.   The smallest possible number of violent acts
     committed by released offenders.

5.   An increase of general community confidence in
     parole administration.

The methods[32] by which the above objectives can be
attained are:

1.   A process for selecting persons;

2.   A system for prerelease planning;

3.   A system for supervision and assistance;

4.   A set of policies, procedures, and guidelines for
     making reimprisonment decisions.

Analytic Applications

Applications of Homans model in the correctional system
are unlimited.   The distribution of activities, interaction, and
sentiments within the internal and external system can very easily
be adapted to the study of the following:

1.   The interaction of the total criminal justice system.
Each segment of the system (police, prosecution, courts, and
corrections) could be taken as an individual unit with its contemporary definition(s) of goals, policies, and procedures.   Each
unit, having been so defined, could then be compared for characteristics of duplication, simplification, elimination, and addition.
Tests for efficiency, effectiveness, and economy of the total system
relative to goals may then be attempted.[33]

The analysis here will develop an explanation of administrative and organization interaction.   The analogy of members
reacting within a small group compared to the units of criminal
justice (police, prosecution, courts, and corrections) reacting as
a small group can be developed.   Understanding the group in terms
of influence, pressure, power, and politics will assist in understanding the individual unit personality.

The external system of criminal justice will become more
visible through available documentation and formalization.   Methodology to gain data relevant to the internal system may require
extreme sophistication of survey sampling, questionnaire, observation, and interview.

2.   Each individual unit of criminal justice can be analyzed
by its activities.

3.   Correction presents a fertile field for analysis.   From
an organization and administrative position, analysis might be
developed along the application of POSDCORB (a mnemonic word
which implies that Planning, Organizing, Staffing, Directing,
Coordinating, Reporting, and Budget represent the essential elements of organization and administration).

Corrections can be studied as a whole or divided into its

subparts for analysis, as follows:

A.   To analyze each system according to its own set of standards and goals, and the identification of personnel within the system.

B.   To identify the disparities in correctional arena: national, state, or local level.

C.   To investigate the centralization or decentralization of the correctional service. Centralization is the combining of activities by functions, with the consolidation of formal structure, central policy, and decision-making. Decentralization can take place by functions, geographic regions, or product division.

D.   A study of costs, in areas of activities, interactions, and sentiments. See Table I for the average daily costs of correctional service.

Table I[a]

The Average Daily Costs of Correctional Service

	Juvenile	Adult
Detention	$11.15	$--
State institutions	9.35	5.24
Local institutions (including jails)	10.66	2.86
Probation	.92	.38
Parole or aftercare	.84	.88

[a] Source: Task Force Report: Corrections, op. cit., p. 194.

See Table II which shows costs without the adjustment to efficiency, effectiveness, and economy.

Table II[a]

National Characteristics of Corrections, 1965

	Average daily population of offenders	Total operating costs	Average cost of offender per year	Number of employees in corrections	Number of employees treating offenders
Juvenile corrections:					
Institutions	62,773	$226,809,600	$3,613	31,687	5,621
Community	285,431	93,613,400	328	9,633	7,706
Subtotal	343,204	320,423,000			
Adult felon corrections:					
Institutions	221,597	435,594,500	1,966	51,366	3,220
Community	369,697	73,251,900	198	6,352	5,081
Subtotal	591,494	508,846,400			
Misdemeanant corrections:					
Institutions	141,303	147,794,200	1,046	19,195	501
Community	201,385	28,682,900	142	2,430	1,944
Subtotal	342,688	176,477,100			
Total	1,282,386	1,005,746,500	----	121,163	24,073

Sources: National Survey of Corrections and tabulations provided by the Federal Bureau of Prisons and the Administrative Office of the U.S. Courts.

[a] Source: The Challenge of Crime in a Free Society, op. cit., p. 161.

E. The following problem areas, [34] which were identified
in the Task Force Report: Corrections, can be adapted to Homans
model for analysis. The statement of the problem sets the direction for further research.

1. The need for across-the-board strengthening of
probation and parole. Basic services such as
probation and parole, which have proven effective,
are still undersupported, both quantitatively and
qualitatively.

2. The need for greater, broader funding of correctional services. Correctional personnel salaries
are low; correctional programs, with few exceptions, must get along on shoestring budgets, un-
trained personnel, overcrowding, and few treatment programs. Insufficient financing has become almost a fact of life to which some correctional people have made a resigned adjustment.

3. The need for a clearer correctional philosophy.
The Nation must decide what it wants done about
offenders. One meeting called this a need to
define the national attitude toward offenders: "Do
we wish to punish or to cure?" Many felt that
the field of correction itself is torn by ideological
conflicts, has failed to develop a workable philosophy
on how best to control crime, and has not achieved
a shared body of knowledge and skills.

4. The need for better public understanding of the
correctional task. Correctional work is hampered
by public ignorance, and many correctional officers
are expending much of their energy in interpreting
their roles--energy that should be used with
offenders and clients.

5. The need for more manpower with which to handle
crime and delinquency. The growing manpower
need greatly exceeds the supply of qualified personnel.

6. The need for increased state-level coordination of
correctional services. This issue was related to
funding, deployment of personnel, programming,
physical facilities, provision of specialized services,
and training and recruitment of personnel.

7. The need for general improvement in the administration of justice. The machinery of justice, on
which correction is dependent, was seen as needing
repair. References were made to the large number

of felons in local jails, unserved misdemeanants,
skewed sentencing practices, abridgment of
constitutional rights of juveniles, bail bond problems,
and undue response to political influences.

8. Training and education. In-service training is a top
   priority, also the need for a national academy for
   correction and regional workshops.

9. Diagnostic services. The number of professional
   personnel available for testing, evaluation, and
   psychiatric and psychological consultation to courts,
   parole agencies, and institutions is insufficient.
   Diagnostic services need to be accomplished by
   expanded treatment resources.

10. Detention. A need for more and better juvenile
    detention centers. Many children are still jailed;
    where detention homes exist, there is often a lack
    of adequate programming, with undue emphasis
    on custody. Detention centers frequently are not
    constructed according to modern standards; few are
    available regionally.

11. Special services. The need for more alternatives
    for control and treatment of the offender, such as:
    vocational rehabilitation, group services, halfway
    houses, foster homes, work release, and camps.

12. Diversification. The need for special kinds of
    physical facilities and programs for the retarded
    or marginally defective offender and the criminally
    insane.

13. Statistical system. There is great need for coordi-
    nated, centralized statistical programs for accurate
    information on volume, costs, personnel, etc.,
    for planning and interpretation.

14. Regionalization. The locating of correctional
    facilities in isolated rural communities.

15. Presentence reports. Decisions affecting offenders
    are being made without benefit of social-psychological
    data.

16. Research. Greater need for, and sharing of,
    knowledge.

17. Adult services: (a) legislation and services
    needed for the misdemeanant offender; (b)
    disparities in sentencing practices; (c) broader
    development of services for addicts and alcoholics;
    and (d) increased need for jail standards relative
    to construction, maintenance, and program.

Change Factors Relative to
The Correctional Arena

Homans model for analysis has been developed as a useful
tool to be applied in conducting research in the correctional arena.
The position has been taken that characteristics of organization
can be explained historically, described contemporaneously, and
predicted futuristically.

An end product of analysis is change. Homans model
handles quite well the inter-relatedness of activities, interactions,
and sentiments. As one is altered, a chain reaction develops,
thereby producing an overall alteration or change.

Change based upon analysis is a unique type of change.
Information is produced through analysis which leads to rational
decision-making. The process by which this evolution comes about
is described by Schein as the "adaptive-coping cycle":[35]

1. Sensing a change in the internal or external
   environment.

2. Imparting the relevant information about the
   change to those parts of the organization which
   can act upon it.

3. Changing production or conversion processes
   inside the organization according to the information
   obtained.

4. Stabilizing internal changes while reducing or managing
   undesired by-products (undesired changes in related
   systems which have resulted from the desired changes).

5. Exporting new products, services, and so on, which
   are more in line with the originally perceived changes
   in the environment.

6. Obtaining feedback on the success of the change
    through further sensing of the state of the external
    environment and the degree of integration of the
    internal environment.

Change, therefore, is a continuing condition, either as a
muddling-through process or as a process of rationality.[36] The
latter, based upon proper information, i.e., analysis, is preferable.

Change is relative to organizational control. Organizations
operating under autocratic controls have more difficulty in accepting change. Democratically oriented organizations have less difficulty in accepting change.[37]

Change is not restricted to economic conditions which
include organizational efficiency, economy, and effectiveness. Nor
is it restricted to cultural conditions. In effect, change is neither
exclusively economic nor exclusively cultural, but a multifactor
effect.[38] The start of change " . . .is to a large degree a
response to the presence of some degree of social disorganization,
caused either internally or externally."[39]

> . . .the analysis of most processes. . .is the
> assumption that the various parts of any social
> system are interdependent, so that changes in one
> sector will be followed by strains which necessitate
> adjustive changes in other sectors if the social system
> is to maintain its viability. This seems to be the basic
> common denominator . . .[40]

To produce organizational change founded upon organizational analysis, the entire system of related activities, interactions, and sentiments must be changed. In essence, it is necessary to change the entire organization and not only the people in
the organization. If it is desired to change the whole or sub-parts
of the correctional arena, the issuance of a new policy, new
procedures or new orders, or retraining or education may not be
the best method(s) to employ. The entire situation must be dealt
with.

> Yet we persist in attempting to change organizations
> by working on individuals without redefining their roles
> in the system, without changing the sanctions of the

system, and without changing the expectations of other
role incumbents in the organization about appropriate
role behavior.[41]

Change involves the individual in the organization setting
in terms of total interaction and of: (1) redefining of role, (2)
changing sanctions, and (3) changing expectations.

Methods for Change

Katz and Kahn have listed several methods for inducing
change, including: the direct use of information, skills training,
individual counseling and therapy, the influence of the peer group,
sensitivity training, group therapy, feedback on organizational
functioning, and direct structural or systemic alteration.[42]

The primary target of change may be the individual
as an individual personality, the interpersonal relationships between members of peer groups, the norms of
peer groups, the interpersonal relationships between
members of an organizational family, the structure of
a role, the role relationships of some segment of
organizational space, or the structure of the organization as a whole. The difficulty with many attempts
at organizational change is that the changers have not
clearly distinguished their targets and have assumed
that the individual or group-level target was the same
as the social-structure target.[43]

Information as a method of change. The use of information
can act as a support mechanism for other methods of change.
Information capitalizes upon the existing forces in a situation, and
is not itself a prime mover. It produces change, therefore, only
if the necessary motivation is forthcoming from other sources.[44]

Individual counseling and therapy. The therapeutic approach
can be used to bring about individual change. This approach can
utilize the conscious and subconscious ability of the individual to
change.

Influence of the peer group. The application of group
process to bring about change is identified by Kurt Lewin and
Rensis Likert.

Sensitivity training. The interaction of small numbers
of people in a group setting, with little direction and little control,
gives the individual insight into his own motivations while responding to the total group process.

Group therapy within organizations. Three conditions may
be necessary for the development of group therapy:

> The first factor is similar to Dewey's old initial
> condition for problem-solving, the existence of a felt
> difficulty. The group must be hurting; its members
> must recognize a severe and painful problem. The
> second factor is group solidarity or cohesiveness.
> Members must have commitment to the group and its
> objectives. Otherwise they will not have the motivation
> to overcome the additional anxieties involved in problem
> solution. The third condition is a state of frustration
> created by the failure of denial and other mechanisms of
> defense to function in their accustomed manner. Groups
> tend to avoid facing up to the basic causes of their
> problems through various devices of avoidance and
> denial. When group members, through the help of a
> consultant or by other means, find that running away
> from the problem gives them no relief, they are ready
> for more realistic exploration. [45]

Feedback on organizational functioning. Feedback retrieves
information from the external system as well as the internal system, and relates to the positioning and identification of activities,
interactions, and sentiments.

Direct structural or systemic alteration. The changing of
external activities.

> . . .the degree of control and regulation of the act-
> ivities of the organization cannot be changed at one
> level without affecting the whole organization. In
> fact, this is characteristic of any systemic property.
> If we are really dealing with an organizational or
> system variable, its manipulation will involve the
> entire organization. [46]

Summary

A conceptual scheme has been developed by which corrections can be viewed in terms of (1) a method of organizational
analysis, (2) corrections and organizational analysis, (3) analytic
application, and (4) change factors relative to the correctional arena.

The main emphasis of corrections was found to be on a foundation other than empirical data. It is apparent that

> more successful correction will develop . . .from further refinement of numerous methods now in use; of classification, group therapy, planned release practice; and careful supervision and guidance . . . (and) to stress the need for versatile programs to meet the diverse needs in the offender population.[47]

Homans model, for organizational analysis, was selected for its versatility and adaptability. Homans model stresses the relationship of activities, interactions, and sentiments all inter-woven with internal and external systems.

A review of the adult correctional model and juvenile model highlighted the relationships, historical development, and present position of the correctional arena.

Homans model was then portrayed to areas of application. Systematically, numerous areas were identified for analysis. And change factors were identified to make adoptive, data which might be developed through analysis.

"The trend is not to strive to attain a single end for all, but to discriminate as nicely as possible between offenders in order to achieve feasible and appropriate goals that are suited to the various types of criminals."[48]

Notes

1. Tappan, Paul W. (ed.), Contemporary Corrections (New York: McGraw-Hill, 1951), p. 11.

2. Homans, George The Human Group (New York: Harcourt, Brace, 1950).

3. Pfiffner, John M. and Sherwood, Frank P. Administrative Organization (Englewood Cliffs: Prentice Hall, 1960). pp. 28-29.

4. Ibid., p. 30.

5. Radcliffe-Brown, A. R. Structure and Function in Primitive Society (New York: Free Press, 1965), Chapter IV "On Joking Relationships."

6. Roethisberger, F. J. and Dickson, W. J. Management and the Worker, (Cambridge: Harvard University Press, 1939); also see Mayo, Elton The Social Problems of an Industrial Civilization, (Boston: Harvard Business School, 1945).

7. Litterer, Joseph A. The Analysis of Organizations (New York: John Wiley & Sons, Inc., 1965), p. 121.

8. Ibid., p. 123.

9. Ibid., p. 123.

10. Ibid., p. 129.

11. Information in this section of the paper was developed from the following sources: The President's Commission on Law Enforcement and the Administration of Justice: The Challenge of Crime in a Free Society (Washington: Government Printing Office, 1967); The President's Commission on Law Enforcement and Administration of Justice: Task Force Report: Corrections (Washington: Government Printing Office, 1967); and National Council on Crime and Delinquency National Survey of Corrections, 1967.

12. Tappan, op. cit., adapted from Chapter I, "Objectives and Methods in Correction".

13. Ibid., p. 4.

14. Task Force Report: Corrections, op. cit., p. 121.

15. Ibid., p. 129.

16. Rosenheim, Margaret K. (ed.), Justice for the Child (New York: Free Press of Glencoe, 1962), p. 3.

17. U. S. Department of Health, Education, and Welfare, Children's Bureau, "Juvenile Court Statistics, 1964" (Washington, D. C.: Children's Bureau, 1965), p. 1.

18. Task Force Report: Corrections, op. cit., p. 143.

19. Ibid., p. 143.

20. Ibid., pp. 150-51. The states which do not have a centralized aftercare system are the following: Alabama, Arkansas, Kansas, Maryland, Mississippi, New Mexico, North Carolina, North Dakota, Pennsylvania, and Virginia.

21. Neumeyer, Martin H. Juvenile Delinquency in Modern Society (New York: D. Van Nostrand, 1964), p. 39.

22. The American Correctional Association, Manual of Correctional Standards (Washington: The American Correctional Association, 1966), p. 98.

23. Task Force Report: Corrections, op. cit., p. 155.

24. Ibid., p. 162.

25. The American Correctional Association, op. cit., p. 43.

26. Task Force Report: Corrections, op. cit., p. 163.

27. Ibid., p. 171.

28. Ibid., p. 179.

29. Ibid., p. 180.

30. The American Correctional Association, op. cit., p. 114.

31. Task Force Report: Corrections, op. cit., p. 185.

32. Ibid.

33. Etzioni, Amitai Modern Organizations (Englewood Cliffs: 1964), see Chapter Two, "The Organization Goal: Master or Servant", pp. 5-19.

34. Ibid., pp. 203-04.

35. Schein, Edgar H. Organizational Psychology (Englewood Cliffs: Prentice-Hall, 1965), p. 99.

36. A problem emerges, which Blau describes as rationality producing irrational results. Regardless of the sophistication of analysis, total information may never be possible because of time, economy, and availability of data. Therefore, a discussion of rationality may suggest a degree of, not complete, rationality. See Peter Blau, The Dynamics of Bureaucracy (Chicago: University of Chicago Press, 1965).

37. Likert, Rensis New Patterns of Management (New York: McGraw-Hill, 1961), see Chapter 2 "Leadership and Organizational Performance," and p. 41-42, 245.

38. Etzioni, Amitai and Etzioni, Eva (eds.), Social Change: Sources, Patterns, and Consequences (New York: Basic Books, 1964), p. 7.

39. Ibid., p. 403.

40. Ibid., p. 403.

41. Katz, Daniel, and Kahn, Robert L. The Social Psychology
    of Organization (New York: John Wiley and Sons, 1966),
    p. 391.

42. Ibid., see Chapter 13, "Organizational Change," for a
    definitive discussion of methodology to induce change,
    p. 392.

43. Ibid.

44. Ibid., p. 393.

45. Ibid., pp. 410-11.

46. Ibid., p. 427.

47. Tappan, op. cit., p. 11.

48. Ibid., p. 5.

VIII. Special Police Problems

Problem #1: Professionalization

1. Morris L. Cogan[1] indicated that 300 years have failed
to bring agreement on a single definition for "profession,"
but that a full fledged profession demands that practitioners acquire an intellectually based technique through
prolonged study. Further, it is a moot question whether
...municipal employees, such as police could maintain
professionalism ...under the conditions of their employment.

2. Criteria by which a profession can be recognized:[2]"(a)
Systematic body of knowledge and skills, oriented to
intellectual pursuit; (b) More or less well established
principles, methods, theories, etc.; (c) A clearly defined
purpose (product), etc.; (d) An esoteric terminology; (e)
Pecuniary profit is not primary objective; and (f) Associations within the field are concerned with standards, accreditation, ethics or certain self-monitoring elements."

3. Professions may be described[3] as occupations which
provide highly specialized intellectual services. They
possess three principal features: (1) A body of erudite
knowledge, a set of attitudes, and techniques which are
applied to the service of mankind through an educated
group; (2) A standard of success measured by accomplishment in serving the needs of the people rather than by
personal gain; and (3) a system of control over the practice
of the calling and the education of its practitioners through
associations and codes of ethics.

4. A professional fireman is defined as any member of the
fire brigade maintained by a local authority who is wholly
and permanently employed on fire brigade duty. This is

155

a misuse of the word professional. Professionalism is specialized intellectual training with direct remuneration. One's skill group training is at some time specialized and intellectual, and qualifies as the sort of specialized intellectual training identified with professional education. It doesn't of itself identify the skill group as a profession.[4]

5. A profession is a vocation or occupation requiring advanced training in some liberal art or science, and usually involving mental rather than manual work, such as teaching, engineering, writing, etc., and especially medicine, law, or theology.

    a. The job of the professional is technical--based on systematic knowledge or doctrine acquired only through long prescribed training.

    b. The professional man adheres to a set of professional norms.

    c. The client to a professional service is peculiarly vulnerable; he is both in trouble and ignorant of how to help himself out of it.

    d. The service ideal is the pivot around which the moral claim to professional status revolves.

    e. Norms covering client relations dictate that the professional be impersonal and objective (limit the relationship to the technical task at hand, avoid emotional involvement) and impartial (not discriminate, give equal service regardless of personal sentiment).

    f. A science, in contrast to a profession, has no clients except, in an ultimate sense, society.[5]

6. Professionalization is accomplished through: (a) prescribed courses of study, standardized and geared to one another in high schools, colleges, and universities; (b) application of prescribed methods in practice teaching, reading, briefing, etc; (c) post-graduate courses, prescribed and administered if a specialized field is selected; (d) internship for application of theory to practice for the purpose of

developing skill; (e) acknowledgment and acceptance of self-imposed ethical standards of professional practice and personal conduct; (f) examination to determine fitness to practice and enter the profession; (g) continuous study and research for improvement and advancement of professional techniques and their application within the profession.[6]

7. The American police has no nation-wide organization[7] and in consequence, many police associations have sprung up all over the country. The Fraternal Order of Police now has lodges in about half the states . . . Many policemen at all levels of government belong to the Fraternal Order of Police, the National Police and Peace Officers' Association, National Sheriff's Association, and other nationwide state, county, or local bodies.

8. In regard to state licensing the Tenth Amendment of the Constitution of the United States reserves to the states and to the people those powers not delegated to the federal government. According to this principle, the authority to organize police forces in the United States rests with the individual states and their subordinate instrumentalities such as cities, counties, townships, and so forth. . . police power rests with all of the people, and their elected representatives create the law which the police enforce. With no single source assigning this authority, one must look to the United States Constitution, United States Supreme Court decisions, and federal statutes--the constitutions, laws, and court decisions of each of the several states . . . to determine how the police are organized and the extent of their authority and duties.[8]

9. Some of the requisites[9] essential in the establishment of a profession are: (1) that an adequate body of technical data exist; (2) that the technical data can be arranged and organized; (3) that a set of standards be met requiring mental training and effort; (4) that a Code of Ethics govern

the conduct of members in their work; (5) that a spirit
of public service exist; and (6) that the persons desiring
to join the profession possess special competence and work
for further advancement of the profession.

10.   Local law enforcement should seek ways and means to
certify or license its membership. It should set academic
standards and regulate the licensing of its members.[10]

11.   Law enforcement is not classified as a profession. It is
under the classification of service workers.[11]

Problem # 2: Abortion

1.   Abortion is defined in criminal law as the miscarriage or
premature delivery of a woman who is quick with child,
when this is brought about with a malicious design or for
an unlawful purpose.

2.   "Every person who provides, supplies or administers to
any woman or procures any woman to take any medicine,
drug or substance, or uses or employs any instrument or
other means whatever, with intent thereby to procure the
miscarriage of any woman, unless the same is necessary
to preserve her life, is punishable by imprisonment in the
state prison not less than two nor more than five years."
--California Penal Code, Sec. 174.

3.   This offense is one requiring a specific intent, the intent
to procure a miscarriage. To sustain a conviction this
intent must be proved.

4.   "Upon a trial for procuring or attempting to procure an
abortion, or aiding and assisting therein . . . the defendant
cannot be convicted upon the testimony of the woman upon
or with whom the offense was committed, unless she is
corroborated by other evidence. -- California Penal Code,
Sec. 1108.

5.   The woman upon whom the abortion is performed is not
an accomplice of the person performing the abortion. --
People v. Clapp, 24 Cal. 2d 835.

6. There are two major classifications of abortions---sponta-
    neous and induced. A spontaneous abortion is simply a
    natural miscarriage. An induced abortion is a pregnancy
    deliberately interrupted by physical, chemical or operative
    means. Classifying an abortion as therapeutic or criminal
    depends upon whether it has been performed legally, where
    the pregnancy has been proved to be injurious to the
    physical and mental health of the mother, or by illegal
    means.

7. The following are some statistics[12] on abortions in the
    United States:

    a. Approximately 18,000 pregnancies are interrupted
        annually for therapeutic reasons.

    b. Three out of ten pregnancies end in abortion.

    c. Approximately a million of these abortions annually
        are illegal.

    d. Between ten and twenty abortions take place every
        fifteen minutes.

    e. 10% of white, unmarried girls in college become
        premaritally pregnant--95% of these pregnancies end
        in abortion.

    f. Nine out of ten artificially induced abortions, whether
        therapeutic or criminal, are procured or prescribed
        for married women over thirty years of age, who
        have three or more children and who have been
        impregnated by their husbands.

    g. There are approximately 2,500 abortions performed
        daily--theoretically one-half to one million are possible
        annually. Of these, less than 500 criminal prosecutions
        are initiated.

    h. Between the years 1946 and 1953 the District Attorney
        of New York County was able to prosecute only 136
        cases.

8.   There are four categories of therapeutic abortions:[13]

    1. Medical

    2. Eugenic

    3. Humanitarian

    4. Socio-Economic

9.   The law of Criminal Abortion: Procurement or attempted
        procurement of an abortion by any means has been
        declared in nearly every state in the union to be a
        possible felony. Exceptions:

    a. To preserve the life of the mother;

    b. To preserve the life or health of the mother;

    c. To save the life of the mother or to prevent serious
        or permanent bodily injury;

    d. When physician is satisfied that the fetus is dead;

    e. Statute requires for violation when the act is done
        unlawfully, or maliciously or without lawful justification.

10.   History of the Law of Abortion:[14]

    a. Earliest records of abortion date back more than
        4,600 years.

    b. Roman law indicated unlawful if within 40-80 days
        after conception.

    c. England, 1803, abortion became a felony.

    d. England, 1929, Child-Destruction statute: must prove
        that the act of abortion was done in good faith.

    e. Abortion is a statutory crime throughout the United
        States with the exception for therapeutic abortion.

11.   Einstoss[15] has indicated that in Los Angeles County 75%
        of the persons prosecuted for performing abortions had
        no formal medical education.

        During the period of August, 1963, to June, 1965, there
        were 13 deaths attributable to criminal abortion in the
        county.

        The number of married women approximately equals the
        number of single women.

From 5 to 8% of the cases involved victims of statutory
rape (females under 18).
One percent involved girls who became pregnant while
under the age of 15.

12. A recent clinical study[16] indicates one abortion takes
place for each 3.6 live births. This computes to
1,200,000 abortions in the U.S. annually; of these only
8,000 are legally performed in hospitals. An estimated
5,000 abortion deaths per year are due to illegal operations.
The method in the first three months of pregnancy is to
scrape the walls of the womb; after three months the
operation constitutes a miniature cesarean. It is among
the simplest and safest of operations when performed in a
hospital. In some European countries, the death rate
for legal abortions is estimated, at its maximum, to be
35 per 100,000, compared to 17 per 100,000 for tonsil-
lectomies. There are no detrimental after-effects, either
physical or psychological. The well-to-do, as a whole,
undergo therapeutic abortion 4 times as often as poor
patients. A significant proportion of abortions involve
married women with several children. The Model Penal
Code composed by the American Law Institute in 1962
recommended that abortion be legalized under the following
circumstances:
1. Physical or mental health endangered.
2. Strong possibility of child being born with serious
mental or physical defects.
3. Pregnancy resulting from incest, rape, or illicit
intercourse with girl under 16 years of age.

13. Methods of Abortion:[17]
1. Direct instrument methods, usually used by professional
abortionists. This type includes curettage, dilation,
sharp instruments, irritants.
2. Chemical methods include purgatives, intestinal
irritants, uterine-contracting substances, poisons taken

in small amounts.

3. Chemicals taken internally: use of different type
   poisons.

14.   Source of complaints:[18]

1. 50% are received through a legitimate doctor at a
   hospital.

2. Overheard gossip of neighbors, also the local druggist.

3. Death: in 10% of the cases where the police are
   confronted with a dead body an autopsy reveals
   evidence of an illegal abortion.

Problem # 3: Labor-Management Disputes

1.   The basic social environment in the United States has
      been hostile to the development of union organization.
      Until 1842 the courts continued to outlaw all union act-
      ivity. Then, in the case of Commonwealth v. Hunt, the
      Supreme Judicial Court of Massachusetts decided that a
      strike was not illegal as such. It had to be proved that
      the workers objectives were bad. After this landmark
      case, the courts tended to judge the legality of strikes
      on the basis of "motive and intent."[19]

2.   The Evolution of Organized Labor:
      A. 1800-1850:
         (1) A combination of employees to bargain with
             employers was judged to be a crime, since they
             were considered as interfering with the natural
             laws of supply and demand.
         (2) During this time we were largely engaged in
             farming, which emphasized traits attached to
             individualism.
         (3) The normal producing unit was one person.
      B. 1850-1930:
         (1) Industrial Revolution; a time of reluctant toleration
             of unions.

(2) Courts' rule of law known as the doctrine of "Means and Ends."

(3) Union principles are lawful, but will examine the activities-strikes, picketing, boycotts, etc.

(4) 1898: Yellow-Dog Contract; applicant for employment had to sign a statement that he did not belong to, or would not join a union.

(5) 1908: court decided nationwide secondary boycotts were in violation of the Sherman Anti-Trust Act.

(6) 1914: Congress passed the Clayton Amendment to the Sherman Act, which ruled that labor was not a commodity of commerce, and unions were not organized in restraint of trade. Restrictions were imposed on the power of the courts to impose injunctions.

C. 1930-1945:

(1) Passage of the Norris-LaGuardia Act of 1932. This opened the era of active support for labor. The act did three things:

    (a)   Stated that collective bargaining should be recognized, in principle, as a part of our national public policy.

    (b)   It held yellow-dog contracts contrary to public policy, therefore unenforceable.

    (c)   It placed severe limitations on the power of Federal Courts of Equity to issue injunctions against union activities.

(2) 1935: National Labor Relations Act or Wagner Act; established the rights of employees to unionize, select representatives and bargain collectively.

(c) Union membership went from 2.5 million in 1932 to 15 million in 1947.

D. 1945-1955:
    (1) Shift in public policy, resulting in the adoption
         of numerous restraints on union activities:
    (2) Actions on the state level:
         (a)   16 states passed laws prohibiting the closed
                or union shop--so-called "right to work"
                laws.
         (b)   21 states provided for strike notice and
                "cooling off" periods.
         (c)   11 states restricted picketing.
         (d)   12 states prohibited secondary boycotts.
         (e)   10 states directed unions to account for
                their finances.
         (f)   6 states lowered the bar against the use
                of the injunction in labor disputes.
    (3) 1947: Taft-Hartley Act; imposed a set of six un-
         fair labor practices upon unions.
    (4) Post-World War II unions felt to have too much
         power.
E. 1955:
    (1) Development in public policy seemed to be
         concentrating on examination of the relations be-
         tween unions and their members.
    (2) Labor-Management Reporting and Disclosure Act
         of 1959.

3.   The world's largest union[20] is the Metallarbeiter-Gewerk-
     schaft (West Germany's Metal Workers Union) with a
     membership of 1,842,800.

4.   The longest major strike was at the plumbing fixtures
     factory of the Kohler Co. in Sheboyan, Wisconsin, which
     was called in April, 1954, and ended eight and one half
     years later in October, 1962. The strike cost the United
     Auto Workers $12 million.[21]

5. Each year 140,000 contracts are negotiated between labor
    and management, 90% of which result in a wage increase
    and are accomplished without violence.[22]

6. Work Stoppages in 1964 indicate the enormity of the
    problem:

Number of stoppages or strikes:	3,655
Average duration in days:	22.9
Workers involved:	1,640,000
Man-days idle:	22,900,000
Average man-days idle per man:	14.0

    Issues involved: Wages; supplementary benefits; hours;
    union organization; job security; plant administration;
    arbitration; grievance procedures; union matters.

7. Labor-management disputes[24] involve management, which
    has at stake investments in production and sales, and
    employees, who have their jobs at stake. Potentially,
    and often in practice, the most difficult problem in police
    administration and operations is created when labor-manage-
    ment relations develop into strikes or lockouts. These
    factors often lead to civil disturbances which result from
    tactics employed by the principals or by the police them-
    selves, or from tensions which develop.

8. "Policemen working a strike tend to fraternize with either
    pickets or management, or both. This practice should
    be avoided so that the officers' perspective will be at all
    times entirely objective and impartial."[25]

9. Any other police position than that of strict impartiality
    is indefensible. It is neither the duty nor the responsibil-
    ity of the police to attempt to settle the basic issues in
    any labor-management dispute.[26]

10. The police role in labor-management disputes has often
    been difficult. The police attitude[27] should be that the
    force exists not to take sides, but to protect life and
    property and to maintain the peace. A public relations

program should make sure that the contacts between the police and the disputing groups are made before trouble develops.

11.   The duty of the police in a strike situation is the job of maintaining law and order.[28] They are not arbitrators of the dispute. They should, however, know as much as possible about the strike in order to police the area effectively.

12.   One way to insure that law and order will be maintained is to have a "meeting of the minds" of all people concerned with the strike. This would include the police as well as the employers and the striking employees. Things to be known at the conference should include: The employer should be aware of the right of the employees to assemble and picket the area. He should be told of the dangers inherent in hiring private guards. On the other hand, the strikers should be aware that the employer has the right to keep his shop going if he can find the help; ingress and egress cannot be impeded around the struck plant; and destruction of the employer's property will not be tolerated.

13.   Picketing:

A.   Peaceful picketing is the lawful congregation of workers on grounds near the premises of the employer with whom they have a controversy.

B.   Peaceful picketing is a right protected by the United States and California Constitution.

C.   Mass picketing or circular picketing is not in itself a violation of the law.

D.   Picketing becomes illegal if it blocks streets and roads or interferes with the free and immediate use of the sidewalk or with ingress or egress to any place of business.

14.   Legal Aspects of Unusual Occurrences (California):

A. Penal Code:

    1. Riot: Section 404 P.C.

        a. Any use of force or violence

        b. Threat to use force

        c. Disturbing public peace

        d. Power of execution

        e. Two or more persons

    1a. Punishment of Riot: Section 405 P.C.

        Every person who participates in any riot is punishable by a fine not exceeding one thousand dollars, or by imprisonment in a county jail not exceeding one year, or by both such fine and imprisonment.

    2. Lynching: Section 405 P.C.

        a. The taking by means of riot of a person from the lawful custody of a peace officer.

    2a. Punishment for lynching: Section 405b P.C.

        Every person who participates in any lynching is punishable by imprisonment in the State prison for not more than 20 yrs.

    3. Rout: Section 406 P.C.

        a. Two or more people advance toward an act which would be a riot if completed.

    4. Unlawful Assembly: Section 407 P.C.

        a. Two or more people agree to do an unlawful act--no advance

        b. Do a lawful act in a boisterous, violent manner.

    4a. Punishment of rout or unlawful assembly is a misdemeanor. Section 408 P.C.

    5. Remaining present at place of riot, etc., after warning to disperse: Section 408 P.C.

        a. Every person remaining after being lawfully warned to disperse is guilty of a misdemeanor.

b. Dispersal order: Section 726 P.C.:

(1) Officer must go among the persons assembled;

(2) Or as near them as possible;

(3) And issue a command to disperse in the name of the people of the State.

    (a) A proper dispersal order would be the following:

       "This is John Doe (stating the Officer's Name), a peace officer of the State of California and Police Officer for the City of "X." I do hereby declare this an unlawful assembly and, in the name of the people of the State of California, I command you immediately to disperse."

    (b) It is necessary that a dispersal order be given before a person can be guilty of a violation of section 409 P.C.

    (c) Guilty as a misdemeanor.

6. Neglecting or refusing to disperse rioters: Section 410 P.C.

    a. Officer must have notice of unlawful or riotous assembly.

    b. If he neglects or refuses to disperse these persons, he is guilty of a misdemeanor.

7. Disturbing the Peace: Section 415 P.C.

    a. Any person who maliciously and willfully disturbs the peace or quiet of any person is guilty of a misdemeanor

B. Most cities have a "Municipal Code" to cover certain areas not mentioned in the Penal Code. Such a municipal code might include the following laws:

1. Blocking the sidewalk--No person shall stand or sit, in or upon any street, sidewalk or crosswalk to obstruct the passage of pedestrians.

   2. Blocking Entrance, Exit, or Approach-- No person
       shall block, impede, or obstruct any public place,
       entrance, or exit.

15. Vocabulary of Labor-Management Relations:
    A. Taft-Hartley Act 1947:
        1. Prohibited secondary boycotts;
        2. Enforcement of collective bargaining;
        3. Guaranteed freedom of speech for employers;
        4. Prohibited closed-shops (hiring of union members
            only);
        5. Gave a company the right to sue a union;
        6. Stated that unions must prepare financial reports;
        7. Placed curbs on jurisdictional strikes;
        8. Prohibited communist union leaders;
        9. Provided a 60-day cooling off period before a
            strike becomes effective.
    B. Labor Contract or Collective Agreement-- An agree-
        ment expressed or implied, between an individual
        worker or union and an employer, under which the
        former agrees to work in return for compensation.
        1. Stipulates a given time period;
        2. Must be renewed;
        3. Under Taft-Hartley Act, 1947.
            a. Either side must give a 60-day notice to
                cancel contract;
            b. During this time (60-day period) strikes or
                lockouts are forbidden.
    C. Collective Bargaining: the means by which a labor
        agreement or contract is negotiated.
        1. The bargaining takes place between management
            or representatives and labor or representatives.
    D. Labor Injunction: a court order secured by management
        in anticipation of a strike, during a strike, or at other
        times commanding labor to do a particular act. How-
        ever, under Taft-Hartley Act, injunctions are only

permitted under certain conditions.

E. Strike: a work stoppage ordered by labor in an attempt to secure or enforce their demands on management.

F. Jurisdictional Strike: a strike called to settle a dispute where two or more unions claim workers in borderline occupations employed in a plant covered by their agreements. This is forbidden by the Taft-Hartley Act as an unfair labor practice.

G. Lockout: management's equivalent to a strike. Management shuts workers out of his plant until an agreement is reached.

H. Boycott: agreement by members of a union to refuse any dealings with a particular employer.
   1. Refusing to buy or handle his products.
   2. Action by an employer's own workers is a primary boycott.
   3. When other unions join in it is a secondary boycott.
   4. Taft-Hartley prohibits any secondary boycott.

I. Picketing: defined as the posting of a person or persons by a labor union at the entrance of a place of business affected by a strike.
   1. Justice William Douglas, in a U. S. Supreme Court decision, declared picketing as "a form of free speech--the working man's method of giving publicity to the facts of industrial life. . . . as such, picketing is entitled to constitutional protection."

J. Mediation: a neutral third party suggests a settlement which the parties to the dispute are not obliged to accept. The neutral party is called the "mediator."

K. Conciliation: the action of a neutral third party who tries to bring about a friendly feeling between labor and management.

L. <u>Arbitration</u>: a quasi-judicial procedure by which the
parties to a controversy agree in advance to submit
to the findings.

<u>Problem #4</u>: <u>Homosexuality</u>

1.   There are two classifications of homosexuals.[29] The "active"
        and the "passive." The active homosexual actively part-
        icipates in homosexual relations. The passive homosexual
        controls his desires and abstains from homosexual activity.
        He might on occasion give in to a temptation but he re-
        covers himself and avoids further contacts as much as
        possible.

2.   Homosexuality and the problem it poses exists all over
        the United States but is most evident in large cities.
        Cities offer established homosexual societies, opportunity
        to meet other homosexuals, and anonymity.

3.   There is no law in any state against being a homosexual.
        The laws which police enforce are directed at specific
        acts. For the most part these laws make it a crime to
        engage in any sexual act which could not result in pro-
        creation.

4.   It is unlawful in California[30] to solicit anyone in a public
        place to engage in a lewd act. Under these laws the
        police are able to make arrests.

5.   Anyone convicted of a homosexual act, in the State of
        California, or any offense involving lewd or lascivious
        conduct, must register with the police. <u>California Penal
        Code,</u> Section 290.

6.   The accompanying social and criminal problems are as-
        sociated with homosexuality:
        (1) Robbery and assault;
        (2) Male prostitution;
        (3) Crimes of violence;
        (4) Venereal disease;

(5) Susceptibility to blackmail;

(6) Servicemen selling services;

(7) Exposure of other persons to perverted practices.

7. Female homosexuality is less strictly regulated than the male homosexual conduct.

8. In New York, in 1950, homosexual conduct between consenting male adults and between boys from 16-21 was reduced to a misdemeanor in the Criminal Code. In the Criminal Code of Illinois, revised in 1961, this conduct is no longer a crime.[31]

9. Definition of homosexuality: Overt homosexuality, technically, when an adult prefers sex relations with his or her own sex, in spite of the availability of potential partners of the opposite sex. Homosexuality becomes a crime, socially considered, when it is practiced in public and offends others for this reason, and when it is used to seduce children or young adolescents.[32]

10. Theories[33] regarding causes of homosexuality: The three well-known theories are that it is an inherited tendency; that it is a result of conditioning or maladjustment, such as unsatisfactory social relations, etc.; or that it is due to a sex hormone imbalance. Kinsey's findings show that 37% of the total male population has had at least some overt homosexual experience, while 4% of white males are exclusively homosexual throughout their lives. Kinsey reports homosexuality among women as 19% reporting such experience.

11. Homosexuality has been recorded[34] in ancient Greece where it was not only tolerated but encouraged. It is reported that during the reign of Louis the 16th of France both men and women in his court engaged in this practice.

12. Laws concerning the homosexual:

(a) Against the law in all places and states, both in public and private.

    (b) Punishment measures vary.

    (c) Laws are less specific than general criminal laws.

    (d) Laws are very seldom enforced because of type of behavior; problems of getting evidence; and a great deal of tolerance both by the police and general public.

    (e) Wolfenden Report (1957), in England, made recommendations that the laws should be changed, and that homosexuality should be defined under law the same as heterosexual relationships.

13. Men who remain permanently homosexual amount to no more than 5%, whereas 50% of homosexual men never give way to their impulses.[35]

14. In countries where homosexuals are not prosecuted or treated as outcasts, sex crime statistics indicate that homosexuals usually do not engage in criminal behavior.[36]

15. 1966: British law passed providing the following:

    (a) Homosexual acts between consenting adults, in private, are no longer criminal.

    (b) Maximum sentence for homosexual acts against a boy under the age of 16 will be life in prison; no change from previous law.

    (c) A homosexual act against a youth between 16 and 21 will be punishable with up to 5 years in jail, while acts of public indecency could bring a two-year sentence.

16. Every person who commits any of the following acts shall be guilty of disorderly conduct, a misdemeanor (California):

    (1) Who solicits anyone to engage in or who engages in lewd or dissolute conduct in any public place or in any place open to the public exposed to public view.

    (2) Who solicits or who engages in any act of prostitution.

    (3) Who loiters in or about any toilet open to the public for the purpose of engaging in or soliciting any lewd

or lascivious or any unlawful act.

(4) Every person who loiters about any school or public
place at or near which children attend or normally
congregate is a vagrant, and is punishable by a fine
of not exceeding five hundred dollars ($500) or by
imprisonment in the county jail for not exceeding six
months, or by both such fine and imprisonment.

Problem # 5: Pornography

1. Pornography is defined[37] as, "originally, a description of
    prostitutes and their trades; hence, writings, pictures,
    etc., intended to arouse sexual desire."

2. Definition: A thing is obscene if, considered as a whole,
    its dominant theme or purpose is an appeal to prurient
    interest. Prurient interest is defined as a shameful
    or morbid interest in nudity, sex or excretion, which
    goes substantially beyond customary limits of candor in
    description or representation of such matters.

3. One method of enforcement against pornographic material
    is an action "in rem," an action against the material
    itself. This method is a statutory action which provides
    for the seizure of the obscene material upon court order;
    for notice and hearing. Applying the community standard,
    the court sits as the conscience of the community and
    rules upon each piece of evidence suspected of being
    obscene. Enforcement can also be by injunction and
    prosecution.

4. The Granahan Committee[38] of the House of Representatives
    turned up informed estimates in 1959 that the commerce
    in filth, considered as a whole, may reach a billion
    dollars a year. In 1960, Postmaster General Arthur B.
    Summerfield estimated obscenity mail order revenues
    at $500 million a year.[39]

5. Model Penal Code sec. 207.10. Obscenity is defined in
    terms of material which appeals predominantly to prurient

interest. Appeal to "prurient interest" refers to qualities
of the material itself, the capacity to attract individuals
eager for a forbidden look behind the curtain of privacy
which our customs draw about sexual matters. The Code
further states[40] that society may legitimately seek to
deter the deliberate stimulation and exploitation of
emotional tensions arising from the conflict between social
convention and the individual sex drive.

6. Obscene material--methods of enforcement:[41]

   (a) Action by seizure of the obscene material;

   (b) Injunction--used especially where there are several
   defendants. The injunction is against the defendants,
   enjoining in the sale, circulation, or distribution of
   obscene material.

   (c) Prosecution--most common, this includes trial, etc.

7. In June, 1957, Justice William J. Brennan declared:
   "Implicit in history of the First Amendment is the
   rejection of obscenity as utterly without redeeming social
   importance. We hold that obscenity is not within the area
   of Constitutionally protected speech or press." The Roth
   test of obscenity states that: (1) material must be patently
   offensive; (2) utterly without redeeming social importance;
   and (3) the dominant theme of it must appeal to prurient
   interest.

8. March, 1966: At Ralph Ginzburg's trial in Federal District
   Court in Philadelphia, the Government pointed out that the
   publisher, in his promotional ads, had promised subscribers
   sexual titillation from reading his publication. The publisher had, in fact, gone to extraordinary lengths to convey
   the idea that the very act of mailing Eros could be a dirty
   joke. Before the Ginzburg ruling, such a mailing would
   not have been a determining factor in an obscenity decision.
   In Ginzburg's conviction, the Court expanded the Roth test
   to include the manner in which the purveyor promoted his
   merchandise.

9.   The Movie Production Code: General Principles--

    (1) No picture shall be produced which will lower the
moral standards of those who see it. Hence the
sympathy of the audience shall never be thrown to
the side of crime, wrong-doing, evil or sin.

    (2) Correct standards of life, subject only to the require-
ments of drama and entertainment, shall be presented.

    (3) Law--divine, natural or human--shall not be ridiculed,
nor shall sympathy be created for its violation.

10. The Post Office Department: The principal law, U.S. Code
Title 18, Section 1461, stated briefly, says that it is
punishable by fine and imprisonment to knowingly cause
the mails to be used to transport obscenity. This law
was originated in 1865, and was amended to its present
form in 1873. A minor additional law (U.S. Code Title
18, Section 1463) makes it illegal to write obscenity on
the outside of mailing wrappers.

11. The Bureau of Customs was established by George Washington in 1789. Its function, under Section 305 of the Tariff
Act of 1930, as amended, is to refer to the courts for
possible forfeiture any material which appears to be
obscene. The court determines obscenity.

12. Definitions:

    (a) "Obscene" means that to the average person, applying
contemporary standards, the predominant appeal of
the matter, taken as a whole, is to prurient interest,
i.e., a shameful or morbid interest in nudity, sex,
or excretion, which goes substantially beyond customary limits of candor in description or representation
of such matters and is utterly without redeeming social
importance.

    (b) "Matter" means any book, magazine, newspaper, or
other printed or written material, or any picture,
drawing, photograph, motion picture, or other pictorial
representation, or any statue or other figure, or any

recording, transcription or mechanical, chemical
or electrical reproduction or any other articles,
equipment, machines or materials.

(c) "Person" means any individual, partnership, firm,
association, corporation, or other legal entity.

(d) "Distribute" means to transfer possession of, whether
with or without consideration.

(e) "Knowingly" means having knowledge that the matter
is obscene.

13. a. General State Laws. Sale or distribution, etc., of
obscene matter:
Every person who knowingly sends or causes to be
sent, or brings or causes to be brought into the state
for sale or distribution, or prepares, publishes,
prints, exhibits, distributes, or offers to distribute,
or has in his possession with intent to distribute or
to exhibit or offer to distribute, any obscene matter,
is guilty of a misdemeanor.

b. Distribution of obscene matter to a minor:
Every person, who with knowledge that a person is a
minor under 18 years of age, or who, while in
possession of such facts that he should reasonably
know that such person is a minor under 18 years of
age, knowingly distributes to, or sends or causes to
be sent to, or exhibits to, or offers to distribute any
obscene matter to a minor under 18 years of age, is
guilty of a misdemeanor.

c. Hiring, employing, etc., a minor to engage in sale
or distribution of obscene material:
Every person who, with knowledge that a person is
a minor, or who, while in possession of such facts
that he should reasonably know that such person is a
minor, hires, employs, or uses such minor to do
or assist in doing any of the acts of sale or distribution of obscene material is guilty of a misdemeanor.

> d. Advertisement, promotion of sale, etc., of matter
> represented to be obscene:
> Every person who writes or creates advertising or
> solicits anyone to publish such advertising or other-
> wise promote the sale or distribution of matter
> represented or held out by him to be obscene, is
> guilty of a misdemeanor.
>
> e. Singing obscene songs, ballads, etc.:
> Every person who knowingly sings or speaks any
> obscene song, ballad, or other words, in any public
> place is guilty of a misdemeanor.

14. Defense:

It shall be a defense in any prosecution for a violation of
these offenses that the act charged was committed in aid
of legitimate scientific or educational purposes.

Problem # 6:   Riot Control

1. Crowd: A large number of persons when collected into a
somewhat compact body without order.

2. Mob: People in a large disorderly group.

3. Suggestions for controlling riots:[42]

   a. Train police in techniques of riot control.

   b. Support the police. Do not permit them to be
   discouraged from taking effective action by fear of
   being "pilloried" by civilian review boards.

   c. Build up contacts in trouble areas to spot developing
   riots early before they get out of hand.

   d. Prosecute rioters promptly so the deterrent effect is
   not lost by delay.

4. The overall strategy of the police is to contain, isolate,
disperse.

5. Tactical formations used in controlling rioters:

   A. Squad line: a defensive formation used for holding back
   a crowd from gaining access to a particular location.
   It consists of a line of police standing side by side to

> hold a surging riot in check.

    B. Squad wedge: an offensive tactic used to split or penetrate a crowd. It is often used in short distances to rescue prisoners or an injured person.

    C. Diagonal formations: used to move or turn a crowd from buildings.

6. Streams of water and chemical agents such as tear gas are most effective as weapons in police conflict with dangerous mobs. Firepower should be used as a last resort.

7. Crowd Control:

    A. Removal or isolation of the individuals involved in the precipitating incident before the crowd has begun to achieve substantial unity.

    B. Interruption of communication during the milling process by dividing the crowd into small units.

    C. Removal of the crowd leaders, if it can be done without the use of force.

    D. Distracting the attention of the crowd from its focal point by creating diversions at other points.

    E. Preventing the spread and reinforcement of the crowd by isolating it.

8. Riots:[43]

    A. Riots are the worst form of unlawful public gatherings and have caused the greatest loss of life and destruction of property, second only to war.

    B. Riots are caused by a number of things, but always are associated with extreme public feeling.

    C. There are several classifications of riots: (1) racial; (2) industrial; (3) catastrophic; (4) celebrative; (5) economic; (6) quasi-political; (7) prison. Quasi-political is the rarest; prison and celebrative the most common.

9. Control of riots and unlawful assemblies:[44]

Reconnaissance of the area, and close observation
of all elements involved in a potential riot, are
necessary precautions in riot control.   They indicate:

A.   Possible magnitude of the riot.

B.   Damage which could be inflicted.

C.   Types of problems the authorities will confront
     in dealing with the group.

This information must be obtained by plainclothesmen
or undercover agents.

Information needed in the riot area:

A.   Fire hazards;

B.   Availability of weapons;

C.   Accessibility of streets;

D.   Type of shops and stores to be protected against
     looting;

E.   Type of people--kind of appeal and approach;

F.   Knowledge concerning the agitators, including
     (1) names; (2) identifying marks; (3) clothing;
     (4) local or strangers; (5) degree of success in
     handling crowd.

Disperse mob and keep it under control afterward.
Arrest leaders as soon as possible. It is important to
have the greatest force on the side of law and order,
such as armored trucks and heavily armored men.
Control is made easier through the use of various
methods of public communication, in particular, sound
trucks and PA systems.

10.   Preventive measures:

A.   Intelligence: Procedures should be established to
     assure that police executives will be informed of:
     (a) signs of tensions; and (b) circumstances that will
     cause the formation of a crowd.

B.   Conferences: When a disturbance seems imminent, the
     city manager or mayor and the chief of police should

           attempt to hold conferences with crowd leaders to
analyze the situation, plan action designed to resolve
the differences peacefully, discuss likely action of
the participants, outline policy in reference to the
police enforcement program, and explain the legal
aspects of the situation so that all may understand
the legality or illegality of probable acts.

11.   Riots are often publicized[45] in a haphazard manner, as in
the case of the Hell's Angels when they took over the
town of Laconia, New Hampshire early in the summer of
1965. Signs were posted on highway telephone poles:
"Come To The Riot--See Weirs Beach Burn Saturday
Night."

           Many preventative measures are used by police, as
indicated by Life's account of the 1965 Laconia, New
Hampshire riot: "Tear gas shells exploded and National
Guardsmen, advancing with fixed bayonets, fired shotguns
loaded with rock salt and No. 6 birdshot into the crowd.
Brawlers and bystanders alike were blinded by gas and
peppered with pellets."

12.   The Army has six basic steps[46] in the control of riots,
each used after the one before it has failed:

    A. Show of force in view of the mob;

    B. Order to disperse;

    C. Advance in a V-shaped wedge to split the mob into two
        sections, bayonets pointed at the mob;

    D. High pressure water hoses and/or tear gas;

    E. Gun fire by sharpshooters directed at leaders;

    F. Full fire power.

13.   Constitutional Aspects:[47]

    A. Civil rights are limitless unless proscribed by state
        or local law.

    B. The courts have said that all rights are not free of
        restrictions for the well-being of others.

C. Crowd control involves the restriction of: freedom of
speech, freedom of assembly, and freedom of petition
(all First Amendment).

14.   Police action across the nation has not been uniform.[48]
In every interracial riot the police have complained of
being under-staffed. The major riots occurring in the
U.S. before those of the 60's were during wartime
conditions during which the police were understaffed.
The majority of the police departments in the U.S. do
not have riot plans.

15.   Normally, violence in a race riot[49] is directed towards
civilians primarily and as an afterthought towards the
police. In many cities across the nation the new 36"
riot baton is replacing the traditional 24" baton. It is
felt that riot squads should consist of men of immense
stature and of a certain type of personality that doesn't
crack and can conceal its bias.

16.   "The Legislature shall provide, by law, for organizing
and disciplining the militia, in such a manner as it may
deem expedient, not incompatible with the Constitution and
laws of the United States. Officers of the militia shall be
elected or appointed in such manner as the Legislature
shall from time to time direct, and shall be commissioned
by the Governor. The Governor shall have power to call
forth the militia to execute the laws of the state, to
suppress insurrections, and repel invasions." --California
Constitution, Art. VIII, Sec. 1.

17.   Counties and municipal corporations are liable for injury
to real or personal property caused by mobs or riots
unless the negligence of the injured person contributed to
the damage.[50]

18.   Riots may become so severe that the military is required
to assist in stopping the disturbance.[51] In this type of situation martial law may be established. A proclamation of

military law does not mean that the laws of the state or
ordinances of the community are suspended. It means
that certain additional regulations may be imposed by the
military authorities for the regulation of order. The
troops enforce the law of the state when civil authorities
are unable to do so. Violators of the law and of the
regulations imposed by the military authorities are arrested
and turned over to the regular civilian courts for regular
judicial proceedings.

19. United States Constitution, Article IV, Section 4:
The United States shall guarantee to every State in this
Union a republican form of government, and shall protect
each of them against invasion; and on application of the
legislature, or of the executive (when the legislature
cannot be convened) against domestic violence.

20. It is the duty of the President to employ Federal troops
to protect the state against domestic violence, when such
aid is requested by the legislature or the governor if the
legislature cannot be convened. --U.S. Code 201, Section
502.

It is the duty of the President to see that the laws of the
United States are faithfully executed. Whenever it is
impracticable by reason of domestic disturbances to en-
force the federal laws within any State or Territory, the
President is authorized to intervene with Federal troops.
--U.S. Code 202, Section 503.

21. Any officer or other person who orders, brings, keeps or
has under his authority or control any troops, or armed
men at any place where a general election is held in any
State, unless such force is for the purpose of repelling
armed enemies of the United States, shall be imprisoned
not to exceed 5 years and fined $5,000. --U.S. Code 55,
Section 794.

22.   The Posse Comitatus Act of 18 June, 1878:

"It shall not be lawful to employ any part of the Army
of the United States as a posse comitatus, for the
purpose of executing the laws, except in such case and
under such circumstances as authorized by the Constitution
or by Act of Congress." This act serves as a restriction
on civil peace officers making use of any part of the
Army to aid in enforcing the law. Federal law makes
it unlawful for an enlisted man to act as a deputy for
civil peace officers. The Posse Comitatus Act does not
prohibit the use of Federal troops where the purpose is
to protect Federal property, nor does it prohibit the use
of troops to assist the free passage of the United States
mail.

23.   New Methods in Riot Control:[52]

A. Cleveland maintains a mobile riot headquarters in a
bus and uses helicopters to direct police and fire
equipment.

B. New York has a specially trained tactical force of
400 men averaging 6 feet in height and chosen for
outstanding physical and mental aptitudes.

C. The new idea is to let angry mobs blow off steam
without letting them get to the point of violence.

D. Chicago has a 600 man force which can be moved
quickly without weakening police protection in other
areas.

24.   Chemical Grenades:[53]

a. Tear gas; b. Nauseating gas; c. White phosphorous;
d. Screening smoke; e. Federal Speedheat grenade;
f. Universal gas candle.

25.   Devices:[54]

A. Sonic devices:

(1) Powerful bull-horns that emit earsplitting blatting
and shrieking noise.

(2) Helicopter, equipped with powerful portable
sound projectors, can hover over a hostile mob
or a menacing crowd.

(3) Sonic riot-buster, a low-vibration sound which
has an extraordinary ability to resonate the human
viscera and thus affect the colon. The result is
the same as a mass attack of uncontrollable
dysentary.

B. A revolving, car-roof mounted flashing spotlight of
such brilliance that it will temporarily affect the vision
of the rioters.

C. A portable system to electrify a car body, a painful,
but harmless shock of high-voltage low-amperage
electricity which will shock rioters bent on over-
turning the vehicle.

D. Tranquilizer darts--used to quiet ring-leaders of a
wild crowd without permanent injury.

E. Ultra-violet material spread on rioters, can lead to
those who leave the riot scene with the use of portable
scanners to pick up particles at special roadblocks.

F. Highly-effective bubble-foam generator which can cover
a 5,000 cubic foot area in 60 seconds. The area will
stay covered for approximately 10 minutes.

G. Patrolmen can carry a hand-sized aerosol can containing liquid tear gas.

H. Policeman's side arms can now be equipped with a
special barrel adaptation that enables firing of various
types of projectiles over considerable ranges. Tear
gas, dye marking, tranquilizing, noise-making and
other projectiles can be fired from this adapter.

Problem # 7: Integration of Police and Fire Services
1. Three general forms of police and fire services:[55]
A. Complete integration of police and fire functions:

(1) The personnel in the public safety department are known as public safety officers who are capable equally of performing police and fire duties.

(2) All public safety officers normally serve on police patrol and are responsible for normal police activities, fire prevention and inspection, and all fire calls.

(3) Specialization is kept to a minimum, although there will be need for certain technicians, investigation officers, fire apparatus operators, and others.

(4) The public safety department is headed by a director whose primary responsibility is to coordinate all police-fire activities.

B. Partial integration:

(1) All officers are trained in both police and fire service, but there are separate divisions of police and fire, and personnel are assigned to each.

(2) A director of public safety heads the department and acts as coordinator between the two services.

(3) The public safety officers assigned to the police division are primarily patrolmen who will assist and cooperate in fire fighting.

(4) The public safety officers who are primarily firemen will be assigned as standby personnel to man the fire apparatus.

(5) The number of such personnel will be kept to a minimum for additional manpower will be secured from public safety officers assigned to police patrol.

C. An integrated department with a volunteer fire department:

(1) This is found in small communities which have never had an organized fire department.

(2) The police force handles the fire while being
integrated by a volunteer fire department.

2. Reasons for integration:[56]

A. Mounting costs of local government.

B. A steady trend toward shorter work weeks for police
and fire employees.

C. Increased demands for police service gives a degree
of urgency to the search for suitable methods of
keeping public safety costs within funds available.

D. Firemen often spend less than one per cent of their
time in fighting fires.

3. The advantages of fire-police integration may be summa-
rized as follows:[57]

A. More trained manpower available for either fire or
police duty.

B. Single hierarchy of command resulting in no duplication and better planning, coordination, public relations, training and communications.

C. Faster and better fire and police services, including
increased fire prevention activities.

D. The public safety officer is usually paid more; he
must know more; his job is more challenging; and
he is more valuable because he is trained to perform
both the police and fire duties.

4. Statistics indicate that fewer men can do more work when
fire and police departments are integrated.[58] The average
number of firemen and policemen in 81 cities of a size
comparable to Oak Park and with separate departments is
99. Oak Park operates with 53 officers and two office
girls.

5. Although the salary is higher, the public safety officer
gives the public more versatility.[59] While the public safety
officer is performing patrol duries, he is at the same
time the equivalent of one extra man on reserve at the
station for fire fighting.

6. The average police officer strength--1.7 per 1,000
   population--has remained unchanged since 1958, despite
   a 58 per cent increase in the volume of crime, a 26
   per cent increase in motor vehicle registrations and
   constantly rising demands for other police services.
   Rapid population growth, increasing population density
   and mobility, as well as the continued refinement of
   individuals' rights and needs require a realistic re-
   examination of community police-fire protection needs.[60]

7. In the United States a person dies in a fire every forty-
   seven minutes. Every day approximately 31 persons die
   in a fire, and 11,315 persons die each year in fires.
   "In light of these facts, it is not surprising that safety
   officials are constantly looking for more and better ways
   of controlling fire, and that many of them believe a closer
   coordination and cooperation between fire and police forces
   seems to be the best way."[61]

8. The Bureau of Governmental Research does not recommend
   that every city integrate its police and fire services.
   It does suggest that they do not dismiss the idea as
   impractical without consideration to the benefits of closer
   police-fire integration.[62]

9. There are approximately 73 known municipalities in the
   United States and Canada which have complete or partial
   consolidation of the police-fire activities.

10. California Penal Code:

    -447a   --Arson: Burning dwelling, house, trailer, etc.

    -448a   --Burning barn, stable, etc.

    -449a   --Burning of personal property.

    -450a   --Burning with intent to defraud insurer.

    -451a   --Attempts to burn property.   Penalty: felony.

11. Pressure Groups and Integration:[63]

    IAFF--International Association of Fire Fighters; most
    outspoken group; opponent against integration.

IAFC--International Association of Fire Chiefs; on record
as having opposed integration for over eighty years.
IACP--International Association of Chiefs of Police. They
have taken no official position on integration. However, they do recognize that this concept of public
safety can no longer be ignored or opposed in an
unalterable manner. Some opposition has been
provided by various local units of the IACP.

12. In Sunnyvale, California, there is a Chief of the Department of Public Safety.[64] The Chief of Police and Chief
of the Fire Department were made captains. All employees of the police and the fire departments became public
safety officers instead of policemen and firemen. After
ten years of integrated police-fire services in Sunnyvale,
California, two characteristics emerged:

A. The crime rate in Sunnyvale was below the national
crime rate average by 15% and below the California
crime rate average by 5%.

B. Sunnyvale had 68% fewer building fires than the average
American city of similar size as illustrated by the
National Board of Fire Underwriters Report.

13. In Elgin, Ill.,[65] twenty-four men were recruited for joint
police-fire service. As the new men were hired for this
service, they were placed in the fire department for
thirty days of training and, thereafter, were given two
weeks of training in the police department, including
formal classroom training programs, and experience in
riding with the regular motor patrol. The men are regarded as police officers except when a fire call is reported.
At that time, they report to the scene of the fire and
come under the fire officer in charge.

14. Those cities that have successfully tried police-fire
integration have a number of factors in common:[66]

A. The cities are relatively small.

B. They are middle or upper income residential communities.

C. The cities are generally part of a metropolitan complex.

D. They generally have no industrial or warehouse facilities.

E. The cities are in rapidly developing areas.

In 1956 only ten communities used total integration of police and fire services. Since that time, 31 communities in the United States and 29 communities in Canada have adopted the program. Of the communities that have integrated police-fire programs, 42% have a population under 10,000. Of the communities that have a population over 10,000, 16% have a population over 50,000.

15. Problems of Integration:[67] Buena Park adopted integration of police and fire in 1953 with a 20-man department and 24 volunteers. Inefficiency, neglect of equipment, and failure to operate in a proper manner stirred the citizens to place a referendum on the ballot in Nov. 1956 election. Integration was defeated by a 2 to 1 vote.

Chico operated under a single director of police and fire for 24 years until 1950.

Fremont terminated integration in 1958.

Hawthorne grew from a one-man police and fire department to a fully integrated status in 1937. On January 1, 1946, the departments separated operationally, but remained under one administrative chief. Complete separation occurred in 1953.

Monterey Park: the integration of Monterey Park did not proceed beyond the appointment of a single administrator and the holding of a number of training periods.

Sanger: the city manager of Sanger has stated that the municipality had never operated on an integrated basis.

The city became known as an adherent of integration when
it failed to appoint a successor to the fire chief who
retired in 1950. A replacement was provided in 1956.
San Marino: between 1950 and 1954 the city council was
unable and unwilling to determine which of the two fire
captains should be appointed chief. The chief of police
was named chief of the fire department, but there was
never an attempt to integrate the two forces.

Problem # 8: Civil Defense and Disaster Planning

1.   A major disaster is any condition that actually threatens
the safety of the City or any area of the City.

2.   Disaster plans must be developed so that every detail of
emergency action and coordination of the various agencies
can create a master effort which is unified and efficient. [68]

3.   During the period from 1950 through 1961 the total expend-
iture by the Federal government for civil defense was
$532 million, although Congress had actually appropriated
$620 million for the purpose. This is less than 30 cents
per year per American. [69]

4.   The federal government will match funds with states and
cities to assist them in building control centers. There
are 51 state and local training facilities located throughout the United States. There is in storage 225 million
dollars' worth of medical and engineering items, in 42
warehouses throughout the country. The warehouses are of
three types: small-capacity, located on a calculated risk
basis in or near principal cities; larger ones located away
from likely target areas; and depot-type warehouses, at
still greater distances from probable targets. [70]

5.   The basic policies set forth below should be followed in
planning and developing the civil defense police services
program, as suggested by the Federal Civil Defense
Administration:

a. The regular staffs of all police agencies within the state should be augmented by trained auxiliary police.

b. Auxiliary police should be carefully selected and properly trained.

c. Auxiliary police should be given uniform police authority throughout the state so that there will be no conflict in the coordination of forces and activities at the scene of emergency, when auxiliaries are assigned to mutual aid or mobile support operations.

d. In mutual aid operation, the head of the local police force in whose jurisdiction the emergency occurs is in command of all police personnel and equipment.

e. In planning for police aid under a mutual aid agreement local police should not be expected to deplete their own personnel and equipment to a point where police operations in their own jurisdictions are endangered.

f. When requests for mutual aid are received, regular police personnel should be dispatched so far as possible, and trained auxiliary police should be assigned temporarily to take their place.

g. In mobile support operations the Governor assumes authority over police forces in the state.

6. Functions of civil defense include:[71]

a. Educating citizens to recognize the siren signals, to understand their meaning, and to know what to do when they are sounded.

b. Teaching citizens how to save lives through first aid, fire fighting, and provisions for shelter, food, and clothing.

c. Preparing volunteers for rescue and aid in time of disaster.

d. Preparing leaders and leadership groups to direct such operations as medical, transportation, communications, radio-logical monitoring, rescue, engineering, welfare, fire, and police.

e. Organizing and coordinating the material resources of government, industry, and commerce to care for the victims of disaster and reduce the effects of disaster.

f. Working cooperatively with all governmental service offices so that all services will be provided during emergencies.

7. Enactments for civil defense mobilization: [72]

a. National Security Act, 1947.

b. Federal Civil Defense Act, 1950.

c. Strategic and Critical Material Stockpile Act.

The above acts show that the federal government has total control of civil defense measures if it so deems. All states follow the federal guidelines for civil defense as outlined in the Model Civil Defense Act and all states have some type of civil defense organization. Model Civil Defense Act provides that:

a. Governor retains direct control over civil defense operation;

b. If disaster is larger than the local area, governor can assume control;

c. States will authorize and direct the local areas to set up their own civil defense program with a director directly responsible to the local authorities.

The police department's plan for civil defense should contain:

a. Provisions for coordination and dispatch for personnel in civil defense emergency;

b. Provisions for cooperation between planning operations and mutual aid with adjacent political sub-divisions in protection and law enforcement areas;

c. Communication between local, state, and federal groups;

d. An inventory of all people available for service;

     e. Provisions for an alternate operations station in case
       the first is destroyed.

8.   Civil Defense Operations[73]

For civil defense, as in the case of disasters, certain of
the normal police functions are expanded and others are
contracted. In addition, however, there are certain civil
defense police operations which supplement even the
disaster requirements:

     a. Emergency mobilization and deployment;

     b. Explosive Ordnance Reconnaissance;

     c. Radiological defense;

     d. Chemical defense.

9.   Disaster Relief:[74]

     a. Local government--should have a civil defense
       force ready and trained.

     b. State government--The governor can call in state
       militia, national guard, Red Cross and, if neces-
       sary, the Federal Civil Defense Administration.

     c. Federal government--goes into action after
       governor has applied to the president for aid
       and president declares the state to be a "Major
       Disaster Area."

Usually there are about 20 major disasters every year.
Federal Disaster Relief Act provides emergency protection
of life and property, and is intended to be supplemental
only.

Civil defense warning systems should be of the following
types:

     a. "Take Cover": A wailing tone or series of short
       blasts for three minutes--indicates possible hostile
       attack.

     b. Alert Signal: A steady sounding of siren or horn
       for five minutes--indicates evidence of impending
       attack.

c. All Clear: No sound on public warning devices.
This should be given over radio and other public
address devices.

10. California Law Enforcement Civil Defense Organization:

a. The state law enforcement coordinator will direct
civil defense operations.

b. Operations will be directed through operational
area.

c. County and municipal law enforcement officials
through their normal command channels will
operate under the direction of the district
commander.

d. County Sheriff:

(1) Operates warning system.

(2) Maintains liaison with state agencies and
municipal agencies within the county.

(3) Develops emergency traffic control plans.

(4) Monitors and reports external radiation
hazards.

(5) Recruits and trains auxiliary forces.

(6) Reconnaissance and reporting of unexploded
ordnance.

11. California:

a. Whenever there is a menace to public health or safety
created by any calamity, any member of the California
Highway Patrol, Sheriff's Department, or police
department may close off the area where the menace
exists for the duration, to any persons not authorized
by such officer to enter or remain within the closed
area. Exception to this rule is any authorized member
of any news service.--Penal Code. Section 409.5.

b. Every person who goes to the scene of any disaster to
observe the scene or personnel coping with the disaster,
when there are emergency vehicles going to or from
the scene of the disaster for the purpose of preserving

life and property, and who impedes such equipment
or personnel, is guilty of a misdemeanor. --Penal
Code. Section 402.

c. Disaster Act 41402: No person shall be prosecuted
for a violation of any provision of this code when
violation of such provision is required in order to
comply with any regulation, directive, or order of
the Governor promulgated under the California Disaster
Act. --California Vehicle Code. Sacramento, 1963.

12. In organizing for a disaster,[75] include in the governmental
agencies: health, fire, police, public works, and building
departments. Non-governmental agencies encompass the
American Red Cross, local Civil Defense units, Chamber
of Commerce members, and the Salvation Army. Also,
the telephone company, power and light company, trucking
and fleet companies, and local hospitals.

Problem # 9: Licensing

1. Government sees licensing as a regulatory device. But
private groups may want this licensing to minimize
competition, thus establishing a monopoly and raising
prices, without having the public welfare in mind.

2. Licenses[76] are required for the operation of certain
business. Examples are druggists, liquor dealers and
real estate brokers. Any person who carries on such
business without a license cannot recover for goods sold
or services rendered. In addition, unlicensed dealers
and professional practitioners may be subject to criminal
penalties.

3. Police departments are required to investigate applicants
for certain types of licenses and to supervise the operations
of licensed persons and places.

4. Even the fact that some licenses or permits are used
partially for revenue devices does not nullify the fact that

the preservation of public safety is the principal reason
why governments issue them.

5.   License: a permission to act; freedom to engage in a
business, occupation, or activity otherwise unlawful,
when permission is granted by competent authority

6.   Regulatory Procedures:[77]

    (a) Rules and Orders--One method is simply to pass
a city ordinance saying "thou shalt" or "thou shalt
not." Reliance for enforcement of ordinance may
be placed upon the police and law departments,
upon a separate regulatory agency, or upon
complaints initiated by the general public.

    (b) Licenses and permits--If a more systematic
enforcement is desired than is likely to be obtained by the first method, persons in the regulated
occupation or activity may be required to secure
a license. This serves two purposes in the
regulated activity: first, to identify for enforcing
authorities all persons engaged in regulated
activity; second, to permit the enforcing authority
to determine whether the applicant for license
is complying with regulations.

    (c) Inspections--Rules and orders may be supplemented
by a regular process of inspection to determine
compliance, and to correct noncompliance.

7.   For costs of collection and for the administration and
enforcement of all laws now in effect or hereafter enacted,
regulating or concerning the use, operation, or registration
of vehicles used upon the public streets and highways of
this State, and for the exercise of those powers and for
the performance of those duties now imposed upon the
California Highway Patrol.--Art. 26, Sec. 2, West's
Annotated California Codes, Constitution Vol. C.

8. The chief of police shall perform any license fee and tax collection services prescribed by ordinance. --Sec. 41607, West's Annotated California Codes, Vol. 36.

9. Non-police and quasi-police Tasks:[78]

   Examples of logical division selection, when the indicated tasks are made a police responsibility, include: the patrol division for the supervision of the animal pound; the traffic division for the supervision of the licensing and inspection of taxicabs and drivers; the juvenile or vice division for the supervision and licensing of amusement places; the detective division for the supervision of weights and measures.

10. Where an act is made criminal by reason of its having been done without a license permit required by law, it is not incumbent upon the prosecution to prove that the defendant did not have a license, since it will be taken as proved that the defendant did not have a license unless the defendant proves that he did have such a license.[78]

11. Department of Alcoholic Beverage Control, Powers and Duties (California):

    The Department of Alcoholic Beverage Control shall have the exclusive power, except as provided and in accordance with laws enacted by the Legislature, to license the manufacture, importation and sale of alcoholic beverages in the State, and to collect license fees or occupation taxes on account thereof. The department shall have the power, in its discretion, to deny, suspend or revoke any specific alcoholic beverages license if it shall determine for good cause that the granting or continuance of such license would be contrary to public welfare or morals, or that a person seeking or holding a license has violated any law prohibiting conduct involving moral turpitude. It shall be unlawful for any person other than a licensee of said department to manufacture, import, or sell alcoholic beverages in this State. --Constitution of California,

Article XX, Section 22.

12. The California legislature returns to incorporated cities
and counties 90% of all license fees paid for the privilege
of conducting business under the Alcoholic Beverage
Control Act. During 1963 over $11 million was returned
to local governments in direct ratio to the number of
licenses located within the incorporated city or county.

13. The Sheriff, board of police commissioners, chief of
police, city marshall, town marshall, or other head of
the police department of any city or county, upon proof
that the person applying is of good moral character, may
issue to such a person a license to carry concealed a
pistol, revolver, or firearm for a period of one year
from the date of the license. --California Penal Code,
Section 12050.

14. The owner of a pharmacy or any person who purchases
a narcotic upon federal order forms, as required under
the provisions of an act of Congress approved December
17, 1914, shall maintain and file such prescriptions in a
separate file apart from non-narcotic prescriptions. The
written order forms shall be preserved for at least three
years after the date of the last entry made and shall
always be open for inspection by any peace officer or
inspector or members of the Board of Pharmacy. --
Division X of Health and Safety Code, Sections 11280 and
11573.

15. Volstead Act of 1917--passed by Congress December 17,
1917; ratified January 29, 1919; became the Constitution's
18th Amendment, or better known as Prohibition. This
Amendment stated: "After one year from the ratification
of this article, the manufacture, sale, transportation of
intoxicating liquors within, the importation thereof into,
or the exportation thereof from the U.S. and all territory,
subject to the jurisdiction thereof for beverage purposes is
thereby prohibited." The 18th Amendment remained until

the 21st Amendment repealed it on December 5, 1933.

Problem # 10: Inspection

1.   Inspection[79] is the process of obtaining facts relating to
persons, things, conditions, and actions by observation,
inquiry, examination, and analysis. Inspection is of two
kinds: (a) a staff inspection made by someone who lacks
direct control over the subject of the inspection; and (b)
an authoritative inspection made by those in direct
command.

2.   "It is unlawful to willfully fail or refuse to comply with
any lawful order, signal, or direction of any traffic officer
or to refuse to submit to any lawful inspection under this
code."--California Vehicle Code, Section 2800.

3.   In some communities the police inspect the security of
establishments when they are closed to business and
check on compliance with laws and regulations of such
licensed enterprises as taverns, bars, dance halls, bowl-
ing alleys, skating rinks, pool halls, and other amusement
establishments.

4.   Inspection records are commonly used by many departments. The use of these miscellaneous forms will depend
on:[80]

      (a) size of the department;
      (b) attention given to specialized activities;
      (c) relative costs of forms and procedures.

Store reports serve a number of purposes:

      (a) They cause the patrol officer to make periodic
           contacts with businessmen on their beat in order
           to obtain the information.

      (b) They assure a periodic inspection of every
           commercial establishment in the city for the
           purpose of detecting and causing to be corrected
           such police hazards as improperly secured or
           barred doors, windows, and skylights; improper

and inadequate interior and exterior lighting; safes
and other valuables in a position where the patrolman is able to see them easily from a window;
and improper handling of cash, either when left
on the premises at night, or when being transported to the bank for deposit.

(c) They provide the residence addresses and telephone
numbers of the proprietor and his assistant should
there by need for locating them in an emergency.
To be fully effective, store report data must be
kept up to date.

5. On August 28, 1965, the 89th Congress adopted the 'Baldwin Amendment.' In essence, by December 31, 1967, a
highway safety program in accordance with uniform standards was approved by the Secretary of Commerce. Such
programs must be: designed to reduce traffic accidents,
deaths, injuries, and property damage resulting therefrom,
on highways on the Federal-aid system. Provisions must
be made for effective record systems, improvement of
driver performance, vehicle safety, highway design and
maintenance, traffic control, and the detection and correction of high accident locations. Legislation requiring
mandatory motor vehicle inspection was one of the requirements stated in the Baldwin Amendment. The proposed
legislation would provide for the inspection of basic safety
items at a minimum cost to the motorist. [81]

Problem # 11: Subversives

1. In 1950, Congress passed the comprehensive Internal
Security Act. [82] This Act set up a Subversive Activities
Control Board charged with determining whether a particular organization is communist "action," communist
"front," or communist "infiltrated." Any such organization
is placed under such disabilities as these:

(1) It must register annually with the Attorney
General.

(2) It must report the names of its officers, the
names of all its members, and identify the
sources of all its funds.

(3) It must label as "communist propaganda" all its
publications sent through the mails or across
state lines.

(4) Members of communist organizations may not
obtain passports, hold elective federal positions,
serve as officers or employees of a labor union
or work in a defense plant.

In 1954 the Communist Control Act went even further by
virtually outlawing the Communist Party as a political
body. Membership in the Communist Party is not illegal,
per se, but Communists are natural targets of the Smith
Act, which makes it a crime to be a knowing, active, and
purposeful member of a group advocating the violent overthrow of the government.

2.   Smith Act--Federal:[83]

In 1940 Congress created a law which makes it a criminal
offense to teach or advocate, "the duty, necessity, desir-
ability, or propriety of overthrowing or destroying the
government of the United States or any other governmental
unit of the United States by force or violence" or to publish
any written matter advocating forcible overthrow, or to
organize any group who teach or advocate such doctrine.
This statute has been used as the principal vehicle for
prosecuting Communists. Its constitutionality was upheld
in Dennis vs. U.S. and Yates vs. U.S.

3.   Crimes of treason against the state:[84]

The constitutions or criminal codes of all the states in-
include the crime of treason against the state, which is
similar to the federal law. However, there have been only

two prosecutions for treason against the state: (1) One as a consequence of Dorr's Rebellion in Rhode Island in 1845; (2) The prosecution by Virginia of John Brown and his associates at Harper's Ferry in 1859.

4. The McCarran Act--Federal:[85]

Known as the Internal Security Act, it declares illegal "for any persons knowingly to combine, conspire, or agree with any other person to perform any act which would substantially contribute to the establishment within the United States of a totalitarian dictatorship" directed from abroad. This Act (1950) and the Communist Control Act of 1954 control registration of Communists and their activities. Although this legislation was passed around 1950, the Subversive Activity Control Board's final order to register was not made effective until 1959. Legal problems were encountered by the Board and the courts. In 1961 a sharply divided Supreme Court upheld the registration provisions, but serious legal and enforcement problems remain.

5. Hatch Act of 1939:

(a) It shall be unlawful for any person employed in any capacity by any agency of the Federal Government, whose compensation or any part thereof, is paid from funds authorized or appropriated by any act of Congress, to have membership in any political party or organization which advocates the overthrow of our Constitutional form of Government in the United States.

(b) Any person violating the provisions of this section shall be immediately removed from the position or office held by him, and thereafter no part of the funds appropriated by any Act of Congress for such position or office shall be used to pay the compensation of such person.

6. California Penal Code, Section 37:

    Treason against the state consists only in levying war
    against it, adhering to its enemies, or giving them aid
    and comfort, and can be committed only by persons owing
    allegiance to the state. The punishment of treason shall
    be death.

7. The House of Representatives Committee on Un-American
    Activities[86] was created in 1938 by a resolution in the
    House of Representatives. It was a temporary investigating
    committee, given a renewal of authority from time to time,
    and ultimately, in 1945, it was added to the list of the
    House's permanent committees.

8. "Subversive organization" means every conspirator,
    association, society, camp, group, political party,
    assembly, and every body or organization composed of
    two or more persons or members which comes within
    either or both of the following descriptions:

    a. Which directly or indirectly advocates, advises,
        teaches, or practices the duty, necessity, or
        propriety of controlling, conducting, seizing, or
        overthrowing the Government of the United States,
        of this State, or of any political subdivision there-
        of by force or violence.

    b. If under foreign control--West's California Codes
        Sec. 35002 and 35003.

9. Any subversive organization which violates any provision
    of this title is guilty of a felony punishable by fine of not
    less than one thousand dollars, nor more than ten thousand
    dollars. Any such violation constitutes a separate and
    distinct offense for each day, or part thereof, during which
    it is continued. --West's California Codes, Sec. 35300.

10. Subvert: To overthrow or destroy something established.

11. Widespread fear of subversion has characterized the past
    fifty years in the United States. The list of Federal laws
    that define treason, espionage, sabotage and similar crimes

has grown long. [87]

12.   Department of Justice: Federal Bureau of Investigation has
       jurisdiction over violations pertaining to the internal
       security of the United States: (a) Espionage; (b) Sabotage;
       (c) Treason.

13.   Methods used for subversion:

       (1) Infiltrate agents into strategic organizations and
           mass media (newspapers, radio, college faculties
           and police and military units).

       (2) Soften up the populace with symbols and slogans.

       (3) Draw together the crowd nucleus.

       (4) Agitate the crowd by use of: (a) External command;
           (b) Internal command; (c) Messengers between
           a and b; (d) Shock guards; (e) Cheering sections;
           (f) Police baiters.

       (5) Manufacture Martyrs--claims of police brutality
           are popular in such campaigns.

14.   Three committees have carried the burden of legislative
       investigations of subversive activities in California:

       (1) The Assembly Relief Investigating Committee.

       (2) The Fact-Finding Committee on Un-American
           Activities.

       (3) The Senate Investigating Committee on Education.
       Scope of the Committee Investigations includes: (1)
       Pro-axis groups; (2) Communism and labor; (3) Communism
       and the schools; (4) Communist front organizations; (5)
       Miscellaneous investigations.

15.   Since its inception, the Communist Party, USA, has been
       unswerving in its allegiance to the Soviet Union, which is
       committed to the goal of world domination by communism.
       Because the United States is the principal deterrent to
       further Communist expansion, the Communist Party, USA,
       is, and will continue to be, a serious threat to our internal
       security. [88]

16.   The Communist underground conspiracy follows three
       important rules:[89]

       (1) Decentralization, with ultimate command resting
           in Soviet Headquarters. Operationally, the under-
           ground is broken up into very small units.

       (2) No records; thus no evidence in case of capture.

       (3) Cover: all agents working underground have a
           cover name, business, family, and general life.

17.   The Red Guards have presented themselves as a working
       machine in the United States. Their doctrine is Chinese
       Communism, and their procedure of operations is going
       through the operations of Tongs (Triad Secret Societies).
       Using Tong Societies that have existed here for over a
       hundred years, they have a source of revenue. Tong
       Societies still are very active in activities such as gambling,
       narcotics (via Mexico-white heroin vs. Mexican-brownish
       heroin), prostitution, Tong Society dues, murder, robbery,
       burglary, illegal stills for liquor, etc.

18.   Ku Klux Klan:[90]

       The officers for any local clan are as follows: Exalted
       Cyclops, president; Klaliff, vice president; Klokard;
       lecturer; Kludd, chaplain; Kligrapp, secretary; Klabee,
       treasurer; Kladd, conductor; Klorago, inner guard; Klexter,
       outer guard; Nighthawk, in charge of candidates; and
       Klokann, a three-member board of investigators, auditors
       and advisors. During the 1920's the membership topped
       four million and extended into such states as Indiana,
       Kansas, and Colorado. Today the membership--most
       strongly concentrated in North Carolina, South Carolina,
       Georgia, Florida, Alabama, Mississippi and Louisiana--
       is well past 10,000 and is growing.[92]

19.   The Black Muslims[91] movement is growing rapidly and is
       nationwide. In December, 1960 there were 69 temples
       or missions in 27 states from California to Massachusetts
       and Florida.

Problem # 12: Organized Crime

1.   Organized crime[93] is a society that seeks to operate out-
      side the control of the American people and their govern-
      ments. It involves thousands of criminals, working within
      structures as complex as those of any large corporation,
      subject to laws more rigidly enforced than those of
      legitimate governments. Its actions are not impulsive
      but rather the result of intricate conspiracies, carried
      on over many years and aimed at gaining control over
      whole fields of activity in order to amass huge profits.

2.   Types of organized criminal activity include:

      (1) Gambling ranges from lotteries, such as "numbers"
           to off-track horse betting, bets on sporting events,
           large dice games and illegal casinos. Gross
           revenue to organized gambling is estimated at $7
           to $50 billion. Profits are conservatively estima-
           ted at about $6 to $7 billion a year. Legal
           betting at racetracks amounts to only $5 billion
           a year.

      (2) Loan sharking, the lending of money at higher
           rates than the prescribed limit, is the second
           largest source of revenue for organized crime.
           Interest rates vary from one to 150% a week,
           according to the relationship with the lender.
           No reliable estimates exist of the gross revenue
           from organized loan sharking, but profit margins
           are higher than for gambling operations, and many
           officials classify the business in the multi-billion
           dollar range.

      (3) Narcotics: The large amounts of cash and the
           international connections necessary for large, long-
           term supplies can be provided only by organized
           crime. Conservative estimates of the number of
           addicts in the nation and the average daily expend-
           iture for heroin indicate that the gross heroin trade

is $350 million annually, of which $21 million
are probably profits to the importer and distributor.

(4) Other Goods and Services: Prostitution and bootlegging play a small and declining role in organized crime operations.

3. Mafia (now called La Cosa Nostra):
La Cosa Nostra is the largest organization of the criminal
underworld in this country, very closely organized and
strictly disciplined.   It is a criminal fraternity whose
membership is Italian either by birth or national origin,
and it has been found to control major racket activities
in many of our larger metropolitan areas, often working
in concert with criminals representing other ethnic back-
grounds.   It operates on a nationwide basis with international implications.

4. Internal Structure of La Cosa Nostra:[94]
Today the heart of organized crime in the United States
consists of 24 core groups ("families") operating as
criminal cartels in large cities across the nation.
The 24 "families" have membership varying from as many
as 700 to as few as 20.   The hierarchical structure of the
families resembles that of the Mafia groups that have
operated for almost a century on the island of Sicily:

(1) Family headed by Boss whose job is to maintain
order and maximize profits.   He can be over-
ruled by national advisory group.

(2) Underboss: collects information, relays information,
takes over for boss when absent.

(3) Consigliere: on the same level as the underboss,
his job is to be counselor and advisor.   He is
often an elderly member.

(4) Caporegima (Lieutenant) act as buffers between
upper and lower personnel.   They are like
supervisors.

(5) Soldati (soldiers) may, for example, operate
particular illegal enterprises.

(6) Employees and agents do the actual work.

In the United States there are 750,000 to 1,000,000 persons
who are influenced or controlled by the Mafia.[95]

5. The Mafia is marked by an ancient code that binds all of
its members to the following tenets:[96]

(1) Reciprocal aid in case of any need whatsoever.

(2) Absolute obedience to the Chief.

(3) An offense against one of the members must be
considered an offense to the entire organization
and must be avenged at any cost.

(4) Never resort to the state's authorities for justice.

(5) Never reveal the names of members of the organization.

6. In Italy, between January 1, 1956, and June 30, 1960,
the number of crimes connected with the Mafia were as
follows: 168 murders, 19 large robberies, 7 major kid-
nappings, and 37 cases of cattle stealing. These are only
the crimes reported to the police. There is reason to
believe that twice this many occur. The Mafia came into
being in an area of feudal estates in the center of Sicily.
The real chief of the Mafia was Don Vito Cascio Ferro.
He was born at Bizacquino in the province of Palermo,
and to him is attributed the dubious glory of having perfect-
ed not only the Mafia's organization but also Italy's underworld in such field as robbery and kidnapping for blackmail.

7. "Organized crime" cannot flourish without crooked cops
and politicians. The now-familiar Mafia, or Cosa Nostra,
is structured like a business corporation,[98] tightly run,
highly disciplined, with diversified interests both underworld (loan-sharking, bookmaking, etc.) and legitimate
(dry cleaning, trucking, restaurants). Prostitution and

bootlegging have become too risky and are losing favor
with the mob, but the importing and distribution of narcotics
at the "wholesale" level remains lucrative. There are
really no believable figures on the extent of organized
crime in the U.S.--mob-run gambling, narcotics, extortion,
or loan-shark or "Juice operations."

8.   Criminal syndicates alone exact several billion annually
through their depredations. Martin Mooney offers the
following graphic estimate (in the 1930's):[99] "Add up
the yearly income of General Motors, U.S. Steel, Hearst
Papers, Radio Corporation of America, the National Bank,
and 25 other powerful business enterprises of the country
and there you have a little over half of what crime and
racketeering earmark for their own coffers each year."

9.   A U.S. Attorney General's Special Group on Organized
Crime reported that the American public spends an
estimated 47 billion dollars a year on all forms of illegal
gambling, a figure that was higher than the national defense
budget. A further estimate is that some 4-1/2 billion
dollars pass hands to some of our public servants each
year; that is, some 513,000 tax-free dollars, each hour
of each day.[100]

10. Meetings of the Grand Council of the Mafia (Semi-Public)
have been held as follows: 1952-53, Florida; 1954, Chicago;
1956, Binghampton; 1957, Appalachia.

11. In 1950 the Senate Committee to Investigate Organized
Inter-State Commerce brought to the public attention the
menace of national organized crime.

12. Organized crime in the last 40 years has taken on new characteristics. The most dangerous criminal gangs today are
not specialists in one type of predatory crime, but engage in
many and varied forms of criminality. The key to successful gang operation is monopoly of illicit enterprises or
illegal operations, for monopoly guarantees huge profits.[101]

13.　One of the most shocking revelations of the Kefauver
Committee was the "extent of official corruption in
facilitating and promoting organized crime." This
corruption was found in state and local government
agencies in four different forms:[102]

(1) Direct bribes or protection payments.

(2) The unusual and unexplained wealth of law
enforcement officials.

(3) The use of political influence and pressure to
protect criminal activities or to further the
interests of criminal groups.

(4) The participation of law enforcement officials
directly in the business of organized crime.

14.　Investigations by the Illinois Criminal Investigation
Commission show that organized crime is a multi-million
dollar operation. Their loan companies collect as high
as 200% interest and usually regard the body of the borrow-
er as collateral.[103]

15.　In the operations where high interest rates are charged
the gang is usually more interested in only taking over
control of the business. This is known as Loan Sharking.
Stock Fraud is the selling of shares of false representation.[104]

16.　Criminal Syndicalism defined: "Criminal Syndicalism"
means any doctrine or precept advocating, teaching, or
aiding and abetting the commission of crime, sabotage,
or unlawful acts of force and violence or unlawful methods
of terrorism as a means of accomplishing a change in
industrial ownership or control, or effecting any political
change. --California Penal Code, section 11400.

17.　Bankruptcies engineered by racketeers may alone be cost-
ing businessmen half a billion dollars yearly.[105]

18.　California is greatly concerned about the numbers and
import of nationally known hoodlums who are actually
crossing the state line to assume at least part time

residence in California or to meet with hoodlums who are
permanent residents of the state to plan strategy for future
moves of the mobs. . .During the past years, Palm
Springs and Los Angeles have become favorite rendezvous
of many undesirable individuals from throughout the
United States.[106]

19.   The two major crime syndicates in this country are the
       Accardo-Guzik-Fischetti syndicate, whose headquarters
       are in Chicago; and the Costello-Adonis-Lansky syndicate
       based in New York. The Mafia is the binder which ties
       together the two major criminal syndicates as well as
       numerous other criminal groups throughout the country.[107]

Problem # 13: Departmental Reserve Officers

1.   Reserves are men held out of action for use in an
      emergency, or for replacing active units.

2.   An auxiliary is an assisting or supplementary group or
      organization, giving aid or support.

3.   A volunteer is a person who enters or offers to enter into
      any service of his own free will.

4.   The regular police, regardless of training and willingness
      cannot alone carry out all the necessary functions without
      added strength. They need a reserve.[108] Properly train-
      ed, such a reserve is a great public relations force.
      California has thousands of reserve policemen in the towns,
      in small cities and even in the great sprawling city of
      Los Angeles.[109]

5.   The "county auxiliary protective units" or vigilantes,
      which were organized by the American Bankers Association,
      represented a quasi-public effort to secure a larger degree
      of police protection for rural banks. Volunteer police are
      necessarily untrained and undisciplined, though they are
      vested with an authority which can be exercised with
      prudence only under the established forms of law.[110]

6.   The administrative heads have expressed their distaste
      for any scheme which involves lending their uniform and
      their name to untrained and undisciplined personnel.[111]

7.   The auxiliary law enforcement units are of three types:[112]

      a)   The Reserve Component is the most commonly
           encountered organization used by paid law enforce-
           ment agencies. All personnel are sworn law
           enforcement officers, and although voluntary are
           governed and directed by the identical policies,
           laws and departmental directives as are paid full
           time officers. In most instances, units of this
           type are uniformed, sometimes armed, and per-
           form either similar or identical duties to the
           career officers.

      b)   The Support Unit is similar to the reserve com-
           ponent with the exception that they may fulfill
           duties other than law enforcement. Members of a
           support unit are usually not as thoroughly trained
           as a reserve officer or deputy and perform duties
           of a less skilled nature. Clerical work, delivery
           of messages, or working in civil defense capacities
           are examples of duties sometimes performed by
           these types of people.

      c)   Special Services Units fulfill duties implied by the
           title, special services. Units of this category are
           special officers or sheriffs' deputies with limited
           powers, and devote themselves to specific and
           limited duty requirements. These units are called
           when their special talents, training, or equipment
           are needed, for example mountain climbing,
           mounted posse, aero squadrons, etc.

8.   It is impossible to foresee every difficulty which may arise
      in the situations for which the plan of operation is prepared;
      therefore, it becomes necessary for the planner to provide

for an adequate number of reserves who will be readily
available when emergencies demand the services of additional men. Usually the mounted patrolmen not engaged in the
plan are used as the reserve force.[113]

9. Civilian workers: Even more damaging to the effectiveness
    of police work is the failure to use civilian manpower
    where it is needed. Eleven percent of America's police
    personnel is civilian, but the great majority of civilians
    work as maintenance men, clerks or stenographers, or
    enforce parking regulations. It is in police staff work
    that civilians can make the greatest contribution. Com-
    munications, records, information retrieval, research,
    planning, and laboratory analysis are vital parts of police
    work that, as often as not, could be performed better
    by civilians with specialized training than by sworn law
    enforcement officers.[114]

10. The organization of police reserves began in the pre-
    depression period as social and political groups. Appoint-
    ments to the police reserve in many communities were
    made as a political favor. The advantages of becoming a
    reserve were many: such persons could carry firearms,
    possess a police badge, enforce the law on their own
    premises, and be generally immune from arrest.
    During the manpower crisis of World War II, the reserves
    were actually organized into a functioning unit to supplement
    the regulars. After the war, these units tended to die
    out. However, when another manpower problem arose
    during the Korean Conflict, the reserve units once again
    came into active participation in police work.[115] Reserve
    exist in a majority of the cities with more than ten-
    thousand population. Reserves have greatly increased
    since World War II.

11. Auxiliary policemen have authority only while in uniform.
    They are not privately employed police, watchmen or

guards. When an auxiliary policeman is off duty and out
of uniform, a regular patrolman must be summoned before
the auxiliary policeman can perform any police function,
in a situation requiring police attention. A minimal amount
of service or training is usually required before the
auxiliary policeman can carry a weapon. The auxiliary
policeman should be continuously trained. Class training
and accompanying an experienced officer on a routine duty
under supervision are usually what is required for training. The auxiliary police organization is separate and
distinct from the regular police force. [116]

12.   Long Beach Reserve Corps Rules and Regulations: The
Chief of Police is responsible, under bond, for the acts
of all members of the Police Reserve when they are
serving the city of Long Beach without compensation. The
Reserve Police Corps was organized for the purpose of
establishing a trained, well-organized group of officers
who will be readily available to assist the Long Beach
Police Department in the protection of life, limb and
property, and to assist in the event of earthquake, tidal
wave, fire, explosion, riot and crowd control, or other
situations requiring additional manpower. The Police
Reserve, except for training purposes, is an emergency
unit only.

13.   Organized in the late 1960's, the Hays, Kansas Police
Reserve,[117] has become a welcome addition to the city's
regular police force. The reservists are called out for
traffic and crowd-control duty during holidays, parades,
celebrations and emergencies. In addition, they perform
yeomen service in investigating traffic accidents. Neigh-
boring communities also request the unit's assistance on
special occasions.

Hays does not, however, allow the reservists to make
arrests as policemen or handle disturbance calls which

might involve violence.

14. Unit Operational Structure of Auxiliary Police Units:

   A. Quasi-Military: authority ranks based on the Armed
      Forces.

   B. Chairman Method: same as A, except chief officer
      is chairman of president.

   C. Directorship: board members choose ranking officers
      and determine policy.[118]

15. In 1959 there were 388,000 persons throughout the country
listed as members of the auxiliary police of civil defense.
In the arming of these auxiliary police there is no standard
practice. Some carry a pistol when on a training exercise,
others a night stick, and still others are unarmed.[119]

16. In some instances, air squadron units, Scuba diving units,
boat flotillas, or rescue squads have been organized as
a part of auxiliary police activities.

A novel variation in the auxiliary police concept has been
developed in Highland Park, Michigan. An unusual increase
in juvenile crime prompted officials in that city of 38,000
to organize a Citizens' Night Patrol, consisting of five
radio-equipped cars with from two to three men in each
car. On duty from 8:30 p.m. to midnight, they exercise
no police power and engage in no police action of any
kind whatsoever. Their function is to "prowl," observe
and report any unusual or suspicious activity by radio
to headquarters, whereupon one or more of five uniformed
patrolmen take over the situation. Members of the Citizens'
Patrol are unarmed and do not leave their cars under any
circumstances. The essence of the plan is that it doubles
the observation power of the patrol force. Officials of
Highland Park report a sharp reduction in the number of
incidents involving juveniles.[120]

17. Disadvantages of Police Reserves:[121] Even when more reserve
officers are uniformed in a distinctive manner, the public

is often unable to distinguish between a regular and a
reserve officer, and for that matter a great portion of the
public are probably not aware that such a thing as a
reserve policeman exists. The unauthorized display of
a firearm, procuring favors with the badge, and immoral
conduct on the part of a reserve officer are often interpreted by the public as representative of the entire department.

The organization of a police reserve has acted, on occasions, to retard the necessary expansion of the department. Several police administrators indicated that, because
they had utilized reserves to a great extent, they were unable to convince the community of the need for additional
officers.

18. Advantages of Police Reserves:[122] "One chief remarked
that he was able to save the city $50,000 per year by
using police reserves, while another commented that his
reserve officers permitted him to replace regular officers
on vacation, sick leave, and non-compensated overtime,
to a total of 25,000 hours per year."

Problem # 14: Mental Illness

1. Mental illness in the community:
According to a 1960 report from the National Association
of Mental Health at least one person in every 10 had some
form of mental or emotional illness which was serious
enough to require treatment for full recovery. It was
estimated that one out of 12 Americans would be hospitalized for mental illness during their lifetimes. The
evidence was conclusive that half of the hospital beds
throughout the country are used for the mentally ill. Also,
it was estimated that 14,100 young people between fifteen
and twenty-four years are admitted to public mental
hospitals yearly for mental illness. [123]

2.   Mental illness statistics:

In the United States there are about half a million patients
in psychiatric hospitals, nearly all of whom are psychotic
and over one-half schizophrenic. This number is greater
than the total number of patients hospitalized for all other
illnesses. One child in every five of grade school age
will at some time in his life need expert help because of
neurosis, personality disorder, or psychosomatic disorder. Another one in twenty will be incapacitated by a
psychosis, but will not be hospitalized. [124]

3.   Section 1367, California Penal Code, states that a person
cannot be tried, adjudged to punishment, or punished for
a public offense, while he is insane. (This does not rule
out civil liability.) Section 26 of the Penal Code defines
those who are not capable of committing crimes as (a)
Idiots; and (b) Lunatics and insane people. An idiot has
a mental age under 3 years; an imbecile a mental age
from 3-7 years; and a moron a mental age of 8-12 years.

4.   Cases which should be brought to the hospital:

A. Any person, not properly cared for, whose
actions are not normal, and who appears to be
in such a mental condition that he needs assistance.

B. The following persons, not properly cared for,
who by their actions indicate that they may be
mentally ill:

1) Those sustaining a serious injury, severe
head blow, etc.

2) Those having a high fever.

3) Those suffering from amnesia.

4) Aged persons suffering from travel fatigue.

5) Epileptics.

6) Escapees from mental hospitals.

7) Parolees from mental institutions and
probationers from the Psychopathic Division

of the Superior Court whose mental
behavior is questionable.

A policeman may use as much force as is necessary in restraining a mental patient. If an officer needs assistance to get the patient under control, he should not hesitate to call for aid. Whenever restraining straps are not available, handcuffs may be used to prevent the mentally ill person from injuring himself or others, but care should be exercised.

5. Psychoses which most frequently result in a missing persons case are dementias caused by organic changes in the cortical brain cell. The presenile psychoses--Alzheimer's disease and Pick's disease--are relatively rare forms of dementia which occur in the forties; the arteriosclerosis dementias may be seen from fifty upward; while uncomplicated senile dementias seldom appear before the age of sixty. The onset of these psychoses is ordinarily gradual. There is an uninterrupted deterioration of mental powers accompanied by defective memory, disorientation, and confusion.

Amnesia, the loss of memory and knowledge of identity, is a rare occurrence even among missing persons cases. Amnesia has its highest incidence in the confections of scenario writers. Of the authentic cases the most frequent cause is battle shock. [125]

6. Bromberg and Thompson report that, of a total of 9,958 prisoners appearing before the Court of General Sessions of New York City and examined between 1932 and 1935, inclusive, only 1.5% were psychotic, 6.9% were psychoneurotic, 6.9% were psychopathic personalities, and 2.4% were feebleminded. Thus 82.3% of the prisoners were classified as normal, although many of them had mild personality defects which contributed to their criminality. [126]

7.   In 1916 Bernard Glueck carried out a study of 608
      prisoners in Sing Sing prison. He found that 59% of those
      examined were feebleminded, mentally diseased, or mental-
      ly abnormal. The feebleminded numbered 28.1%; 12% were
      insane or mentally deteriorated; 18.9% were classified as
      psychopathic.

      One of the pioneers in dealing with the feebleminded
      delinquent was Dr. Henry H. Goddard. In his book of
      case histories, The Criminal Imbecile, written as early
      as 1915, he shows that persons so intellectually impaired
      could not, in justice, be held accountable for their
      crimes.[127]

8.   There are at least five meanings of the word "insane" or
      "insanity" in legal issues:[128]

      1)   the lack of capacity to make a valid contract
           or deed;

      2)   lack of testamentary capacity (ability to make a
           valid will);

      3)   the degree and type of "insanity" required to
           nullify capacity to commit crime;

      4)   fitness for commitment to a mental hospital;

      5)   incompetency (suitability for guardianship).

9.   Any person committed to a state hospital is disqualified as
      an elector and is disqualified from voting or from holding
      office. --California State Constitution, Article 2, section 1
      (51).

      The Department of Motor Vehicles shall not issue or renew
      a driver's license to any person who is insane . . . or
      when it appears by examination or other evidence that such
      person is unable to operate a motor vehicle upon a highway
      safely because of physical or mental defect or lack of
      skill. --California Vehicle Code, section 12805 (c) (f).

      The Medical Correctional Institution shall have as its
      primary purpose the receiving, segregation, confinement,

observation, diagnosis, care and treatment of young men
subject to the custody, control and discipline of the
Director of Corrections or Youth Authority who are
affected by (1) mental disease, disorder or defect; or
(2) psychopathic or sociopathic personality as evidenced
by inability to adjust to free community life or regular
institutional programs; or (3) any chronic disease or
condition requiring medical or surgical care. --California
Penal Code, section 6126.

10. The term insanity is frequently used in reference to
psychotic patients. This is a social and legal term rather
than a medical one and denotes mental disorder so severe
that the individual is judged to be unable to manage his
affairs, perform his social duties and responsibilities, or
be held accountable for his actions. [129]

11. Section 705, Welfare and Institutions Code, California:
Whenever the court, during the hearing on the petition,
is of the opinion that the minor is mentally ill or if the
court is in doubt concerning the mental health of any such
person, the court may order that such person be held
temporarily in the psychopathic ward of the county hospital
for observation and recommendation concerning the future
care, supervision, and treatment of such person.

12. California follows the McNaughton test (Queen v. McNaughton (1843) 4 St. Tr. (N.s) 847, McNaughton's Case 1843),
10 Clark 8 Fin. 200, 8 Eng. Rep. 718) in determining
whether the defendant was sane at the time of the commission of the crime, when this issue is raised by the
plea of not guilty by reason of insanity. The McNaughton
test provides "that at the time the accused committed the
act he was laboring under such defect of reason, from
disease of the mind, as not to know the nature and quality
of his act, or, if he did know it, that he did not know
that he was doing what was wrong" (People v. Nash, 52

Cal. 2d 36; People v. Gorshem, 51 Cal. 2d 716).
On the trial of the issue raised by the plea of not guilty
by reason of insanity there is a rebuttable presumption
that the accused was sane at the time that the crime was
committed.   The accused has the burden of proving his
insanity by a preponderance of evidence (People v. Dean,
158 Cal. App. 2d 572). [130]

13.   Mental deficiency is a state of mental retardation or
incomplete development, existing from birth or early
infancy, as a result of which the person is unable to meet
the social expectancy of society. [131]

14.   The definition of mentally ill persons as used in the Welfare
and Institutions Code, California, means persons who come
within either or both of the following descriptions:

   A.   Who are of such mental condition that they are
         in need of supervision, treatment, care, or
         restraint.

   B.   Who are of such mental condition that they are
         dangerous to themselves or to the person or
         property of others, and are in need of supervision,
         treatment, care, or restraint.

15.   The Ganser Syndrome is an hysterical reaction not confined
to criminals, characterized by the person's failure to
answer even simple questions correctly.   Hysterical
symptoms may include convulsions, paralysis, disturbance
of gait, rigidity, tremors, and anesthesia.   The Ganser
syndrome may appear in the setting of a schizophrenic
illness or other psychosis. [132]

16.   Definitions:

Neurosis (psychoneurosis): mild functional personality disorder in which there is no gross personality disorganization
and in which the patient does not ordinarily require hospitalization.

Phobia: irrational fear; the individual may realize its
irrationality but nevertheless be unable to dispel it.

Psychosis: severe personality disorder involving loss of
contact with reality and usually characterized by delusions
and hallucinations. Hospitalization is ordinarily required.

Delusions: false beliefs which the individual defends
vigorously despite logical absurdity or proof to the
contrary and despite their serious interference with
his social adjustment.

Hallucinatory reactions: the patient perceives various
kinds of strange objects and events without any appropriate
"external" sensory stimuli. He may hear voices telling
him what to do or commenting upon or criticizing all of
his actions. Occasionally messages are received from
God or from some organization telling the patient of great
powers that have been conferred upon him or of his
mission to save mankind. [133]

Psychosomatic: very real organic symptoms and mal-
functions, in part, caused by psychological processes. [134]

Manic depressive:--Generally delusions of grandeur.

Paranoia: a false belief that others are persecuting him.

Anxiety: a feeling of impending danger, and expressed
by some nervous reaction.

Apathy: the inability to express any emotion at all.

Impulses: the person will have a strong urge to do certain
acts, which are beyond his control. [135]

17.   Insanity and Crime: [136]

Ohio recognizes insanity as a defense for crime because an
unsound mind cannot form the necessary criminal intent.
However, the defense of insanity places the burden of
proof on the accused, and he has to establish it by a
preponderance of the evidence. When a defendant sets up
the defense of insanity for his crime, he must satisfy
the following requirements:

1) That, at the time of committing the crime, he did not know the difference between right and wrong.

2) That, if he did know the difference between right and wrong, he was acting under an irresistible impulse and was unable to control himself.

3) That he did not know the act was contrary to the laws of God and man.

18. Functional psychotic disorders, personality and character disorders, sociopathic personality disturbance:[137] inability to conform to prevailing social standards, lack of social responsibility.

1) Antisocial reaction--impulsive, unable to profit from experience, lack of real loyalty.

2) Dissocial reaction--criminals from abnormal environment with good ego strength.

3) Sexual deviation--wide range of sexually deviant.

4) Addiction--alcoholism or drug addiction.

19. Conduct Disorders:[138]

A. Delinquency and criminal behavior:

1. Cultural deviance--a product of a particular sub-culture which sanctions activities that are considered antisocial or inadequate by the larger society.

2. Delinquency areas--important factor in the rate of juvenile delinquency is the degree of social organization prevailing in the area.

B. Psychopathic Personality:

1. Criminal individuals who suffer from a psychological disorder which interferes with the process of socialization.

C. Deviant Sexual Behavior:

1. Homosexuality.

2. Sexual perversions leading to crimes of violence.

        D. Chronic Alcoholism:

           1. Some people are especially vulnerable to alcohol through physical constitution or a particular array of psychological problems.

20. The Welfare and Institutions Code, 5047, California, provides that anyone may file a petition in the Superior Court alleging that there is a mentally ill person in the county who is in need of care. If the petition is filed with good intent, the following persons cannot be rendered liable, criminally or civilly:

    1) Any peace officer.

    2) A probation officer.

    3) A physician attending a patient.

    4) A physician attached to a public hospital or institution where the person is a patient.

    5) A legal guardian.

Whenever a mentally ill person commits a felony he must be charged with the appropriate Penal Code violation and must be booked at the division of arrest. In this instance the suspect should not be transported to the Hospital Division since this would strengthen any plea of not guilty by reason of insanity he might make later. It is not within the province of the policeman to adjudge a felon's sanity; that is within the jurisdiction of the court only.

21. Section 5880 of the Welfare and Institutions Code, California, states: When any person becomes so mentally ill as to be likely to cause injury to himself or others and to require immediate care, treatment, or restraint, a peace officer, health officer, county physician, assistant county physician who has reasonable cause to believe that such is the case, may take the person into custody for his best interest and protection and place him as provided in this section. Upon application in writing which states the circumstances under which the person's attention was

called to the officer or others, the person believed
mentally ill may be admitted and detained in quarters
provided in any county hospital or state hospital.
The person may be detained for treatment for a period
not to exceed 72 hours, excluding weekends and holidays.
Within the 72 hours the person shall be discharged from
the institution unless a petition of mental illness is
presented to a judge of the superior court, and the court
issues an order for detention, or unless the person is
admitted as a patient under any other law.
Qualified persons in a county or state hospital may refuse
to admit any person apprehended under provision 5880 and
the person shall be entitled to release and transportation
to his residence or another facility for further care if
requested.

22. The state may establish custody and restraint of: mentally
ill persons, insane persons, chronic inebriates, and other
persons of unsound mind.

23. Psychopathic personality may be defined as a neurotic
character disorder in which the patient acts out his neurotic
conduct in his everyday conduct. Alcoholism resulting in
delirium tremens, alcoholic hallucinations, dementia or
Korskoff's Psychosis may relieve a suspect of criminal
activity. [139]

24. Statistical studies indicate that psychopathic personalities
and mentally deficient persons represent a significant
proportion of criminals. Schizophrenia appears as the
most statistically significant psychosis in relation to
criminal behavior. [140]

25. Mental patients (mostly psychotics) occupy almost one-half
of all the hospital beds in the United States. This figure
requires some explanation, however, as psychotic patients
may be hospitalized for several months or even years,
whereas nonpsychiatric patients are hospitalzed on the

average for about two weeks.

The actual incidence of psychoneurotic disorders is difficult to determine, but it has been conservatively estimated that 10,000,000 or more people in the United States today could be classified as psychoneurotic.[141]

26.   About half of all suicide attempts that an officer handles are not really attempts at suicide, but are attempts to gain sympathy, with no real intention of taking their lives.[142]

27.   Problems of nomenclature greatly increase the difficulty of comparing research results from one country to another. Only a small percentage of psychosomatic and neurotic ailments are diagnosed and treated.

Prior to age fifteen, very few persons are hospitalized for mental illness.

As of the mid-nineteen sixties, 200,000 persons were confined in public institutions in the United States. The cost was $400,000,000 per year.

In the United States, in 1965, there were approximately 300 public and 250 private hospitals for prolonged care of mental patients. During any given time there were approximately 575,000 patients in them. Eighty-five per cent of the patients are in state mental hospitals, 10% in the veterans' hospitals, and 2% in private hospitals.

Short term patients are now being taken by general hospitals. In a year more than 200,000 psychiatric patients are admitted and discharged.

28.   If a court jury finds a defendant insane, all trial proceedings must be suspended until he becomes sane. The court must, in the meantime, commit the defendant to a State hospital for care and treatment. Criminal charges may then be dismissed, but the commitment order will remain in full force, until he becomes sane. --Section 1370, California Penal Code.

29. Deviant Sexual Behavior:[143] Delinquents and psychopaths
     often include deviant sexual behavior in their repertory of
     rebellion against social standards, but their disorder
     centers upon the rebellion rather than upon sexual satisfac-
     tion. In some cases such behavior may be the sole depart-
     ure in a person who in all other respects reflects the
     standards of his society.

30. Methods:[144]

     Eighty-five per cent of the mentally ill in England are
     willing to go to a hospital voluntarily, whereas in this
     country the figure is far closer to two or three percent.
     This is due primarily to their fear of the unknown. Thus
     an officer's reassurance of a patient is well worth the
     effort.

     If it is necessary to take the patient against his will, he
     should be approached from both sides and his arms and
     legs grabbed simultaneously. Sometimes a patient will
     quiet down when he is restrained. In fact, he may be
     glad that the police saved him from himself.

     It is never a good idea to lie to the patient. The officer
     should tell him that he is being taken for his own good,
     which is true.

     The uniform of the officer is a great advantage. In our
     culture, it breeds respect and also fear on the part of
     wrong-doers. This fact is not lost to the mentally ill
     person who may be afraid of the officer, and yet at the
     same time respect him.

     In some instances the officer may note that there are
     apparently other mentally ill people in the family. This
     actually may be the case, but there is nothing the officer
     need do, except, perhaps, report it to the proper author-
     ities.

     When policies permit, the officer, in his report, should
     give a detailed account of what happened at the time of
     apprehension.

Naturally, he should bring a doctor into the picture as quickly as possible, because time may be a very important factor.

Problem # 15: Public Relations

1.   Public relations has a myriad of definitions, but from a practical point of view, it can be reduced to a formula: an effective operating program + public understanding = public support. Without public support, there is no progress.
Essential elements:[145]

   a) The public should be kept informed.

   b) A good public relations program should be well planned.

   c) Representatives of news media should be given correct and exact information, with adequate background.

   d) Program, or agency, "overselling" should be avoided.

   e) A year-round plan of public relations should be maintained and should not be resorted to only in times of strife.

   f) Plans should be developed and staff trained specifically for handling of "spot" news.

2.   In the planning of an effective public relations program, it is generally agreed that a four-point approach should be followed:[146]

   a) A study to discover what are the public relations problems and their respective proportion.

   b) The adoption of sincere policies of management, business or institutional, as the basis of a sound program.

   c) The drafting of a detailed program that will earn public approval and support.

    d) Perhaps most important, telling the public
relations story in frank and convincing terms
to all interested publics.

The basic objective of a good public relations program is
to bring about better public understanding which in turn
develops public confidence.

    a) Obtain the understanding and good will of the
public. It cannot be overemphasized that
accomplishment of this objective requires the
agency to perform a function the public wants done
and to do it well.

    b) Public attitudes must be determined, evaluated,
and used in the formulation of correctional
policy and action.

    c) Inform and instruct the public regarding the
purpose, the program, and the operations of the
institution and department.

    d) Educate the public to the proper use of the
correctional facilities, resources and program.

    e) Overcome misconceptions of the public; provide
information which permits the public to adopt a
positive point of view.

    f) Maintain harmonious relations with other units
of government.

    g) Provide for the integration of the correctional
facilities, institutions, and the field units within
the communities.

3.   Public relations; definition:[147]

Public relations in law enforcement involves the activities
that the various law enforcement agencies undertake in
carrying on their work with the public. These activities
are planned and conducted so as to give the law enforcement
service a good reputation with the public and establish
the service as one that functions in the public interest.

Public relations comprises the sum total of all the contacts, attitudes, impressions, activities, policies, and opinions that are involved in the relationships between the public and law enforcement agencies.

Essential attributes of an officer: Public relations activities must begin inside the department, but success depends upon the impression created in the community. The attributes in the following list, though by no means complete, are considered to be essential for an officer.

a) Open-mindedness: Officers should guard against forming opinions in advance of the handling of any complaint or situation. Citizens judge the law enforcement department not by the number of arrests, but by the services rendered. All the statistics in the world will not change the opinion a person forms of a police agency if his call for assistance--possibly the first he has ever made-- does not receive the attention he thinks it merits.

b) Tolerance: No officer can afford to be intolerant of the attitude, interest, or problems of the subject or complainant. Tolerance depends upon understanding. Each officer, therefore, should constantly attempt to keep informed regarding the attitudes and problems of others.

c) Fairness: Law enforcement officers should not be biased in regard to any individual, group, or situation. They are servants of all the public and should not give more service to one segment than another.

d) Patience: The officer must learn to be patient. His impatience may be felt by other persons and the purpose of the investigation thereby defeated.

e) Compassion: The officer must be compassionate; he must feel the unhappiness or suffering of another. Sincerity is the keynote toward establish-

ing the support or confidence upon which law
enforcement work is dependent.

f) Self-assurance: This trait is apparent when the
officer knows his job and knows that he knows his
job. Genuine self-assurance springs from an
inner knowledge of truth, sincerity, and normal
development of the personality.

g) Courtesy: Courtesy presupposes an attitude of
desiring to please or desiring to serve. The
officer who willingly gives his best to the department and to the public, and who recognizes his
function as a peace officer, usually is courteous.
But the officer who is conscious only of his own
importance and his desire to show authority has
great difficulty in adopting a courteous manner.

Among other attributes desirable in the officer are:
sincerity, honesty, courage, good health, a businesslike
manner, a willingness to serve, loyalty, and ethics.

4.   Basic principles of public relations:
Law enforcement departments must avoid public resentment. The friendship and confidence of the American
people cannot be obtained if police action is unfair and
unreasonable. Good will must be established. By performing small courtesies and special services, all impartially
rendered, officers can go far toward improving their standing in the eyes of all those with whom they come in
contact or who observe their actions. Law enforcement
must establish a reputation producing fear and respect in
the criminal element, while at the same time avoiding any
trace of fear in the minds of the law-abiding public. In
order to accomplish this police purpose, it is necessary
for law enforcement officers to establish a reputation for
truth, honesty, and public service. [147]"Public relations

is the art of analyzing, influencing, and interpreting a person, idea, group or business so that its behavior will conform to the greatest degree possible with the public interest."[148]

5. The goals of a public relations program, in general, are:[149]

    a) Public understanding: This is primarily an educational goal. It presupposes that an informed citizenry is basic to effective law enforcement.

    b) Public confidence: This is primarily a psychological goal. It involves the building of citizen trust and respect for the policemen and police department.

    c) Public support: Such support may take many forms, such as compliance with the law, assistance in police investigations, and backing of measures to improve the police service.

    The public relations program includes internal and external phases:

    a) Internal phases are the policies or administrative actions whose primary effects are internal. They include employee relations as they effect public relations and preparation of police for personal contacts with the public.

    b) External phases are those policies or administrative actions which primarily involve people outside the department. These include press relations, exhibits and demonstrations, preparation of printed reports, speeches, and so on.

6. Many of today's attitudes about police and police work are influenced by three factors:[150]

    a) American hostility toward government.

    b) Low esteem earned by corrupt police departments; this affects all police departments.

    c) The expanding nature of police work.

7. The police chief must be the central figure in all the

publicity, to make sure that the publicity will not lose its effect or become merely occasional or sporadic; a public relations bureau should be established to educate the public.

Whenever possible, the policeman should cultivate friendly relations with the press if this can be done without violating department rules. The average person forms his opinions of the efficiency of the police department in part from the public press.[151]

8.   The public has very little to say about police policies. In the main, small pressure groups, led by a small number of people, yield most influence upon such policies. It is incumbent upon the administrator to seek out these groups and try to influence them.[152]

9.   It is up to the police to gain the confidence of the public. Merchants, residents and all other people with whom the police come in contact must know that the police are out to help them and can be trusted. To do this, the police officer must have a sincere desire to help the public. He can't put up a false front.[153]

10.   Abraham Lincoln said: "Public sentiment is everything. Without it nothing can succeed. Consequently, he who molds public sentiment goes deeper than he who enacts statutes or pronounces decisions. He makes statutes and decisions possible or impossible to be executed."[154]

11.   Public relations in police service encompasses all of the relationships that exist between the police and the public that they serve.[155]

12.   The job of public relations officer involves organization: development of means to prepare press releases, scheduling assignments to special activities, and institution of controls and follow-up to insure that planning and organization are not nullified by indifference on the part of the policemen who must carry out the program.[156]

13.   How can a negative opinion be changed to a positive one?
      This problem is usually handled on two levels. First,
      the officer in the field must be made aware of public
      relations, and must put forth a conscious effort to improve
      these relations. Secondly, the police administration must
      determine the true condition as far as public relations and
      the police image are concerned, and then make some
      positive plan to correct or improve the conditions as they
      exist.[157]

14.   The police department that operates under a cloak of
      secrecy breeds community distrust. It must be a part of
      the community and not apart from it.
      Rapid population growth and changing social conditions in
      our communities make it imperative that the chief establish
      an intensive and continuing program designed to carry the
      police message to the people.[158]

15.   The responsibility of public relations should be assigned
      to one person and commensurate time should be allotted
      for the performance of this duty.
      Studies have shown that there is a relationship between
      occupation, age, education, and the police image.
      Of all the general types of occupations, students, profes-
      sionals, and housewives seem to have the lowest opinion
      of policemen in general. For students the department could
      conduct seminars open to the general student body in which
      students' feelings could be brought out into the open and
      logically debated. For professionals, an advisory committee
      might be formed from their ranks, in which they could
      present their views, and from which some good ideas might
      originate. Speakers should be made available to professional
      organizations to acquaint them with not only the problems
      in the field, but with the progress that is being made.
      For housewives, daytime TV programs about law enforce-
      ment, and professional in quality, could be scheduled to

familiarize them with the "new breed" of law enforcement officer.

The police image is quite high with the very young and the very old. This may be due to the protection factor. The higher the education the lower is the opinion of the policeman, according to a study made in Los Angeles. This is understandable when it is realized that as the educational level of the population rises, so does the tendency for people to question existing institutions and conditions. Education stimulates the desire for improvement and better conditions, and promotes a dissatisfaction with the status quo. Presenting these people with a picture of a new and progressive department would do much to help correct the police image in this group. [159]

16. Importance of Los Angeles police traits as seen by 3100 citizens:[160] (1) Appearance; (2) Education; (3) Physical condition; (4) Training.

Evaluation of the Los Angeles Police Department by 3,100 citizens indicated that:

a) 47.6% think their department is about on an average with other large police departments.

b) 27.6% maintain that it is one of the very best in the country.

c) 10.4% feel that it is below standard.

d) 14.4% admit that they do not know how LAPD compares with other large departments.

Most frequently mentioned adverse comments regarding the attitudes of Los Angeles policemen included: discourtesy, prejudice, over-bearing or superior attitude, lack of cooperation and indifference, sarcasm or belligerence.

The good citizens of the community no longer feel a sincere alliance with the police against thieves and burglars because, today, the multitude of regulations and traffic laws developed by our modern civilization have made lawbreakers of us all.

17.   Steps toward improving public relations:[161]

    1. Establishment of a team of speakers available to clubs and organizations.

    2. Bicycle safety programs where awards are given out by the police.

    3. Sponsorship of youth organizations such as Police Explorer Scouts, Police Athletic League.

    4. Placing of frequent exhibits in the windows of downtown stores and at fairs to show latest equipment and developments.

    5. Holding open house at the department and giving guided tours.

    6. Publishing information pamphlets on crime prevention, juvenile laws, etc.

    7. Producing an annual pictorial report that will show in pictures what the department has done for the community during the past year.

    8. Conducting shotgun and rifle safety courses for the youngsters of the community.

    9. Giving ample publicity to officers who are of minority races.

    10. Improving the service at the complaint desk and on the complaint phone.

    11. Creating a well-organized police reserve, made up of citizens of all walks of life.

    12. Making the police officer dress smartly.

Problem # 16: Minority Group Relations (See Appendix G for Community Organizations)

1.   Minority groups today can be objectively distinguished by one or more of four different characteristics: race, nationality, religion, and language.

The term "minority groups" has come to be applied to those groups in the United States who face certain handicaps, who are subject to discrimination, and who are objects of prejudice from most other people.

A group is a minority group if it is the object of prejudice
and discrimination by the dominant groups and if the
members think of themselves as a minority.
Over a third of America's population consists of minority
groups. Over half of the minority population consists of
white Catholics. About 10 per cent of the total American
population is Negro. Less than 4 per cent is Jewish.
Catholics, Negroes, and Jews, in that order, are the
largest minorities.
Discrimination is usually considered under four general
categories: in economic relations, in law, in politics,
and in social relations.
The sources of intergroup discrimination and prejudice
may be placed in five categories: power conflict, ideological
conflict, racism, social structure, and individual psychology. [162]

2. General principles in minority group relations:[163]

   a. Impartiality--Every person should be treated in an
       impartial manner, and without regard to his
       minority group.

   b. Employment of members of minority groups--
       Every applicant for a police position should be
       treated on an equal basis; that is, on his own
       merits and not on the structure of his group.

   c. Contact with minority groups--Such contact should
       provide two-way communication, with leaders of
       the minority groups expressing ideas for improve-
       ment of law enforcement work among minorities,
       and with police officials and personnel making
       suggestions to minority group leaders designed to
       educate and guide.

   d. The press and minority groups--Greater contact
       should be made by the law enforcement agency
       with the minority press.

    e. Public relations with minority groups--Talks by police officers to service groups and youth groups is necessary to build good public opinion.

    f. Observation of symptoms of trouble--(1) Get the facts; (2) Publish facts; (3) Cooperate with press; (4) Utilize the use of information channels.

3. We look upon a minority group as a social collectivity of persons who, because of their physical or cultural characteristics, are singled out from the others in the society in which they live for differential and unequal treatment, and who regard themselves as objects of collective discrimination. The existence of a minority in a society implies the existence of a corresponding dominant group with higher status and greater privileges. Minority status carries with it the exclusion from full participation in the life of the society.[164]

4. In keeping with democratic trends in Negro-White relations in the country, the Atlantic City Council set a precedent in 1948 by appointing eight Negro officers to the police force. Since then more than 350 uniformed Negro policemen have been employed in 54 cities in 11 states. In 1944 the International City Managers Association sponsored a police "program to prevent disorder and to improve relations between different racial, religious and national groups." A "police training bulletin based chiefly on the results of experimentation on the polygot community of Richmond, California" is circulated by the Department of Justice of that state; similar courses of instruction are offered in police departments in Minneapolis, St. Paul, Youngstown and elsewhere; and a "guide" for their police departments in the United States has been sponsored by their official association.[165]

5. Equal protection under the law was set forth both as principle and an objective in the Declaration of Independence,

in the Constitution, and in subsequent amendments to that
document.

6.   Important terms:[166]

Pluralistic--a pluralistic minority is one which seeks
toleration for its difference on the part of the dominant
group. Although the pluralistic minority does not want
to merge its total life with the dominant groups it does
demand for its members a measure of economic opportunity
and political equality.

Assimilation--the goal of a group to lose itself within
the larger whole. The dominant group must be willing
to accept such absorption.

Secession--independence from the dominant group (cultural
and political).

Militancy--goal is to reach beyond secession, assimilation,
and tolerance (beyond cultural, political and economical
autonomy). The militant minority has set domination over
others as its goal.

7.   The President's Crime Commission[167] recommends that in
each police precinct in a minority-group neighborhood there
should be a citizens' advisory committee that meets regularly with police officials to work out solutions to problems
of conflict between the police and the community. It is
crucial that the committees be broadly representative of
the community as a whole, including those elements which
are critical or aggrieved.

In an opinion poll conducted for the President's Crime
Commission, it was found that 23% of all white people
thought that the police were doing an "excellent" job of
enforcing the law, while only 15% of nonwhites held that
view. At the opposite end of the scale, 7% of whites
thought the police were doing a "poor" job, as contrasted
with 16% of nonwhites.

The opinion poll for the President's Commission also
found that 63% of whites and 30% of nonwhites thought the
police were "almost all honest." One percent of whites
and 10% of nonwhites thought the police were "almost
all corrupt."

It should be a high-priority objective of all departments
in communities with a substantial minority population to
recruit minority-group officers, and to deploy and promote them fairly. Every officer in such departments
should receive thorough grounding in community-relations
subjects. His performance in the field of community
relations should be periodically reviewed and evaluated.

8. U.S. Constitution, Amendment XIV, Section 1: All persons
born or naturalized in the United States, and subject to
the jurisdiction thereof, are citizens of the United States
and of the State wherein they reside. No State shall make
or enforce any law which shall abridge the privileges or
immunities of citizens of the United States; nor shall any
State deprive any person of life, liberty, or property,
without due process of law; nor deny to any person within
its jurisdiction the equal protection of the laws.

9. While the federal courts were continuing to issue orders
of desegregation the Congress of the United States made
no supplementary moves to further the desegregation process
until 1957, when the Civil Rights Act was passed. Its
main provisions were:[168]

    a. The establishment of a Commission of Civil
        Rights to study denials of the right to vote, to
        collect information concerning the denial of equal
        protection of the laws, and to appraise laws and
        policies of the federal government with respect
        to equal protection.

    b. To empower the Attorney General to seek court
        injunctions against interference with the voting

rights of any individual.

   c. To establish a Civil Rights Division in the Department of Justice.

10.   Estimated numbers of minorities in the United States:[169]

Negroes (1960)	18, 871, 831
Jews (1960)	5, 531, 500
Mexicanos (1953)	3, 000, 000
Puerto Ricans (1960)	903, 000
American Indians (1960)	523, 591
Japanese (1960)	464, 332
Chinese (1960)	237, 292
Filipinos (1960)	176, 310

11.   Ethnic Groups: collections of people with certain commonly held characteristics, including: religion, racial origin, national origin, and language and cultural traditions, traits and customs.

12.   In a study of a California police department, 100 officers were asked what percentage of their arrests for drunkenness were of persons of Latin descent; the estimate was about 60%. In reality the percentage was 29%. The interfactor in the study was that the estimates did not change with the degree of education. In this department the educational level was quite high, ranging from high school graduation to several masters degrees. Equally interesting was the fact that there were several officers in the sample who were of Latin descent, and their estimates were in the upper range.[170]

13.   The Philadelphia Commission on Human Relations has worked closely with the city police department and an advisory committee to develop a human relations training program for policemen. The Commission in 1960 reported that the following objectives should be sought in human relations training:[171]

   a. To develop in police officers an appreciation of

the civil rights of the public.

b. To develop in police officers the ability to meet, without undue militance, aggressiveness, hostility, or prejudice, police situations involving minority groups.

c. To develop in police officers an adequate social perspective.

d. To develop in police officers an acceptance of integrated situations.

14.   Organized movements for better race relations generally date from the end of World War II. During 1946, several cities began an active program, including the training of police, designed to lessen inter-racial friction.

Many citizens, and particularly members of minority groups, seem to believe that the Police Department is a punitive agency and exists for the purpose of punishing people.[172]

15.   It might be advisable to organize within the department a highly trained unit whose members are assigned to work with minority groups and in the areas where racial conflicts may be expected to develop.

Research has been undertaken to indicate illusory nature of the view that certain racial groups are more criminal than others.[173]

16.   The National Conference of Christians and Jews was responsible in the 40's for getting the police and minority groups together to talk about their problems and to exchange ideas on how to correct the situation. NCCJ established local regional and national institutes for this purpose.

A National Institute on Police Community Relations held at Michigan State University in East Lansing was sponsored by the NCCJ and was held for the first time in 1955.

17.   Racial disturbances are caused primarily by unhealthy
        social conditions. Any farseeing program to prevent
        such conflicts must ultimately be concerned with elimi-
        nating the cause of the trouble. No agency of govern-
        ment can be more effective in furthering good race re-
        lations and in preventing riots than the police.
            Where standards have been professionalized, the police
        are taught to approach the problem as friends of the
        people in their district. They form committees of
        citizens to cooperate with them. They encourage youth
        groups and promote beneficial social activities. They
        consider good training courses for themselves as a
        necessity and strive to understand the diverse types of
        people within the neighborhood.[174]
            Indicators of rising tensions in the minority community:
        a. an increasing number of rumors, together with
            an increase in their sensational character.
        b. an increasing number of incidents or threats
            of violence.
        c. increasing activity of race-agitating organizations.
        d. disintegration of relations between minority groups
            and the police department.
        e. an increase in labor unrest.
        f. minority reaction to the increasing tension as
            reflected in the minority press.

18.   Other Signs of Trouble:[175]
            Minority group riots never happen suddenly or without
        warning. They are the product of tensions that accumulate
        over a period of time. The following are other indicators
        of threatening or rising tensions:
        a. Growing distrust of law enforcement by minority
            groups.
        b. Increase in number of complaints of police
            brutality.

    c. An increase in altercations on streetcars and
       buses and in other public places.

    d. The holding of protest meetings.

    e. An increase in the number of gang fights by
       juveniles that involve majority and minority
       groups.

    f. Raids on neighborhoods, or party-crashing.

    g. Threats and attacks on the private property of
       others.

    h. The appearance of inflammatory or derogatory
       signs, pamphlets, or leaflets; an increase in the
       circulation of "hate" literature.

19.   Training of an officer:[176]

     Professional knowledge and training are essential in the
field of human relations. An officer should have a
practical working knowledge of:

    a. The psychological and sociological aspects of
       minority group prejudice, its nature, causes,
       and manifestations.

    b. The essential facts of racial, religious, national,
       and cultural differences among people. The
       psychology of minority group behavior and
       attitudes.

    c. Basic facts of social and economic conditions under
       which minority groups live in the community.

    d. How to recognize the symptoms of rising tensions
       among groups which create potential civil disturb-
       ance conditions.

    e. Practical police methods, based on experience, of
       reducing tensions and preventing routine police
       incidents from assuming proportions of a riot.

    f. A thorough understanding of the powers, duties,
       and limitations of a peace officer.

20.   Handling a Riot: some of the lessons police have learned
       in handling a riot include:[177]

       a.   Immediate recognition by the police of an unusual
            and dangerous situation and quick report to head-
            quarters.

       b.   Speedy mobilization of the police force.

       c.   Rapid effective steps, planned in advance, to
            prevent curiosity seekers or potential rioters
            from entering the trouble area.

       d.   Special precautions against excessive use of
            force, insistence on diplomatic and impersonal
            action, and use of Negro policemen.

       e.   Large reinforcements held in reserve but quickly
            available if needed.

       f.   Cooperation of neighborhood leaders.

       g.   Personal appeals to rioters by high officials.

       h.   High officials in direct command of efforts to
            restore order, staying on the job until it is
            finished.

A police department is in the best position when it
maintains a policy of absolute impartiality and when that
policy is carried out in the attitudes, statements, and
actions of individual members.

Problem # 17: Personnel

1.   In recent years, there has been great progress in the
       development of executive talent in the world of business
       and industry--but almost no attention given to this matter
       in the sphere of law enforcement.[178]

2.   The Vollmer system of police administration, one of the
       major contributions of the century to crime control,
       attracted international attention.   The Vollmer police
       system is complex and involves many factors, but most
       important are the high entrance standards that have been
       established to recruit.[179]

3.   Police Certification in California:[180]

certifications proposed: Basic, Intermediate, Advanced.
The qualifications for a certification consist of various
combinations of (a) formal academic training of a fully
accredited nature, leading to regular course credit and
degrees in colleges and universities; (b) short-course
and institute training; and (c) police experience.

4.   Traditionally, the police services have required their
administrators to rise from the ranks. This policy,
coupled with low entrance requirements, has led to a shortage
of professionally trained leaders. Until recently, college
trained people have been reluctant to enter the lower
echelons of the police service, but the trend has changed,
and as more and more college trained people are proving
themselves capable of rising to the top, they, in turn,
are encouraging college graduates to enter the public
service.[181]

5.   Types of Training:[182]

    (1) Cadet Training--designed for recruits, such
           programs vary in length.

    (2) In-Service Training--a refresher course for
           uniformed personnel who have had cadet training
           and practical field experience. It is a more
           advanced and concentrated type of training.

    (3) Specialized Training--courses are available on a
           nonscheduled basis, usually varying in length from
           one to two weeks.

6.   Crime Commission Recommendations:[183]

    (1) Each municipality, and other jurisdiction responsible
           for law enforcement, should carefully assess the
           manpower needs of its police agency on the basis
           of efficient use of all its personnel and should
           provide the resources required to meet the need
           for increased personnel if such a need is found to
           exist.

       (2) Police departments should recruit far more
           actively than they do now, with special attention
           to college campuses and inner-city neighborhoods.

       (3) The ultimate aim of all police departments should
           be that all personnel with general enforcement
           powers have baccalaureate degrees.

       (4) Police departments should take immediate steps
           to establish a minimum requirement of B.A. de-
           gree for all supervisors and executive positions.

       (5) Police salaries must be raised, particularly,
           by increasing maximums.

       (6) Police salaries should be considered separately
           from those of other municipal departments.

       (7) A period of 12-16 months should be required for
           probation and evaluation of recruits.

       (8) Inflexible physical, age, and residence recruitment
           requirements should be modified.

       (9) Ability should be stressed in promotions.

      (10) Screening of candidates to determine character
           and fitness should be improved.

7.   In small cities the median annual pay for a patrolman is
       $4,600; in large cities it is $5,300. Typically, the
       maximum salary for nearly all positions is less than
       $1,000 over the starting salary. A special agent of the
       Federal Bureau of Investigation begins at $8,421 a year
       and, if he serves long enough and well enough, can reach,
       without promotion to a supervisory position, $16,905.
       Formal police training programs for recruits in all
       departments, large and small, should consist of an absolute
       minimum of 400 hours of classroom work spread over
       a four to six-month period so that it can be combined with
       carefully selected and supervised field training. [184]

8.   Among cities of 10,000 population and over, 21 years has
       become the minimum age for acceptance on the police force,
       and more than half of the cities require high school gradua-

tion. In some cities, however, standards are lower--
an eighth grade education or simply the ability to read
and write. Elimination of unsuitable candidates is
achieved in many cities through the use of tests and
examinations. Intelligence tests may be used in large

cities.

A new trend that promises much for the professionalization of police is the establishment of courses by
universities leading to a certificate or degree. In 1959,
more than 56 universities and colleges in 19 states offered 128 programs of different police training. The number
of police officers who complete such programs is a very
small percentage of the total. However, the trend is
growing, both towards an increase in institutions offering
courses and in the number of students enrolled.[185]

9. In 1960 the State of California created a Commission on
Peace Officers Standards and Training. The minimum
standards it prescribed for selection are as follows:[186]

   (1) Citizen of the United States.

   (2) Minimum age of twenty-one years.

   (3) Fingerprinting of applicants with a search of
       local, state, and national fingerprint files to
       disclose any record.

   (4) No convictions by any state or federal govern-
       ment of any crime the punishment for which could
       have been imprisonment in a federal penitentiary
       or state prison.

   (5) Good moral character as determined by a thorough
       background investigation.

   (6) Graduation from high school or a passing of the
       General Education Development Test indicating high
       school graduation level, or a score on a written
       test on mental ability approved by the commission
       and equivalent to that obtained by the average

school student.

(7) Examination by a licensed physician and surgeon.
Only those applicants shall be eligible for appointment who are found to be free from any physical,
emotional, or mental condition which might
adversely affect performance of his duty as a
peace officer. The applicant shall possess normal
hearing and normal color vision. He must possess
normal visual functions and visual acuity not less
than 20-40 vision in each eye without correction
and corrective to 20-20 in the better eye and not
less than 20-25 in the lesser eye.

(8) All interviews shall be held by the hiring authority
or representative, or representatives, to determine
such things as the recruits' appearnace, background
and ability to communicate.

These standards were set after careful deliberation by
experienced law enforcement personnel. They are sub-
scribed to by 90 per cent of California's law enforcement
agencies.

10.   Internal Affairs:[187]

To be effective, a law enforcement agency must achieve
public confidence, and to this end, the Internal Affairs
Division has been a potent force. The citizens of a
community must know that their justifiable complaints
against the police department will receive action.
Also, to be effective, a law enforcement agency must
preserve internal morale against the malicious attacks of
a small segment of the public. To this end, the Internal
Affairs Division has earned the gratitude of many officers
whose names and reputations have been the subject of
unwarranted vilification.

11.   To maintain an effective police personnel program certain
concepts must be followed:[188]

    (1) A classification of positions--a grouping of positions based upon certain qualifications so that a descriptive title may be given.

    (2) The administration of a compensation plan that provides attractive salaries, and for salary advancement.

    (3) The recruitment and selection of employees on a competitive basis.

    (4) An effective employee relations program.

    (5) A program for promotion based upon the merits of the employees.

    (6) A fair system for evaluating job performance.

    (7) An intensive in-service training program on a continual basis.

    (8) Development of an effective method for maintaining discipline in the department which should include recognition of outstanding performance as well as punishment for improper conduct.

12. In many instances an effort is made to bridge the artificial gap between patrolman and detective by assigning the patrolman who engages in the close pursuit of an offender to any later investigation which may be conducted by the detective force.

Many ambitious and qualified youth must spend years in the lower ranks and grades, in the course of which they acquire no practical experience or training in administration and leadership, before they can hope to share the responsibilities and enjoy the prerogatives of high command. [189]

13. Problems of Promotion: [190]

    (1) Promotion is limited to about 8 to 20 per cent of all employees who enter at the bottom of the scale.

    (2) Specifying the classes from which promotions may be made can be difficult.

    (3) There are conflicting opinions about the weight

to be given for length of service (seniority) and
the selection of men for promotion.

(4) In filling the higher posts in the department there
are differences of opinion, and practice, concerning the relative value of making promotions
entirely from within the department or opening
the top positions to competition by qualified
nonresidents.

Notes

1.   Cogan, Morris L. "The Problem of Defining a Profession",
     Annals of the American Academy of Political and Social
     Science, Vol. 297, January, 1955.

2.   Radelet, Louis "Implications of Professionalization of Law
     Enforcement for Police-Community Relations, " Police Chief,
     July-August, 1966.

3.   Encyclopedia Americana Vol. 22, p. 632, 1962.

4.   Aron, T. J. "Education and Professionalism in American
     Law Enforcement, " Police, Nov. /Dec. , 1965, p. 37-41.

5.   Wilensky, Harold L. "The Professionalization of Everyone, "
     American Journal of Sociology, September, 1964.

6.   Leonard, V. A. Police Organization and Management,
     The Foundation Press, Brooklyn, 1951.

7.   Chapman, Samuel G. Police Heritage in England and
     America, Michigan State University, East Lansing, 1962.

8.   Ibid.

9.   Taff, Charles Management of Traffic and Physical
     Distribution, Third Edition, Richard Irwin, Homewood,
     Ill. , 1964, p. 24.

10. Mirich, John and Voris, Eugene "Recognition of Local Law
     Enforcement as a Profession: the Time has Surely Come!"
     Police, March-April, 1965, p. 42-44.

11. Goldfield, Edwin Dept. of Commerce, Bureau of Census,
     Statistical Abstract of the U.S., 1965, 86th Annual Ed.;
     pp. 230-232.

12. Gebhard, Paul H. Pregnancy, Birth and Abortion, Institute for Sex Research, Indiana University.

13. Sands, M. S. Therapeutic Abortion Act, 1966, p. 285.

14. Williams, G. The Sanctity of Life, 1957, p. 146-248.

15. Einstoss, Ron "Study Finds Most Abortionists Lack Medical Training," The Los Angeles Times, February 13, 1967.

16. Lader, L. Abortion, Bobbs-Merrill, 1966.

17. O'Hara, Charles E. Fundamental of Criminal Investigations. Charles C. Thomas: Springfield, Illinois, 1963, p. 479-480.

18. Ibid.

19. Northrup, Herbert R. Government and Labor, Illinois, 1963.

20. McWhirter, Norris Guinness Book of World Records, Bantam Books, New York, 1964.

21. Ibid.

22. Wibick, J. B. "U. S. Economy an Overview," Current History, 49:1 (July, 1965).

23. Monthly Labor Review, U.S. Department of Labor, June, 1965.

24. International City Managers' Association. Municipal Public Works Administration. Chicago: The Association, 5th ed., 1957, p. 68.

25. Los Angeles Training Bulletin, Los Angeles Police Department, Los Angeles, Calif., 1960.

26. Municipal Police Administration, Fifth Edition, pp. 432-433.

27. Ibid., p. 479.

28. Clift, Raymond A Guide to Modern Police Thinking. Cincinnati: The W. H. Anderson Co., 1956, p. 182-183.

29. Payton, Patrol Procedures, 1964, Los Angeles, Calif., p. 231.

30. Duffy, Clinton T. and Hirshery, Al Sex and Crime, Doubleday, New York, 1965.

31. Hibbert, Christopher The Roots of Evil, Little Brown, Boston, 1963.

32. Cameron, Norman Personality Development and Psychopathology, Houghton Mifflin, Boston, 1963, pp. 662-663.

33. Johns, Edward, Sutton, Wilfred and Webster, Lloyd. Health for Effective Living, Third Edition, McGraw Hill, New York, p. 117.

34. Clift, Raymond, A Guide to Modern Police Thinking, W. H. Anderson, 1956.

35. Berg, Charles and Clifford, Allen The Problems of Homosexuality, The Citadel Press, New York, 1958.

36. Woetzel, Robert K. "Do Our Homosexuality Laws Make Sense, " Saturday Review, 46:23-26, October 9, 1965.

37. Municipal Police Administration, p. 311.

38. U. S. Congress, House Committee on Post Office and Civil Service, Hearings, Obscene Matter Sent Through the Mail, 86th Cong., 1st Sess., 1960.

39. Kilpatrick, James Jackson The Smut Peddlers, Avon Book Division, Hearst Corporation, New York, 1960, p. 15.

40. Murphy, Terrence Censorship: Government and Obscenity, Helicon, Baltimore, 1963.

41. International City Managers' Association, Municipal Police Administration, Published by I. C. M. A. Chicago, 1961, pp. 313-314.

42. U. S. News and World Report, 57:80-1; Oct. 12, 1964.

43. Clift, R. Guide to Modern Police Thinking, Cincinnati, 1956, pp. 191-199.

44. Ibid.,

45. Life, "Come to the Riot", July 2, 1965, pp. 88-89.

46. Diamond, Harry "Crowd and Riot Control", Police, 8:59, May, April, 1964.

47. McCarthy, W. P. "Constitutional and Legal Aspects of Crowd Control, " Police, 9:50.

48. Grimshaw, Allen D. "Action of the police and the Military in American Race Riots, " Phylon, 24:271, Fall, 1963.

49. Bishop, Jerry E. "Police vs. Riots" Wall Street Journal,
    164:12, July 28, 1964.

50. Witkin, B. E. Summary of California Law, San Francisco,
    The Recorder Printing and Publishing Co., 1960, vol. 2,
    p. 1218.

51. Aaron, Thomas J. "A Military Force to Police
    My Community," Law and Order, Vol. 13, No. 12,
    December, 1965, p. 96.

52. "New Methods in Riot Control," U.S. News, Vol. 61:
    August 8, 1966, pp. 39-40.

53. Woods, Sterling A. Riot Control, Military Service
    Publishing Co., Harrisburg, Penn., 1952.

54. Zacks, Robert "Fantastic Devices to End Riots,"
    Nation's Business, Chamber of Commerce of the
    United States, July, 1966, pp. 63-64.

55. Municipal Police Administration by the International City
    Managers Association, 1961, pp. 62-63.

56. Ibid.

57. Morris, Robert B. "Fire-Police Integration,"
    The American City, Oct. 1959, p. 122.

58. Detzer, Carl, National Municipal Review, Vol. XLVI, No. 6,
    June 1957, pp. 287-288.

59. Roan, Peter F. "Iowa City Sees Logic in Fire, Police
    Integration," The American City, M., 1959, pp. 216-217.

60. "Strengthening Law Enforcement", Congress Revue,
    March 1965, p. 3.

61. Clift, Raymond E. A Guide to Modern Police Thinking,
    W. H. Anderson, 1956.

62. Bruce, Howard I. A Survey: Police-Fire Integration in the
    United States and Canada, Ohio, 1961.

63. A Survey: Police-Fire Integration in the United States and
    Canada. Cleveland, Ohio: Cleveland Bureau of Govern-
    mental Research, 1961, pp. 65, 67.

64. Jessup, J. A. "Ten Years of Sunnyvale's Combined Police
    and Fire" American City, Vol. 75, No. 4, (April 1960)p.188-91.

65. American City, "Elgin, Ill., Likes Joint Fire-Police
     Service", Dec. 1958, 73:18.

66. Fairholm, G. W. "Where Police-Fire Integration Works"
     American City, Vol. 77, No. 4, (April, 1962), pp. 161-163.

67. Bruce, Howard P. F. I. A. Survey: Police-Fire Integration
     in the United States and Canada, Cleveland: Cleveland
     Bureau of Governmental Research, 1961.

68. The Police Yearbook 1965. International Association of Chiefs
     of Police.

69. Martin, Thomas Strategy for Survival, Tucson: University
     of Arizona Press, 1963, pp. 262-3.

70. Baker, George Walter (ed.) Behavioral Science & Civil
     Defense, National Academy of Sciences.

71. Johns, Edward, Sutton, Wilfred and Webster, Lloyd
     Health for Effective Living. McGraw-Hill, New York,
     1962, pp. 424-425.

72. More, Harry, Jr. and Barnwine, Henry "Police Role in
     Civil Defense," Police, 1:12, July, 1966.

73. International City Manager's Association, Municipal Police
     Administration, Published by I. C. M. A. Chicago, 1961,
     pp. 431.

74. Education for National Survival. U. S. Dept. of Health,
     Education, and Welfare, U. S. Government Printing Office,
     1956.

75. Clift, Raymond E. Police and Public Safety, W. H. Anderson
     1963.

76. Conyngton, Thomas Business Law, 6th Ed. (Roland Press,
     New York, 1964.)

77. Municipal Management Practices. International City Managers'
     Association, Chicago, 1958, p. 397.

78. Frick, Charles W. California Criminal Law, Los Angeles:
     Legal Book Store, 1961, p. 62.

79. International City Managers' Association, Municipal Police
     Administration, Chicago: I. C. M. A., 1961, pp. 110-111.

80. International City Managers' Association, Municipal Police
Administration, Fifth Edition, Chicago, 1961, pp. 394-395.

81. Wechter, Harry L. "The Case for Compulsory Motor
Vehicle Inspection, " Law and Order, Vol. 14, No. 4,
April, 1966, pp. 82-84.

82. Irish and Prothro, The Politics of American Democracy,
Prentice-Hall, New Jersey, 1963, p. 207.

83. Packer, Herbert "Offenses Against the State, " Readings
in Criminology and Penology, ed. Dressler, David
New York: Columbia University Press, 1964, p. 370.

84. Ibid., p. 367.

85. Ferguson, John and McHenry, Dean The American Federal
Government. New York: McGraw-Hill, 1963, p. 144.

86. Carr, Robert K. The House Committee on Un-American
Activities, Ithaca, New York: Cornell University Press,
1952, p. 1.

87. Ferguson, John H. and McHenry, Dean E. Elements of
American Government, Fifth Edition, p. 103.

88. Hoover, J. Edgar A Study of Communism, Holt, Rinehart
and Winston, New York, 1962.

89. Burrham, J. The Web of Subversion, John Day, New York,
1954.

90. Randall, William Pierce The Ku Klux Klan, A Century of
Infamy. Chilton Books, New York, 1965, p. 236.

91. Lincoln, C. Eric Muslims in America (Beacon Press,
Boston), 1961, p. 4.

92. "The FBI's Secret War Against the Ku Klux Klan", Reader's
Digest, January, 1966.

93. The Challenge of Crime in a Free Society. A Report by the
President's Commission on Law Enforcement and
Administration of Justice, Washington: U.S. Government
Printing Office, 1967, p. 187-190.

94. Ibid., p. 192.

95. Martin, Raymond V. Revolt in the Mafia, New York, 1963.

96. Parker, Wm. H. Parker on Police. Charles C. Thomas,
    Publisher, 1957, p. 51.

97. Pantaloone, Michele The Mafia and Politics, New York,
    Coward-McCann, 1966.

98. Stolley, Richard B. "A Crisis Worse than Anyone Imagined
    Report, " Life, February 24, 1967, p. 24-25.

99. Barnes, Harry Elmer New Horizons in Criminology.
    New York: Prentice Hall, 1952, p. 29-35.

100. "Organized Crime, Gambling, and Law Enforcement, "
     Police, March-April, 1964.

101. The International City Manager's Association, Municipal
     Police Administration. 5th Edition, 1961.

102. American Bar Association Commission on Organized Crime,
     I, pp. 16-18.

103. "Chicago Squeeze: Illinois Criminal Investigation Commission
     Hearings, " Newsweek, 67:34-5, January 24, 1966.

104. "New Ways Gangsters Muscle into Business, " Interview,
     F.M. Vinson, Jr. Nations Business, 53:62-5, August,
     1965.

105. Vinson, Fred M. "New Ways Gangsters Muscle into
     Business, " Nations Business, 53:62-5, August, 1965.

106. Special Crime Study Commission on Organized Crime,
     Sacramento, California, 1953.

107. Dressler, David (ed.) Readings in Criminology and
     Penology. Columbia University Press, 1964, p. 48.

108. Ashenhust, Paul Harvey Police and the People. Illinois:
     Charles C. Thomas, 1956.

109. Ibid.

110. Smith, Bruce Police Systems in the United States. New
     York: Harper & Bros., 1949.

111. Smith, Bruce. The State Police. New York: Macmillan,
     1925.

112. King, Everett M. The Auxiliary Police. Springfield:
     Charles C. Thomas, Publisher, 1960. pp. 28-29.

113. Vollmer, August, Peper, John and Boolsen, Frank
     Police Organization and Administration. California
     Department of Education, Sacramento, 1951, p. 48.

114. The Challenge of Crime in a Free Society. A Report by the
     President's Commission on Law Enforcement and
     Administration of Justice. U.S. Government Printing
     Office, Washington, 1967. pp. 111-112.

115. Gourley, G. D. Patrol Administration. Springfield,
     Illinois: Charles C. Taylor, 1961.

116. Municipal Police Administration, Auxiliary Personnel.
     Fifth Edition. International City Managers Association,
     1961., pp. 423-26.

117. Lucas, H. E. "Public Safety Police Reserve Lends Valuable
     Aid," The American City, Vol. 78, No. 2, Feb. 1963,
     p. 20.

118. King, E. M. The Auxiliary Police Unit. Springfield, Ill.:
     C. C. Thomas, p. 3.

119. Smith, Bruce Police Systems in the United States.
     New York: Harper & Brothers, 1960. p. 102.

120. Leonard, V. A. Police Organization and Management.
     Brooklyn: The Foundation Press, 1964. p. 82.

121. Gourley, G. Douglas Patrol Administration. Springfield,
     Illinois: Charles C. Thomas, p. 51.

122. Ibid., p. 51.

123. Jones, Edward, Sutton, Wilfred, and Webster, Lloyd.
     Health for Effective Living. McGraw-Hill, New York,
     1962, p. 94.

124. Cameron, Norman Personality Development and
     Psychopathology. Houghton Mifflin, Boston, 1963, pp. 5-8.

125. O'Hara, Charles E. Fundamentals of Criminal Investigation,
     1966, pp. 156-157.

126. Caldwell, Robert G. Criminology (Roland Press, 2nd Edition.
     New York, 1956), pp. 234-244.

127. Barnes, Harry Elmer and Teeters, Negley K. New
     Horizons in Criminology (Prentice Hall, 2nd Edition,
     New York, 1952) pp. 113, 229-235.

128. Overholser, Winfred. The Psychiatrist and the Law.
     New York: Harcourt Brace, 1953, p. 61.

129. Coleman, James C. Abnormal Psychology and Modern Life.
     Third Edition. (Scott, Foresman: 1964) p. 262.

130. Fricke, Charles W. California Criminal Evidence.
     (Los Angeles: Legal Book Store, Publishers, 1964),
     pp. 243-244.

131. Caldwell, Robert G. Criminology (Roland Press, 2nd Edition.
     New York, 1956). pp. 234-244.

132. MacDonald, John Psychiatry and the Criminal, Charles C.
     Thomas, Illinois, 1958.

133. Coleman, James C. Abnormal Psychology and Modern Life.
     Third Edition, pp. 264, 666-669.

134. Merton and Nesbit. Contemporary Social Problems. 2nd
     Edition. Harcourt, Brace and World, 1966.

135. Payton, George T. Patrol Procedures, 1966.

136. Clift, R. E. A Guide to Modern Police Thinking.
     Cincinnati, 1956.

137. Diagnostic and Statistical Manual. Washington, D.C.:
     American Psychiatric Association, 1952.

138. White, R. W. The Abnormal Personality. New York, 1964.

139. MacDonald, John. Psychiatry and the Criminal. Charles C.
     Thomas, Illinois, 1958.

140. Vedder, Clyde. Criminology. New York: Holt, 1953.

141. Coleman, James C. Abnormal Psychology and Modern Life.
     Third Edition.

142. Payton, George T. Patrol Procedures, 1966.

143. White, Robert W. The Abnormal Personality. Roland Press,
     Third Edition, 1964.

144. Rowland, Lloyd W. "Care is Necessary in Apprehending
     the Mentally Ill, " FBI Law Enforcement Bulletin,
     30:3-5, Jan. 1961.

145. State Board of Corrections. Minimum Jail Standards.
      Sacramento: State Printing Office, 1963.

146. A Manual of Correctional Standards, "Public Relations and
      Information, " pp. 116-119.

147. Peper, John P. Public Relations for the Law Enforcement
      Officer. Sacramento: California State Department of
      Education, 1963.

148. The Encyclopedia America, pp. 769-773.

149. International City Managers' Association. Municipal Police
      Administration. Chicago: I. C. M. A., 1961.

150. Ibid. p. 474.

151. Lowenthal, Max. The Federal Bureau of Investigation.
      New York: William Sloane Associates, 1950.

152. Holladay, Roy E. "The Police Administrator: A Politician, "
      Journal of Criminal Law, Criminology and Police Science,
      53:526, December 1962.

153. Holcomb, Richard L. Police Patrol. Springfield, Ill.:
      Charles C. Thomas, 1957.

154. Melvin, Colonel Maurence. Law and Order. "Chronology
      of a Day in Police Public Relations, " March 1967, p. 13.

155. Wilson, Orland. Police Planning. Springfield, Ill.: Charles
      C. Thomas, 1962, pp. 253-254.

156. Municipal Police Administration. Fifth Edition, 1961.

157. Payton, George T. Patrol Procedures. 1964.

158. The Police Yearbook, 1964. International Association of
      Chiefs of Police, Inc. p. 224.

159. Payton, George T. Patrol Procedures. 1966.

160. Gourley, Douglas. Public Relations and the Police.
      Springfield: Charles C. Thomas, 1953, p. 48.

161. Payton, George T. Patrol Procedures. Los Angeles: Legal
      Book Store, 1964. pp. 293, 299.

162. Merton and Nisbet. Contemporary Social Problems. New
      York: Harcourt, Brace and World, 1966.

163. Municipal Police Administration. International City Managers'
     Association, 1961.

164. Gittler, Joseph B. Minorities in America. New York:
     John Wiley & Sons, 1956.

165. Cole, Stewart G. and Cole, Mildred W. Minorities and the
     American Promise. New York: Harper & Bros., 1954.

166. Merton and Nesbit. Social Trends and Problems.

167. President's Commission on Law Enforcement and Adminis-
     tration of Justice. The Challenge of Crime in a Free
     Society. Washington, D.C.: U.S. Government Printing
     Office, 1967.

168. Marden, Charles. Minorities in American Society. New
     York: American Book, 1962.

169. Ibid.

170. Payton, George T. Patrol Procedures, 1964.

171. Commission of Human Relations, Summary of Report of
     Police Human Relations, 1960, as quoted in Municipal
     Police Administration.

172. Ashenhust, Paul. Police and the People. Illinois: Charles
     C. Thomas, 1956.

173. Mays, John. Society and the Social Structure. London:
     Faber and Faber, 1963.

174. Fineberg, S. A. Punishment Without Crime: What You Can
     Do About Prejudice. New York: Doubleday, 1949.

175. Peper, John P. Public Relations for the Law Enforcement
     Officer. Sacramento: California Department of Education,
     1963.

176. Ibid.

177. International City Managers' Association. Municipal Police
     Administration. Fifth Edition, 1961.

178. Germann, A. G. Police Executive Development. Illinois:
     Charles C. Thomas.

179. Leonard, V. A. Police Organization and Management.
     Brooklyn: Foundation Press, 1951.

180. Germann, A. C. Police Executive Development, Illinois:
     C. C. Thomas, 1962.

181. Germann, A. C. Introduction To Law Enforcement.

182. Boolsen, Frank and Peper, John. Law Enforcement Training
     in California. Sacramento: California Department of
     Education, 1963.

183. President's Commission on Law Enforcement and Adminis-
     tration of Justice. The Challenge of Crime in a Free
     Society. Washington: Government Printing Office, 1967.

184. Ibid.

185. Caven, Ruth Shonle. Criminology. New York: Thomas Y.
     Crowell, 1962.

186. Blum, Richard H. Police Selection. Illinois: Charles C.
     Thomas, 1964.

187. Wilson, O. W. Parker on Police. Springfield, Illinois:
     Charles C. Thomas, 1957.

188. International City Managers' Association. Municipal Police
     Administration. Chicago, 1961.

189. Smith, Bruce. Police Systems in the United States. New
     York: Harper and Brothers, 1940.

190. International City Managers' Association. Municipal Police
     Administration. Chicago, Illinois, 1961.

IX: The Future of Policing

1. Modern technology can make many specific contributions
    to criminal administration. The most significant will
    come from the use of computers to collect and analyze
    the masses of data the system needs to understand the
    crime control process. Other important contributions
    may come, for example, from:[1]

    (1) Flexible radio networks and portable two-way
        radios for patrol officers;

    (2) Computer assisted command-and-control systems
        for rapid and efficient dispatching of patrol forces;

    (3) Advanced fingerprint recognition systems;

    (4) Innovations for the police patrol car such as mobile
        teletypewriters, tape recorders for recording question-
        ing, and automatic car position locators;

    (5) Alarms and surveillance systems for homes, business
        and prisons;

    (6) Criminalistics techniques such as voice prints, neutron
        activation analysis and other modern laboratory
        instrumentation.

2. More and more the contributions of scientific technology
    are being harnessed by the police. For example, the drunk
    driver's intoxication can now be measured by a portable
    machine that measures amounts of alcohol in the blood
    of the suspect.

3. In Detroit, on one of the expressways there is a series
    of fourteen television cameras, each covering a distance
    of 3.2 miles in length. A control officer can immediately
    spot an accident, can move all traffic off that lane through
    the use of signals, can lower the speed limit in the same
    manner, and can dispatch officers to the scene. Also,
    a closed-circuit television system is being developed for

264

crowded metropolitan intersections, where a controller
can coordinate traffic signals to comply with maximum
traffic movement. In Toronto, Canada, a system auto-
matically controls all 500 traffic signals in the city's
business district. The signals are hooked up to a central
digital computer triggered by vehicle detectors buried in
the pavement. In Los Angeles, 50 intersections have been
guarded for several years by stop-go signals controlled
by computer.[2]

4. A psychologist from the University of Chicago has done
much experimentation with the dilation and constriction of
the pupil of the eye. His purpose is to explain how the
mental activity of the brain affects the size of the pupil.
His tests seem to be successful, and the results may be
a relevant aid to the criminal investigator.[3]

5. The Fresno Police Department has made an advance with
mug shots. These, usually black and white, are now being
processed in color by the department. In this manner skin
tone, scars, eye and hair color and blemishes are noticeable, thus aiding a puzzled witness's memory.[4]

6. Nonlethal Weapons: A patrol officer, in meeting diverse
criminal situations, has a limited range of weaponry--either
the short range nightstick or the potentially lethal handgun.
If an officer feels that his life is threatened, he may have
to shoot, with the attendant risk that the suspect or innocent
bystander may be killed. If a suitable nonlethal weapon
were made available, it could supplement the officer's
present arsenal and possibly serve as a replacement for the
handgun.

Crime Labs: Establishment of laboratories is needed to
serve the combined needs of police departments in metropolitan areas, and for the expansion of research activities.
Voice prints and photographic developments will expand the
ability to detect and apprehend criminals.

"Every medium and large sized department should employ a skilled lawyer full-time as its legal advisor. Smaller departments should arrange for legal advice on a part-time basis."

"Police departments should commence experimentation with a team policing concept that envisions those with patrol and investigative duties combining under a unified command, with flexible assignments to deal with the crime problems in a defined sector."

"Each metropolitan area and each county should take action directed toward the pooling, or consolidation, of police services through the particular technique that will provide the most satisfactory law enforcement service and protection at the lowest possible cost.[5]

7.   Alert studies of the community's socio-economic factors will present insight into possible future problems necessitating police participation.[6]

8.   Computers are used for record keeping, design of buildings, or design of organizations, control of various functions such as traffic lights at intersections, and simulation of actual events by using formulas. One area in which law enforcement is not presently using computers is the area of simulation. The computer could simulate a burglary situation, or predict where a burglary will happen, or how to handle the burglary.

9.   The police may have to redesign their function. They may have to view themselves not so much as policemen, but as social agents who are helping the population.[7]

10.   Personnel Standards: It is likely that municipal police departments over the years will set higher personnel standards for all ranks from patrolmen through chief. What may be a trend is illustrated by the Berkeley, California Police Department requirement that all entering patrolmen must have completed two years of college education. In many other cities, although the education

requirement is not that high, the examinations and
investigations have been tightened up in an effort to
secure higher caliber personnel. The educational level
of the population as a whole is rising, and it follows that
police department requirements will also rise.[8]

11. Although professional training is now becoming the vogue
     and many police administrators are proud of the number
     of men on the force who have had, or are taking courses,
     another attitude prevails. The highly trained graduate
     with a bachelors degree is not always welcomed. He
     does not fit into the usual practice of starting a recruit
     at the bottom, on the beat, and working up. The
     graduate is ready for a top position when he comes on
     the force. He is usually younger than the men in equiv-
     alent positions and usually lacks any practical experience
     in police work. He is regarded with dislike as well as
     with fear or suspicion.[9]

12. In general, the policeman of the future[10] must be well
     trained, be especially conscious of his public relations
     role, be prepared to specialize, and be sufficiently moti-
     vated, with all that this implies in terms of pay and work-
     ing conditions. At a more important level, policemen
     must be motivated by a desire to take an important and
     respected place in society. In short, there must be
     further advancements toward professionalization of the
     police service.
     Crucial in the future will be the determination of the
     relative importance of police work to other aspects of
     local government. It is clear that urban growth has
     created a new need for expansion of all services, not
     just police, and the undertaking of entirely new services
     with a call on municipal revenues. The priority to be
     given to police needs, among all the demands on municipal
     resources, will be a central issue that must be faced by

departmental and city administrators and the elected
representatives of the public.

13. Central services in identification, in criminal statistics,
and in communications and training are a necessary feature
for enhancing the work of police departments.
While the changes of the next 30 years may not be as
great as they have been in the last 30 years, it is certain
that the future urban crime pattern will be closely tied
to more and denser concentrations of people, and mobility
whether by automobile or air vehicle.[11]

Notes

1. President's Commission on Law Enforcement and Adminis-
tration of Justice. The Challenge of Crime in a Free
Society. Washington, D. C.: U.S. Government Printing
Office, 1967.

2. Leonard, V. A. The Police of the 20th Century, 1964.

3. Hess, Eckhard, H. "Attitude and Pupil Size,"
Scientific American, April 1965, pp. 46-54.

4. Morton, H. R. Chief of Police of Fresno Police Department,
"Modus Operandi in Color," Police Chief, Vol. 31, No. 1,
(January, 1964), pp. 42-44.

5. The Challenge of Crime in a Free Society, pp. 233-295.

6. Frost, Thomas   A Forward Look in Police Education,
Charles C. Thomas, Springfield, Illinois, 1959, pp. 64-65.

7. International City Managers Association, Municipal Police
Administration, Chicago, Ill., Published by ICMA, 1961,
pp. 507-516.

8. Municipal Police Administration, ICMA, 1961.

9. Caven, Ruth Shonle, Criminology (Thomas Y. Crowell, New
York 1962) p. 288.

10. The Challenge of Crime in a Free Society.

11. Smith, Bruce   Police Systems in the United States.
Harper & Brothers, New York, 1940, pp. 327-507.

Appendix A

Law Enforcement Code of Ethics[1]

As a Law Enforcement Officer, my fundamental duty is to serve mankind; to safeguard lives and property; to protect the innocent against deception, the weak against oppression or intimidation, and the peaceful against violence or disorder; and to respect the Constitutional rights of all men to liberty, equality and justice.

I will keep my private life unsullied as an example to all; maintain courageous calm in the face of danger, scorn, or ridicule; develop self-restraint; and be constantly mindful of the welfare of others. Honest in thought and deed in both my personal and official life, I will be exemplary in obeying the laws of the land and the regulations of my department. Whatever I see or hear of a confidential nature or that is confided to me in my official capacity will be kept ever secret unless revelation is necessary in the performance of my duty.

I will never act officiously or permit personal feelings, prejudices, animosities or friendships to influence my decisions. With no compromise for crime and with relentless prosecution of criminals, I will enforce the law courteously and appropriately without fear or favor, malice or ill will, never employing unnecessary force or violence and never accepting gratuities.

I recognize the badge of my office as a symbol of public faith, and I accept it as a public trust to be held so long as I am true to the ethics of the police service. I will constantly strive to achieve these objectives and ideals, dedicating myself before God to my chosen profession . . . law enforcement.

Interpretation and enforcement of this code may prove difficult. Some have suggested a more realistic code less concerned with ideal or utopian concepts. What is needed is a practical document which is enforceable.

[1]Adopted, 1956, The Peace Officers' Association of the State of California

Appendix B

The following is an analysis of two cases with role interaction. The role of each actor can be developed by the
reader in terms of his own perceptions and expectations.
The reader's own feelings or attitudes might further be
refined by asking: "What would I do if I were in that
actor's position?"

Case I

The demotion of Deputy Chief Inspector Goldberg. [1] Two
factors are delineated in this study: (1) the responsibility of a high
ranking police administrator in enforcing gambling laws against
bingo games; and (2) the discretionary problem in enforcing the law
by police.

Background. In 1954 Goldberg was a deputy chief inspector
in the New York Police Department. The police department did
not enforce gambling laws against bingo games conducted by
religious, fraternal and charitable organizations, unless complaints
about this activity were addressed to the police by the public. Even
when a complaint was received the usual procedure was to take no
action. However, the state Penal Code, which is the primary law
for the city and state, indicated that the State Constitution clearly
outlawed such games, and under section 1370 of the Penal Law
anyone who operated a bingo entertainment was guilty of a misdemeanor and subject to two-year imprisonment or a fine of not
more than $1,000 or both.

Action. The following characteristics describe the police
department prior to the action taken by Goldberg:

1. Officers were encouraged to use discretion in enforcing
and interpreting state and municipal laws.

2. Public resentment was being voiced against the police
department's variable enforcement of the law.

3. The police department had been shaken by a grand
jury investigation which uncovered police association with organized

270

Appendices   271

bookmaking which grossed twenty-million dollars a year.

4. Disagreement existed between the Patrolman's Benevolent Association and the appointed commissioner and top sworn
administrative officer over the latter's attempts to set policy to
encourage enforcement of laws and decrease officer discretion.

5. It was informal department policy to take no action
against church bingo games although these games were in violation
of state law.

Goldberg was responsible for the enforcement of moral
and gambling laws. He was in charge of a special 122-man Public
Morals Squad. His immediate superior was Chief Inspector Condon.
Goldberg has been described by persons within and outside the
department as honest and incorruptible.

Goldberg was informed by departmental memorandum of
gambling activity at various churches in the area. He immediately
informed the churches that they must stop bingo activity, and that
if they failed to do so after a reasonable period of time he would
enforce the gambling law. Goldberg informed Condon of his
intentions. Condon advised that he take no enforcement action.

Despite the objections of Condon and the general attitude
of the department, Goldberg enforced the bingo gambling laws.
He was criticized by the department in the newspapers as not
representing the true attitudes of the department. The public
criticized the department for advocating variable standards in enforcing the law. The situation received much publicity, and all
concerned divided on one side or other of the issue. Goldberg
was demoted by the commissioner, reverting back to his civil
service position of captain.

Results. Responding to the publicity and the general
opinion of the news media that "the only fit place to change a law
is in the legislature and not in the police department, " the police
department instituted a major enforcement effort, closing down all
bingo games. Goldberg was restored to his original rank and
continued until his retirement from the department at age 64. An
amendment was passed by the state legislature authorizing legal

jurisdictions to take action in legalizing charity bingo games.

Conclusions and criticism. Table I consists of an array
of elements which can be used as a measuring device in viewing
decisions. General criticism would focus on the variability of law
enforcement standards in the New York community. Informal
department policy advocated the non-enforcement of certain types
of gambling violations. The department's own value system was
used in place of Penal Code law which defined gambling violations.
Goldberg decided not to follow informal procedure and to enforce
gambling laws. Several questions can be asked: Why did Goldberg
decide against informal department policy when he had followed
it for thirty-six years of service? Was there a conflict between
Goldberg's religious values and those of the community? (This
was not brought out in the case study.)

Officers were encouraged to use discretion in enforcing
and interpreting state and municipal laws, and this was felt to
give too much power and opportunity to substitute individual police
values for legialative Penal Code values.

Case II

Moses on the green. [2] Robert Moses was Commissioner
of the Parks Department of the City of New York in 1956. He had
a reputation as an irresistible force, and was often criticized for
his determination to advance projects to better the welfare of the
city according to his own concepts and whatever the opposition.
Moses was dynamic, strong willed, possessed an independent
income, and was a figure of some importance in the city.

Background. Moses proposed, as Commissioner of the
Parks Department, to convert a half-acre of Central Park into
a parking lot for a privately owned restaurant which was authorized
to function on city property. A news item appeared in The New
York Times stating that a parking lot was going to be constructed
adjacent to the restaurant. No public action was taken at this
time.

Action. Three months later when men and equipment were
being moved onto the site to begin surveys, the public began object-

ing conversion of the site into a parking lot. The main objections came from the mothers in the area who used the proposed parking lot as an area to stroll, push their baby carriages, and supervise their children's play. The area was grass covered and spotted with trees. Approximately twenty mothers organized interested prominent residents of the area to participate in the protest, and elected one of the leading figures as the spokesman of the group. Petitions were circulated in protest against the park's conversion to a parking lot. Newspapers were notified and resentment grew. Moses attempted to stop the protest by stating his position to the news media, but opposition grew until thousands of residents in the area were involved. On the day that actual construction was attempted a group of irate neighbors stood on the construction site endangering themselves to the degree that work had to cease. Moses vowed that construction would continue, and the citizen group vowed that it would not. An injunction was filed by the citizen group to halt construction temporarily and a suit was filed against Moses and the city by the citizen group. The matter was brought into the New York Supreme Court while the preliminary injunction prevailed.

Moses was supported by the Mayor, but the city council divided. One councilman crusaded for the citizen group and proposed legislation which would prevent the destruction of natural park beauty.

Results. The Mayor was placed in a position where he had to select one of three alternatives in behalf of Moses: (1) appeal the temporary injunction to a still higher court; (2) agree to a date for a trial on the merits of a permanent injunction; or (3) drop the whole matter, letting the injunction stand. The Mayor decided on the third course of action. Moses made a press statement that the city would take over the paving contract for the site and build a playground for children. Moses' reputation as invincible in pursuing his goals was dented to some degree in reversing his position on the parking lot.

Conclusions and criticism. See Table I for results.

TABLE I

A MEASURING DEVICE IN VIEWING DECISIONS

		Goldberg	Moses
1.	Selection of alternatives based on conscious and subconscious deliberation about the means selected to achieve specific ends.	implied	implied
2.	Means were not separated from ends.	implied	implied
3.	Ends were formally defined in terms of policy statements of organization.	no	yes
4.	Attitude to appease rather than maximize.	no	no
5.	Ignored the interrelatedness of behavior and means-ends.	yes	no
6.	Decision made with relatively simple rules of thumb.	yes	yes
7.	Conformance with the personal interests, values, and benefits of the decision-maker.	yes	yes
8.	Decision meet the value yardstick of superiors.	no	yes
9.	Decision is acceptable to those who are affected as well as those charged with its implementation.	no	no
10.	Possess reasonability in its context.	yes	yes
11.	Contain built-in justification which will furnish an excuse and avenue of retreat.	no	no

Notes

1.   Bock, Edwin A. (Ed.) State and Local Government: A Case Book (University of Alabama Press: The Inter-University Case Program, 1963), pp. 229-62.

2.   Ibid., pp. 25-35.

Appendix C
Sample Organization Charts
Of Some Larger City Police Departments

GOVERNOR

BOARD OF POLICE COMMISSIONERS
- Secretary to the Board
- Office of the Purchasing Member

CHIEF OF POLICE

ASS'T CHIEF OF POLICE

- Admin. Analysis Division
- Budget & Finance Division
- Personnel Division
- Medical Division
- Public Relations Division
- Intelligence Unit
- Police Academy
- Computer Center
- Planning & Research Division

Bureau of Inspections
- Chief Deputy Inspector
  - Inspections Division

Bureau of Field Operations
- North Area Command
  - Districts
    - Fourth
    - Fifth
    - Sixth
    - Seventh
    - Eighth
- South Area Command
  - Districts
    - First
    - Second
    - Third
    - Ninth
- Spec. Oper'ns Command
  - Divisions
    - Tactical
    - Prisoner Processing
    - Juvenile

Bureau of Investigation
- Ass't Chief of detectives
  - Divisions
    - Laboratory
    - Homicide Arson
    - Spec. Serv.
    - Vice, Robbery, burglary

Bureau of Services
- Divisions
  - Communication
  - Motor Serv.
  - Records & Identification
  - Supply
  - Building & Canine Training

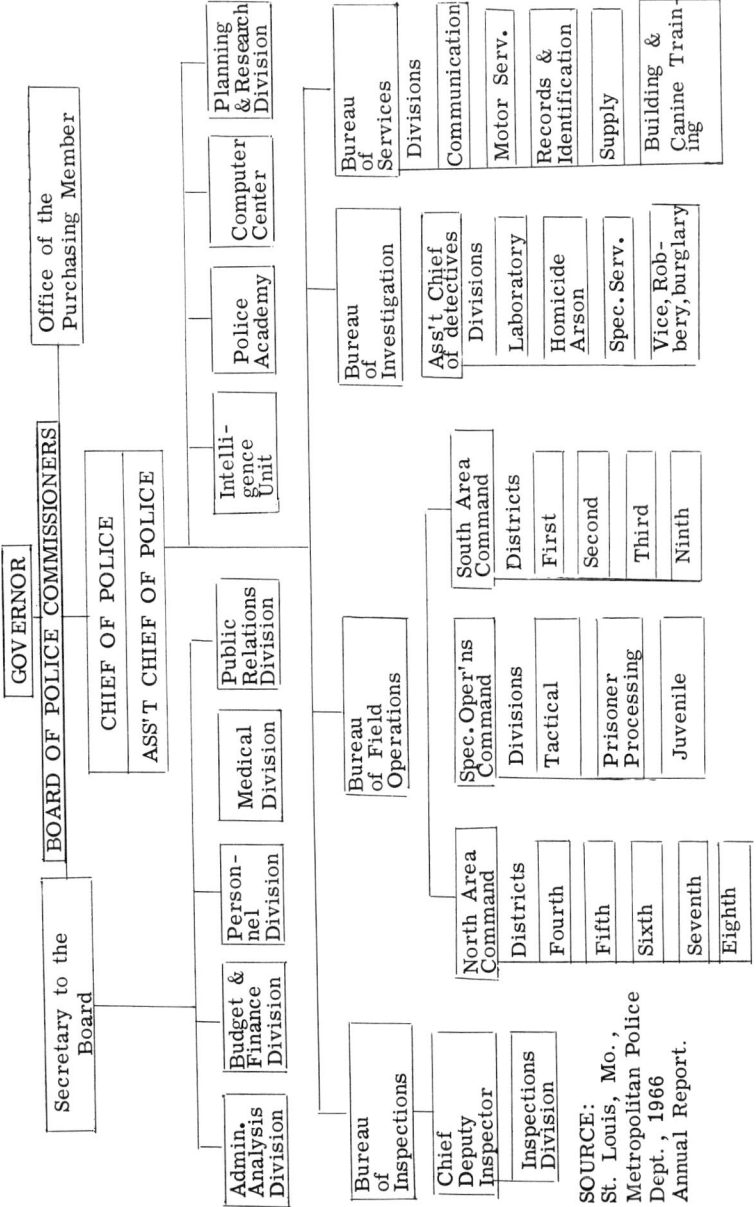

SOURCE:
St. Louis, Mo.,
Metropolitan Police
Dept., 1966
Annual Report.

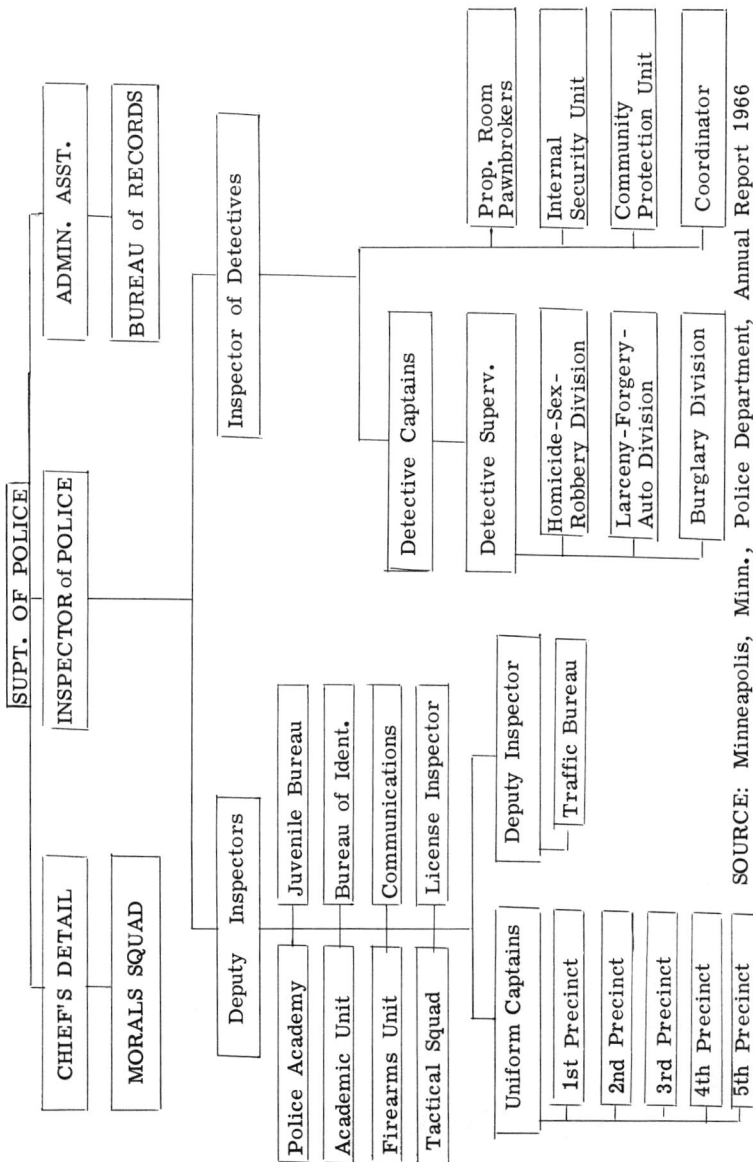

SOURCE: Minneapolis, Minn., Police Department, Annual Report 1966

Board of Police Commissioners

Investigators

Chief of Police

Press Relations Officer

Inspectional Staff

Insp. Administration of Discipline

Personnel & Training Bureau
- Personnel Division
- Training Division

Technical Services Bureau
- Communication Div.
- Records & Ident. Div.
- Motor Trans. Div.
- Supply Div.
- Property Div.
- Valley Serv. Div.

Bureau of Administr'n.
- Coord. of Community Relations
- Admin. Vice Div.
- Business Off. Div.
- Intelig. Div.
- Internal Aff. Div.
- Planning & Research Div.
- Public Info Div.

Patrol Bureau
- Patrol Div. Area 1
- Patrol Div. Area 2
- Patrol Div. Area 3
- Patrol Div. Area 4
- Patrol Div. Area 5

Traffic Bureau
- Accident Inv. Div.
- Parking & Intersect.
- Traffic Enf. Div.
- Traffic Serv. Div.

Bureau of Corrections
- Central Jail Div.

Detective Bureau
- Specialized Divs.
- Geograph. Det. Divs. Area 1
- Geograph. Det. Divs. Area 2

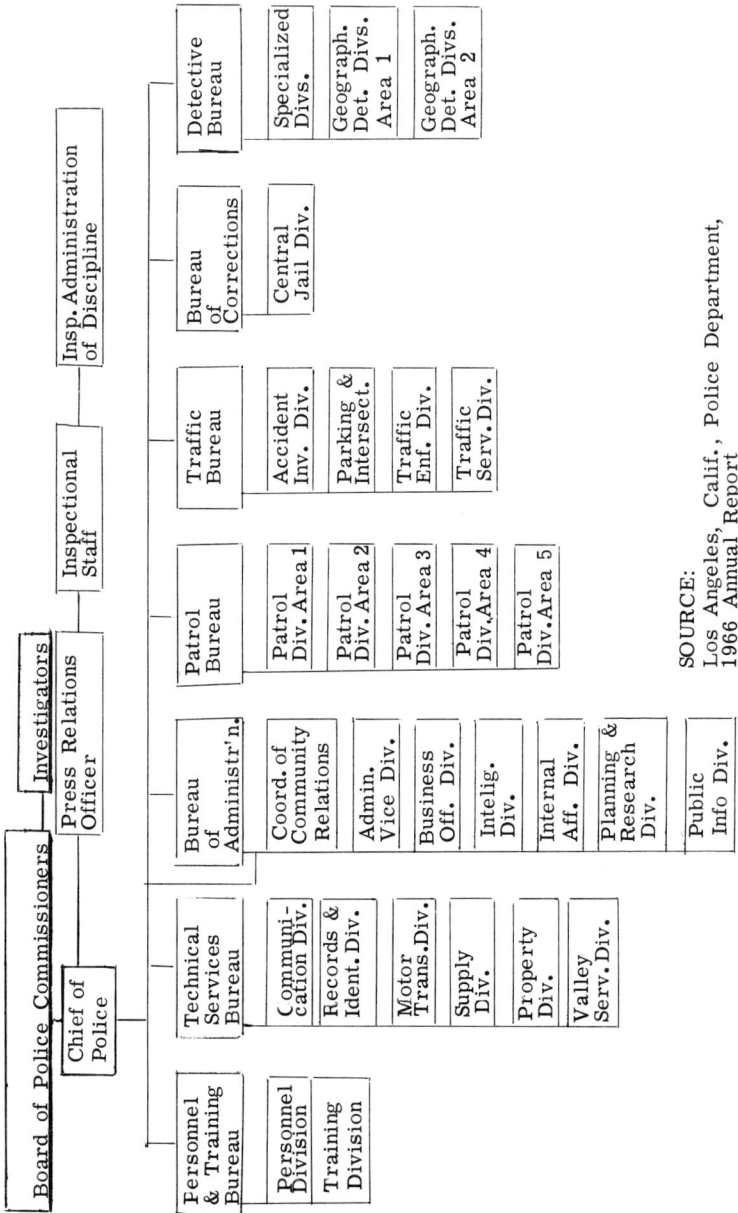

SOURCE:
Los Angeles, Calif., Police Department, 1966 Annual Report

CHIEF

- Medical & Surgical Bureau
- Special Investigation Unit
- Executive Officer
- Chief's Office Staff

Line Functions

- Bureau of Patrol Inspector
  - Evening Commander
  - Night Commander
  - Ports & Harbors Unit
  - Deputy Inspectors
    - 1st Dist.
    - 2nd Dist.
    - 3rd Dist.
    - 4th Dist.
    - 5th Dist.
    - 6th Dist.
- Bureau of Criminal Inv. Commanding Officer
  - General Invest.
  - Scientific Ident. Unit
  - Scientific Laboratory
  - Narcotic Unit
  - Auto Theft
  - Case Prep. Fraud Unit
  - Homicide Unit
  - Tactical Unit
- Bureau of Traffic Commissioner of Traffic Con.
  - Enforcement Unit
  - Flow Reg. Unit
  - Accident Invest.
  - Mounted Unit
  - Traffic Office
  - Two Truck Unit
- Youth Aid Bureau Commanding Officer
  - Juvenile Unit
  - Women's Unit

Staff Functions

- Bureau of Admin. Serv. Commanding Officer
  - Personnel Division
  - Inspection Planning Res. Div.
  - External Aff. Div.
- Bureau of Tech. Services Commanding Officer
  - Detention Division
  - Property & Supply Div.
  - Motor Trans. Div.
  - Communication Div.
  - General Records & Stats. Div.

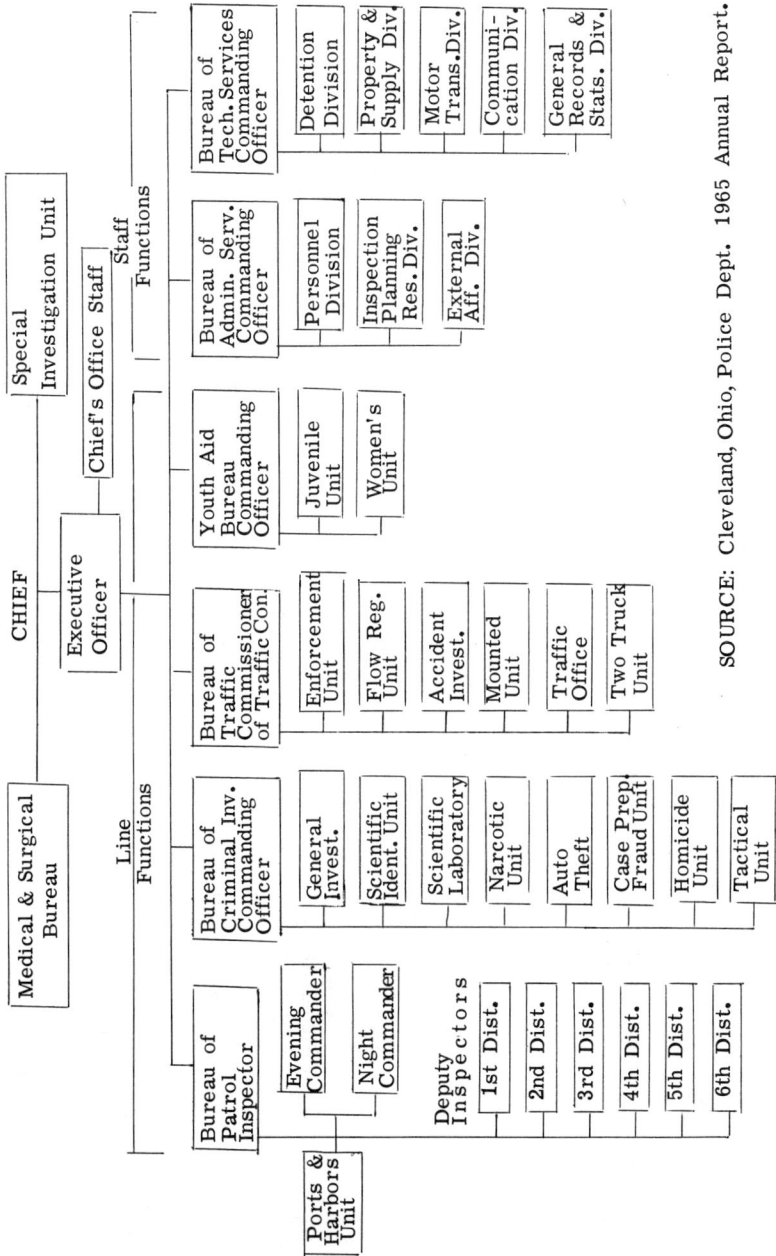

SOURCE: Cleveland, Ohio, Police Dept. 1965 Annual Report.

POLICE COMMISSIONER

INSPECTIONAL SERVICES DIVISION

PLANNING & RESEARCH DIVISION

Administrative Bur.

Operations Bureau

Services Bureau

Community Relations Division

Fiscal Affairs Division

Internal Investigation Division

Personnel Division

Training Division

Patrol Division

Traffic Division

Criminal Investigation Division

Youth Division

Central Records Division

Communications Division

Laboratory Division

Property Division

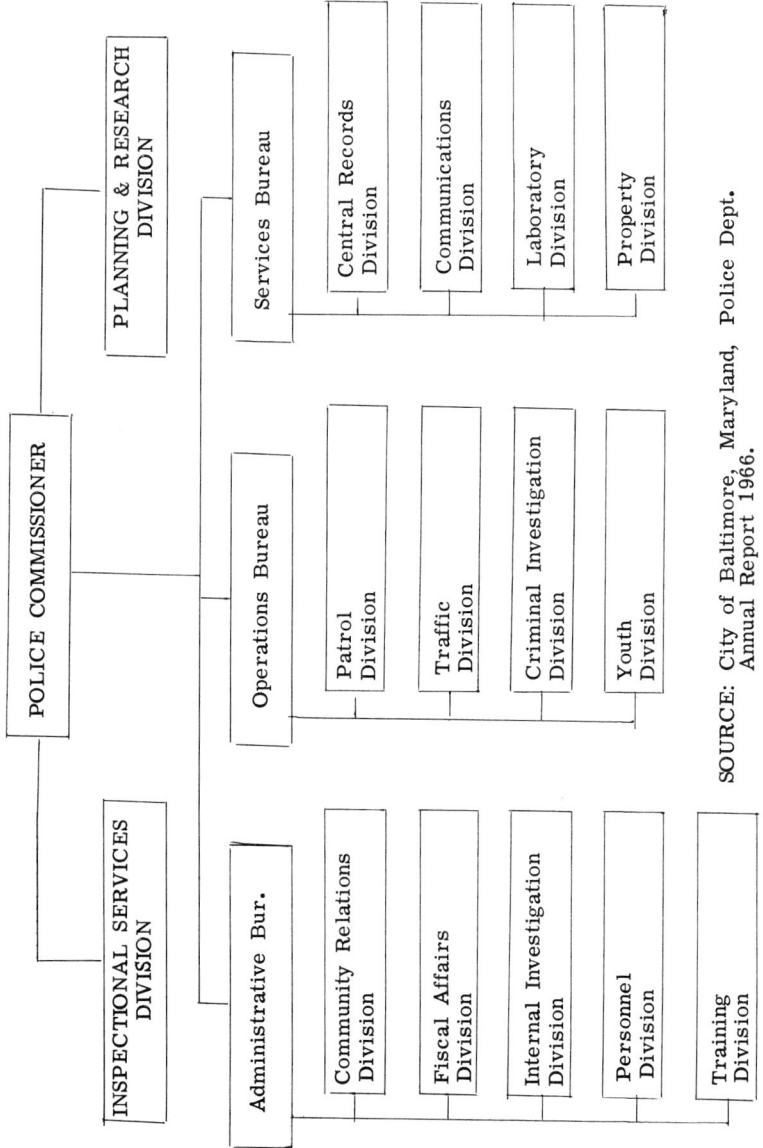

SOURCE: City of Baltimore, Maryland, Police Dept. Annual Report 1966.

MAYOR — Police Commission — Chief of Police

- Commission Secretary
- Community Relations Unit
- Planning & Research Bu.

Under Chief of Police:
- Asst. Deputy Ch. of Police
- Deputy Chief of Police
- Comp. Insp. & Welfare
- Intelligence Unit

Traffic Bureau
- Patrol
- City Prison
- Mounted Unit
- Dog Unit

Patrol Bureau

Administr. Bureau
- General Office
- Correspond.
- Permits & Registr'n.

Personnel Bureau
- Personnel Records
- Investig'ns
- Police Academy
- Police Range
- Underwater Rescue & Recovery Unit
- Chaplains
- Surgeon
- Personnel Sergeant

Criminal Information Bureau
- Bureau of Identif.
- Records & Complaints
- Statistical Section
- Central Warrant Bureau

Juvenile Bureau
- Investigative Details
- Delinquency Prevention
- Juvenile Records
- Dance Hall Inspection
- Bicycle Inspection

Special Services Bureau
- Gambling Detail
- Narcotics Detail
- Prostitution Detail
- Violations of A.B.C.

Inspectors Bureau
- Investigative Details
- Auto
- Burglary
- Fraud
- Gen. Works
- Homicide
- Missing Pers.
- Pawn Shop
- Robbery
- Crime Prev.
- Crime Lab.
- Mobile Crime Lab.
- Bureau of Photography

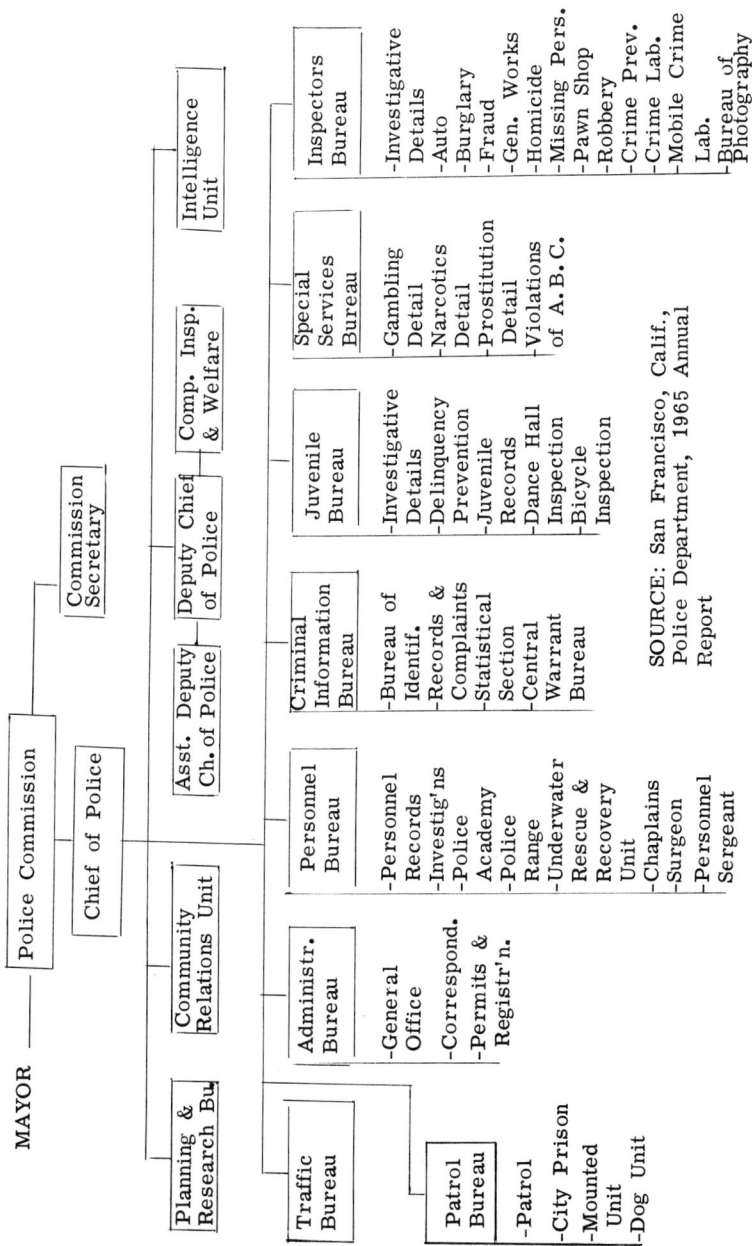

SOURCE: San Francisco, Calif., Police Department, 1965 Annual Report

Appendix D

Planning and Research

Resource material should be available for obtaining data
which is not directly obtainable from the agency records. A listing
of resource materials should include but not be limited to the
following:

1. Law enforcement bibliographies, indicating past
   and current literature in the field of criminal justice.

2. Uniform Crime Reports of the United States.
   Annual reports of statistical data on crime trends,
   rate, location, police employee data, offenses cleared
   and arrests.

3. Publications of the Attorney General of the United
   States.

   a. Annual Report of the Attorney General of the
      United States.

   b. Opinions of the Attorney General.

   c. Annual Report of the Office of Administrative
      Procedure.

4. Publications of the Supreme Court of the United
   States.

   a. Daily Journal.

   b. Slip Opinions.

5. Census Bureau publications. Bulletins issued on
   housing, population, agriculture, business, manufact-
   uring, industries, governments, and specific social
   and economic characteristics of particular geographic
   areas.

6. Readers' Guide to Periodical Literature. This
   subject index to periodicals has been published since
   1905.

7. International Index to Periodicals.

8. Public Affairs Information Service. Lists books, pamphlets, periodical articles, government documents and other library materials in economics and public affairs. Published since 1913.

9. Index to Legal Periodicals. Started in 1907.

10. Cumulative Book Index. Since 1928. A complete bibliography of works in English with exception of government documents, maps, sheet music, and paperbound editions.

11. Facts on File. Weekly news digest with cumulative index.

12. Dictionary of American Politics. A comprehensive book dealing with politics in any form, from political terms to slogans.

13. Statistical Abstract of the United States. Since 1878. A standard summary of statistics on social, political, and economic organizations of the United States.

14. Municipal Year Book. Details on current activities and practices of cities throughout the United States.

15. Dictionary of Sociology.

16. Encyclopedia of Social Science. An analysis of the social sciences with major sections on politics, economics, law, anthropology, sociology, penology, and social work.

17. Sociological Abstract. Contains sections on applied sociology and methodology.

18. Encyclopedia of American Government.

19. American Jurisprudence. Pleadings and practice forms keyed to substantive law in the United States.

20. New York Times Index. Summarizing and classifying of news.

21. Geographically annotated codes, such as West's Annotated Codes of California.

Additional resource data should include textbooks, law books, standard dictionaries, and almanacs. State and municipal publications should also be added as required.

Appendix E

Community Organizations

African Communities League
An educational group which also works in various social
and charitable programs. The group provides money to
Negroes so that they can attend school. The group's
stated doctrine advocates both the uplifting of Negroes
and the brotherhood of all men and God.

African Patriotic League
The main work of this group is in uniting Negro businessmen and the various community political and social leaders. The group's major goal is to unite the Negro community at all social and economic levels for the betterment of all concerned.

Alcoholics Anonymous
A volunteer membership organization offering assistance
to individuals with alcoholic problems who have a sincere
desire to stop drinking. Volunteer workers serve or
sponsor new applicants. Groups are made of people who
had alcoholic problems but have found solutions to their
difficulties and are anxious to help others.

All Nations Boys Club and Community House
This organization provides group work programs for all
ages, including preschool children, boys and girls aged
8 - 18, parents and senior citizens.

All Nations Foundation
The basic goal of this organization is to correct malpractice problems. They work with responsible persons
in positions of authority and with informal leaders in the
community. They try to maintain counselors in the role
of social workers who work with various coordinating
councils. Their various involvements have helped create
relationships between troubled people and social workers
and help them understand their rights and obtain justice and
fulfill their place in society. United Way, Methodist
Church, and donations are the source of funds.

All Peoples Christian Center
Settlement House Program to further Christian Community
Service, interracial understanding and brotherhood. Opportunities for playgrounds, athletic teams, clubs, interest groups for youths (cooking, dancing, crafts), movies,
libraries, winter weekends, and summer camps, day camps,

tutorial program for elementary and junior high students,
day nursery for pre-school children of employed mothers.
No restrictions.

American Civil Liberties Union
A national organization whose membership consists of all
ethnic and economic groups, it is financed by private
contributions with no financial support of any governmental agency. It is concerned with the individual's civil and
legal rights as defined by the Constitution.

American Council To Improve Our Neighborhoods
This group encourages activities in urban renewal and the
breaking up of slums. They work with and through other
national organizations and interested citizens. They
provide staff assistance and consultation on local programs
and problems, and publish views and research findings
on community affairs.

American Friends Service Committee
The major concern of this religiously oriented group is to
promote nationwide brotherhood. The major work of this
group is in trying to prevent violence and civil disobedience
by providing leadership and enlistment programs which
advocate brotherhood and nonviolence in the civil rights
movement. It is sponsored by the Society of Friends
Church (Quaker), and is financed solely by private contributions. "Material aids" program provides clothing,
medical supplies and other needs for overseas relief and
rehabilitation.

American Jewish Committee
The Committee works to combat antisemitism and to solve
community problems.

American Missionary Association
One program of this group is in the educational field.
The group participates in a program to educate young
people in meaningful skills so that they can become
economically solvent.

American Youth Hotels
This organization sponsors inexpensive educational and
recreational outdoor travel opportunities, primarily by
bicycle or on foot along scenic trails and by-ways. It
maintains 99 overnight accommodations in the United
States.

Anti-Defamation League
The main objective of this organization is to develop
recruitment and inservice programs specifically designed

to illustrate minority problems that affect the police.
The organization is also concerned that police departments
be aware of certain social problems and how they affect
law enforcement. Their activity not only focuses on training in law enforcement, but also on recruitment from
minority groups; The deployment of minority group officers
is also a concern of this group. Important in the deployment of minority group officers (as seen by this organization) is the opportunity for rotation within the department. This organization is very involved with courses
as taught by police personnel.

Assistance League of (Community Name)
This organization offers case work service to families
and individuals to enable them to utilize their own capacities and the community's resources to solve their
problems. Activities include family centered counseling,
marital counseling, parent-child relationships, social adjustment of individuals, unmarried parenthood, and
consultation regarding community resources. In addition
to case work service, which includes direct treatment of
children and adolescents, family therapy is available as
part of total agency program. Limited financial assistance is available as part of the treatment plan. This
agency is nonsectarian.

(Name of State) Association For Health And Welfare
A statewide membership organization whose purpose is to
bring together individuals and organizations interested in
improving health and welfare. This organization also
conducts conferences and supplies information to the state
legislature pertaining to health, welfare and recreation.

Association for the Study of Negro Life and History
The primary concern of this group is the needs and goals
of the Negro in America. They are studying and creating
a group tradition for the American Negro which is necessary for improving Negro morale. The Negro is seen
by this group as a unique individual because of his historical and social traditions. The group does not believe
that the Negro has an inferior biological inheritance.

Attendance Service
Services provided in direct alliance with law enforcement
agencies include: (1) Issuance of required work permits;
(2) Liaison between public schools and law enforcement
agencies such as probation department, juvenile court,
and California Youth Authority; (3) Counseling in home
school adjustment; and (4) Aid in enrollees from camps
and institutions.

Big Brothers, Inc.
Seeks to help individual boys who do not have a father or
adequate male influence and who are in need of personal
guidance to make a satisfactory life adjustment. This is
accomplished through the personal interest and companionship of a volunteer man under supervision of trained,
professional caseworkers. Formula of one man--one boy
relationship is based on the concept that all boys need the
friendship, companionship, guidance, and supervision of
a mature responsible male during their formative years.

Big Sister League
A nonsectarian home for young women over 18 years with
social or personality problems. They may be single or
married, pregnant, accompanied by new-born babies, or on
probation or parole. The professional staff works cooperatively with agencies referring clients. Community resources are utilized for employment, educational, medical,
and psychiatric referrals. Group activities and home-
centered educational and recreational programs are offered.

Black Anti-Draft Union
A militant organization to demonstrate against the war in
Vietnam and alleged police brutality. This group feels
that no Negro should be drafted or have to serve his
country because in their opinion Negroes are not afforded
full rights in this country.

Black Muslims
A radical, racist, and religious group. Their great
appeal is to militancy and a "freedom now" attitude on
civil rights. They have the sympathy of many people,
although they number little more than 10,000. They feel
they are blackmen in a whiteman's world. The Muslims
publish the newspaper Muhammed Speaks.

Black Panther Political Party
This organization consists of various people of the black
communities including intellectuals and militant Negroes.
The group describes itself as a political party and is
concerned with the conditions of the black community.
They state their goal is to have politics and politicians of
the black community represent the will of the people of
that community. The group is considered negative towards
police-community relationships.

(Name of Community) Board of Police Commissioners
The civilian board is charged with overall responsibility
for establishing the policies for the police department. It
is responsible for the broad supervision of the department
and for seeing that its policies are followed. In discharging

its duties, the board should have a significant role in the improvement of the department's police-community relations program.

Boy Scouts of America
Their group activities are to promote, through organization and cooperation with other agencies, the ability of boys to do things for themselves and others, to train them in scoutcraft, reliance, and kindred virtues, placing emphasis upon the scout oath and law for character development, citizenship training, and physical fitness.

Boys Club
The Boys Club works with underprivileged and privileged children, and with the Probation Department and the Police Department. They have guidance oriented programs in plastic works, metal works, swimming classes, cooking classes, and gymnastics. The club is open to all boys from the ages of 7 to 18. During the summer months they have travel camps, short camping trips, and day camp for the younger boys.

Catholic Big Brothers, Inc.
A child welfare agency giving counseling and guidance to Catholic boys between the ages of 8 and 18 years and to their parents through professional caseworkers. Boys from fatherless homes are assisted by trained volunteer Catholic men who through individual interest and friendship help assure proper development. When indicated, psychological, medical, and psychiatric examinations are secured.

Catholic Conference For Interracial Justice
The group analyzes current trends in civil rights and publishes papers and booklets on civil rights problems. It also sponsors radio broadcasts and holds an annual convention.

Catholic-Courts Community Development Project
Directed to a specific neighborhood unit in order to lift significantly the level of individual and family social and economic self-sufficiency. The development of neighborhood organization, based on indigenous leadership and focussing on solution of local problems, is the principal goal of the project.

Catholic Welfare Bureau
Provides social services to families, children, and single women. It provides temporary financial assistance, which may be given to persons ineligible for public assistance. Information and referral to social services under public and private auspices are provided.

Centro Hispano
A Latin-American coordinating center for a wide network
of information, using mass media communications. It
assists individuals with problems of employment, immigration, health services, personal counseling, referrals,
vocational guidance, and job development forums. It
encourages local artists and maintains drop-in coffee
houses.

Cleland House of Neighborly Service
With emphasis on community responsibility, this agency
provides opportunities for individual and social adjustment.

Commission on Human Relations
The Commission is a county organization with many branch
offices. It has established a special committee to sum-
marize the problems of community relations and look for
possible solutions to such problems. The commission has
founded lecture groups, work groups, and study groups to
discuss and review ethnic group reactions with the police.

Community Alert Patrol
The object of this group is to act as a buffer between
police and community action and to control aggravated
incidents in the community. The Community Alert Patrol
tries to help with the problems that arise due to various
contacts between the police and the community. It also
tries to ease tensions between various organizations while
trying to protect the community against abusive police
action. The patrol also observes police activities as the
police carry out their duties.

Community Church
Its object is to develop dialogue between the police and
community, and to promote small relations committees
through other organizations. Advisory committees are
maintained in the precincts and in existing groups which
convey community feelings to the police.

Community Coordinating Councils
Local community councils provide a cross section of
community leadership through which interests, needs,
and problems can be identified, classified, and acted on
cooperatively. As autonomous community groups they are
concerned with improving family life, promoting good
citizenship, and meeting the needs of youth and adults
through developing adequate facilities and services.

Community Planning Council
 This cooperative citizen agency plans programs in health, welfare, recreation, and allied fields for better community living. It promotes quality and efficiency of public and private social agencies for preventing and reducing social ills; assesses human needs; develops and mobilizes resources for resolving community problems; promotes integrated services and maintains liaison with local and county-wide civic, economic, social and physical planning agencies and organizations.

Community Relations Conference of (City Name)
 A voluntary coordinating body of agencies and organization having an interest in the betterment of intercultural, interfaith, and interracial relations. The conference serves as a coordinating, clearance, referral, and counseling organization with standing committees on research, education, employment, housing, membership, awards, law enforcement, radio and television, extremist groups, farm labor problems, and immigration.

(Name of County) Community Services Department
 Responsible for assisting the coordination on a county-wide basis of the work of community or public agencies, committees, or councils engaged in activities designed to prevent juvenile and adult delinquency. Recommendations may be made to and received from agencies, councils, community groups or the Board of Supervisors on all matters pertaining to the diminution of delinquency.

Community Volunteer Office
 Any person who is interested in giving time in a volunteer capacity is eligible for service. Services provided are a referral bureau for volunteers who wish to give their time helping in agencies. The bureau fills requests from these agencies, plans projects for clubs and organizations, maintains a community calendar of events, plans and supervises an annual tour of community organizations.

(City Name) Community Welfare and Family Service, Inc.
 This group is concerned with professional family casework for problems in marriage, parent-child relationships, and individual adjustment. Participation in community planning, family life education and specialized social work services to disadvantaged families is stressed.

Community Welfare Council
 A federation of public and private social agencies promoting cooperative planning and coordination in health, welfare and recreation. They provide information regarding social welfare needs.

Congress of Racial Equality (CORE)
> Although CORE'S programs are numerous and diversified, their main objectives are to eliminate racial discrimination by means of investigation, negotiation and occasionally nonviolent direct action. The national CORE program advocates peaceful integration and cooperation among police, the community in general, and the Negro population.

Correctional Guidance Service
> Provides professional correctional counseling, nonsectarian, for legal offenders. Casework and group counseling are provided at a midway center, a residential treatment program conducted in cooperation with State Department of Corrections and concerned primarily with rehabilitation of unemployed parolees who have no family; limited to adult males.

Council of Churches
> The Council promotes churches, individuals and organizations to provide religious education, institute chaplaincy education, and action relating to the community.

Council of Integrated Neighborhoods (COIN)
> This organization is composed of nine "stabilization" groups within the interracial community in Los Angeles County. Membership is open to all neighborhood resident groups which are dedicated to maintaining and developing integrated neighborhoods. While COIN is involved in many community activities, its efforts in the field of police-community relations are limited to programs aimed at reducing and controlling tensions between law enforcement and the community. This is done by attempting to establish clear lines of communications between law enforcement and the community.

Council of Jewish Women
> A Girls Service Bureau provides parent-child counseling services for girls from 6 through 18 years of age and for their families. Girls who need casework help in their personal and interpersonal relationships or in their social adjustments are eligible. Psychiatric consultant available.

Council of Social Agencies
> This organization makes referrals to organizational and governmental bodies for aid.

Council on Mexican-American Affairs
> One of the main activities of this council is to meet with parents and to talk about police-community problems. They attempt to help solve these problems, to give people an opportunity to "let off steam, " and to create a mutual

understanding between Mexican-Americans and law enforcement. This Council meets monthly. The effort to help
solve the police-community problems is only one phase of
a multi-faceted program to help improve the standing of
Mexican-Americans.

Delinquency & Crime Commission
This organization maintains a liaison officer on the Metropolitan Council, who attends meetings of the council. The
commission works on whatever the Board of Supervisors
deems necessary, but on occasion the commission has been
involved in projects to create better understanding between
the police and the community.

Department of Industrial Relations
Anyone who feels he has been discriminated against in
employment or housing due to religion, race, national
ancestry, or national origin is eligible for service.
Services provided include investigation of complaints.
Commissioner determines adjustment where indicated.

(Name of County) District Attorney
The District Attorney's office has a special unit which is
charged with investigating alleged misconduct of police
officers. Citizens who feel that they have been subjected
to police brutality can lodge complaints with this section
of the District Attorney's Office and be assured that the
matter will be thoroughly investigated.

Economic Development Agency
To create new permanent job opportunities for residents of
area; guide community groups in starting community
facilities projects; assist local businessmen through a Small
Business Committee which will advise and refer them to
proper agencies for training and financial aid; guide community groups in starting training and adult education
programs; organize community to work with immigrants
to help their entry into urban life.

Economic and Youth Opportunities Agency
Administers many projects which better police-community
relations: Teen Post, Youth Training Employment Project,
Escape String, and the Newcomers Center.

(Name of City) Economic Development Agency
The agency's goals are to create new permanent job
opportunities for residents of the area; guide community
groups in starting community facilities projects; help guide
community groups in starting training and adult education
programs; organize community to work with immigrants
to help their entry into the labor force and to adjust to the
environment of urban life.

Economic Negro Union
>This organization helps Negroes get jobs. It works at
times with the police to further job placement.

Economic Opportunity Act Implementation
>This organization participates in the implementation of the
Economic Opportunity Act objectives. The organization
assigns special community relations agents to various
poverty areas.

Episcopal Church Home for Children
>Residential care, in a cottage type facility, for boys and
girls showing moderate social or emotional disturbances.
Children must be able to attend public school and to live
in an open environment. Children are accepted from
public and private agencies and directly from parents.
The program also includes recreational supervision, casework service and treatment, and psychiatric consultation.

Exchange Club
>A service club to promote American citizenship, athletics,
boys clubs, and crime prevention. In order to accomplish
the goals of the organization, there must be some sort
of consultation with the police in areas of crime and
delinquency. By working closer with the department, these
people get a first rate human relations view of the department.

Fair Employment Practice Commission
>This state agency was formed in 1959 to promote the right
and opportunity to obtain and hold employment without
discrimination because of race, religious creed, color,
national origin, or ancestry. This organization has the
authority to see that injustices in the field of employment
practices are corrected by means of legal action. This
agency also helps to inform young people of local manpower
needs, and how to qualify for a position.

Family Service Department
>Provides casework services to families and individuals
including financial assistance on a constructive basis. Also,
services to men and women in jails and in correctional
institutions and their families. It acts as parole sponsor
and advisor. It also provides missing persons service,
Christmas planning for families and individuals, and emergency housing for women and their children.

Federation of Community Coordinating Councils
>This organization has no specific law enforcement projects,
but due to its work with youth welfare and in crime prevention, it must have programs concerned with community and

police relations. Policemen are members of many area councils. The main objective of this organization is to aid in the solving of various community problems. There is a staff to work specifically with youth, and they try to set up meetings with the police to effect better understanding.

Five Acres

Residential group placement with a treatment purpose, nonsectarian, interracial, for boys and girls 7 through 11. Eligibility according to staff evaluation of use of services by children and parents. Children are not eligible when their physical, intellectual, or emotional problems cannot be helped by group living experience in an open setting. Cottage groups consist of eight children or less. Social casework services are offered children and parents or other relatives on individual basis. Children are selected by agency psychiatrist.

Freedom Now Party

This organization is political in nature and advocates racial separation and self-help for Negroes. Total support of black power and separation from white society are seen as the salvation of the black man. The major work of this group is in convincing poor Negroes to shop only at businesses owned by Negroes.

Goodwill Industries

Offers temporary employment; employment of the physically handicapped who cannot work in industry; training of handicapped; and employment of those handicapped by reason of age.

Hard of Hearing Society

The Society offers social rehabilitation and aid to hard of hearing children, through scholarship funds, sending hard of hearing children to camp, and providing hearing aids to deserving persons.

Head Start

Head Start is a pre-school program providing funding to delegate agencies for units sponsoring Head Start sites for children entering kindergarten within the next year and who reside in disadvantaged areas. Major goals: to develop children's self image, provide success experiences, increase verbal and conceptual skills, and involve parents and children in a positive learning experience.

(Name of County) Health Department
> Basic public health service to control preventable disease
> is offered to anyone who lives in the county Health Depart-
> ment area without regard to race, religion, financial
> status, or legal residence in the County.
> Services include: Alcoholic Rehabilitation Clinic, Cardiac
> Diagnostic Clinic, Child Development Clinic, Control of
> Communicable Disease, Chronic Disease Control, Dental
> Care, Family Planning, Health Officers' Clinics, Im-
> munization Service, Maternal and Child Health, Mental
> Health, Nutrition Service, Occupational Health, Public
> Health Disaster Service, Public Health Education, Public
> Health Nursing Service, Public Health Social Work, Radio-
> logical Health, School Health, Tuberculosis, Venereal
> Disease, Vital Records.

Home
> Homelike residence for working girls between 18 and 24
> who need casework counseling for personal reasons, social
> adjustments or job placement and who would benefit
> emotionally through group living.

Home For Children
> Cottage type residential home for boys and girls aged 6
> to 12, with serious emotional disturbance and behavior
> problems. Children attend public school; small classroom
> on grounds for a few with severe school adjustment
> problem. Treatment service for children and families
> by staff psychiatrist, psychologist, caseworkers and group
> workers. Recreation and craft program. Interracial and
> nonsectarian.

Human Relations Bureau
> The Bureau was established to assist in assuring all
> citizens the opportunity for full and equal participation in
> the affairs of the community and to promote public health,
> welfare and security.

Human Relations Commission (City Name)
> The Commission has a subcommittee especially interested
> in Police Community Relations. They are involved in
> attending police community relations meetings and listening
> to complaints of police brutality, developing training
> programs which will prepare officers to deal with conflict
> situations in constructive ways, and bettering relations
> between minority groups and the police department. The
> commission also forms junior police clubs as an aid to
> better community relations.

Indian Center Inc.
        The Service Center for American Indians assists in the
        adjustment to urban living and in job placement, housing,
        medical care, legal aid, etc. The service center inter-
        prets to other agencies the unusual or unique problems
        faced by the American Indians from the government
        reservations. The service plans group activities for the
        Indians and sets forth unbiased information on Indian
        affairs.

Indian Welcome Center
        This agency welcomes Indians of all faiths coming into
        the area and provides information and guidance.

International Institute
        Promotes the social integration of persons foreign in birth
        or parentage. Individual services include family case-
        work, technical services, problems in citizenship, and
        cooperation with other agencies where problems of language
        and culture are involved.

Japanese-American Citizens League
        In 1930, this association was begun for the welfare of
        citizens of Japanese birth.

Jewish Community Relations Committee
        The Committee of JCRC has a Social Action Council that
        discusses police-community relations. The JCRC has
        sponsored yearly conferences, both citywide and regional,
        on community relations, and has made speakers available
        on a multitude of subjects including police community
        relations. The committee has also provided in-service
        training on community relations for teachers in the public
        schools, and has provided speakers to police training
        programs.

Lawyer Reference Service
        It refers the poor to members of the Bar Association who
        are willing to serve them for a fee within their means.
        Those who are destitute and have a worthy cause are also
        assisted by the Lawyer Reference Service.

League Of Women Voters
        They maintain workshops concerned with problems that
        the police are involved with. They try to look at the
        department, not at the solution. If a solution comes
        forth, they try to get it from other groups involved.

Malpractice Boards
        The object of these boards is to take complaints against
        the police departments and certain officers, to evaluate the

evidence, and if necessary to present the complaint to
the board of police commissioners.

The Messengers
This group, although unofficial in civil rights action groups,
is interested in building race pride through enlightening
Negroes about their historical background in Africa.

Mexican-American Community Development (MACD)
The organization exists for Mexican-American and Spanish-
speaking people. Services include casework and referral
services. Community workers in outlying areas will
perform individual services to members of their community,
and will seek out problems and concerns of the people.

Mexican-American Opportunity Foundation
This group functions to give deserving Mexican-Americans
opportunities they may not otherwise receive. They
primarily work in the field of employment. This foundation develops on-the-job training for unskilled people.

Mexican-American Political Association
An organization for the political, social, educational, and
economic betterment of Mexican-Americans and all other
Spanish-speaking Americans through political action.

Midnight Mission
Temporary, institutional care for unattached and transient
men. Food, lodging, laundry, and employment.

National Association for the Advancement of Colored People
The National Association for the Advancement of Colored
People was founded in 1910. This group uses the court
as a means to achieve, through legal stress or lawsuits,
its goals. Goals include: 1. abolition of forced segregation; 2. equal opportunities in education, employment,
public accommodation; 3. voting rights, housing; 4. equal
rights under the Constitution. This is the most effective
civil rights group.

National Conference of Christians and Jews
The NCCJ provides consultant assistance for the police-
community relations program with two major projects
currently in the planning stage. They also provide major
police-community relations institutes focusing on the
responsibilities of citizens to work with police to reduce
tensions.

National Safety Council of (City Name)
     Program: Serves business, industry, and legal agencies
     in accident prevention efforts, with emphasis on traffic
     safety, industrial safety, home and off-the-job safety.
     It cooperates with all responsible community organizations
     in development of accident prevention programs and supplies
     films and distributes all safety materials published by the
     National Safety Council.

Neighborhood Adult Participation Program (NAPP)
     The main objective of the organization is the supervision
     of adults aged 21 and over, residing in poverty areas, in
     sub-professional positions with public and nonprofit agencies
     and schools in their community. Aides work for 16 months
     at $4,000 annually, gaining work experience and job skills
     and initiating new career positions within existing agencies.
     NAPP aides help bring agency to which they are assigned
     into closer communication with people being served.   Fee:
     none. Funds: federal.

Neighborhood Council
     An agency for two-way communication between citizens and
     government. It makes known to city and county agencies
     what community needs and concerns may be, and encourages
     these services to meet these needs.

Neighborhood Legal Service Centers
     In addition to keeping the office open evenings and week-
     ends, emergency 24-hour services are offered to civil
     and criminal cases not handled by the Public Defender.

Neighborhood Legal Services Society
     The Society provides legal help for persons in conflict
     with law enforcement officials, provides a speakers bureau
     to public schools on subjects including police-community
     relations, and keeps in close contact with the police.

Neighborhood Youth Association
     Provides a social group work service, through small
     groups, for youth aged 9 to 15 years who have difficulty
     in adjusting to school, home and community. Groups
     discuss problems and, with group worker, plan activities
     geared to meet their particular needs. Groups are referred
     from school personnel, juvenile officers and their social
     agencies.

Neighborhood Youth Corps
     Eligible youths between the ages of sixteen and twenty-two
     who are out of school, unemployed, or from low income
     families are employed on a part-time basis by nonprofit
     agencies or departments of the government via the State

Employment Service. Vocational counseling, job supervision and advisement are given by the employment service.
Youth Corps are supported by the United States Government anti-poverty funds.

Neumeyer Foundation
The development and support of experimental programs
related to social programs is a responsibility of this
foundation. This program aids understanding and curbing
of problems which might arise in the community.

Operation Bootstrap
A private, nonprofit, job-training center. Courses taught
include some phases of police work.

Operation Escape
A two-phase program designed to help predelinquent gang-
youths redirect their behavior and attitudes in more
socially acceptable ways.

Opportunities Industrialization Center
The organization provides training classes for men and
women and assists in preparation for law enforcement
tests.

Organization For Community Action
The main objective is to respond to the needs of the
community through coordinating various neighborhood
improvement groups and working with the school board
and the police department.

Parent Teacher Association
PTA involves parents and teachers working together to
help the school and its students. It helps the police
by encouraging their human relations programs in association with school activities and in-school programs. Their
interest is generated because of their desire for the safety
of their children.

Police Malpractice Center
This organization is a branch of the American Civil
Liberties Union, to assist citizens in making complaints
against, and seeking action to correct police wrongs.

Police Malpractice Complaint Center
The Center assists people in filing valid complaints against
the police department concerning police malpractices.

Project Action
> Project Action assists in prevocational and vocational training, job counseling, and job placement for youth 14 years and up. Preference is given to probationers and parolees. Counseling on legal problems is provided. Fees: none. Funds: contributions, fees from Vocational Rehabilitation Service for VRS trainees.

Project Tutor
> This program takes care of children with problems in basic subjects such as reading and math. This project tries to help these children do better in school by assigning them a tutor to work with individually twice a week. Each tutoring session is supposed to last an hour, during which tutor and tutee may talk and play, as well as study together. A sound relationship between tutor and tutee is all that many students need to catch up with their class and realize their potential.

Public Defender
> Legal representation in the Municipal Court is given to persons charged with misdemeanor offenses who are unable to afford the services of a private attorney. Legal advice regarding civil matters is given.

Salvation Army
> A federation of services provide field service, religious and recreational activities of youth and adult groups; material relief, rehabilitation and casework services to families and individuals; services to men and women incarcerated in detention and correctional institutions.

Self-Leadership For All Nationalities Today (SLANT)
> A police-community relations program is only a small segment of this organization's total activity program. SLANT has set up several "talk" programs in order to encourage a better dialogue between the police department and the community.

Special Service For Groups Inc.
> Serves youth who are delinquent or in immediate danger of becoming delinquent, and their families. The youth come to SSG's attention through referrals by the California Youth Authority which gives notification of boys released from CYA institutions, and by juvenile officers.

State Industrial Relations Department: Fair Employment Practices Division
> This division of the industrial relations department administers, enforces, and generally promotes the purposes of the State Fair Employment Practices Act and the Rumford

Fair Housing Act. It seeks to eliminate discrimination
in employment or housing opportunity against any person
because of race, color, religion, national origin or
ancestry. Unlawful employment practices include discrimination in hiring, promotions, discharge, or pay,
in treatment of job seekers by employment agencies, and
in admission to membership of unions.

Suicide Prevention Center
Persons with problems involving suicide are helped with
management of the crisis, treatment planning, and then
referred to appropriate agencies. Consultation with
agencies and professional personnel is invited. Agency
emphasis is on training, research, and community suicide
prevention techniques.

Teen Post Program
Located in areas which are designated as poverty areas,
or in areas where there is a high possibility of social
tension, this federal program is integrally involved in
numerous programs. While the primary responsibility
centers around job information, educational programs
(guest speakers), and recreational activities, the Teen
Post program is also an attempt to improve the relations
between the Teen Post youngsters (so-called hard to
reach youngsters) and the police. This improved relationship is accomplished through casual drop-ins by uniformed
law enforcement officers, guest speakers from law enforcement, and more formalized programs.

Temporary Alliance Of Local Organizations
The TALO is an all-Negro group which aims at promoting
harmony between police and the Negro community. Police
are invited to many of the functions involving community
relations. Meetings can be held whenever the need arises
to gain the total community's support and interest. Some
printed material in pamphlet form is available concerning
public relations.

Travelers Aid Society (Name of City)
Offers casework services to individuals and families who
need help with problems resulting from or related to
movement whether for social, economic, or psychological
reasons. This would include travelers, newcomers who
have not yet established roots in the community, people
temporarily in the community, and local residents in
difficulty elsewhere. It gives individualized information
and direction services to the traveling public and strangers
in locating friends and relatives, and suggestions regarding
housing and community resources.

United States Bureau of Family Services
        Works in all areas of the United States to improve the
        condition of poor people and their children.

United States Commission on Civil Rights
        The federal program is now working to achieve racial
        balance in schools throughout the country.

United States Government, Interior Department, Indian Affairs
Bureau
        Provides assistance to enrolled American Indians who
        voluntarily leave Indian Reservation areas to establish
        homes and full-time employment elsewhere. Service
        includes administration of vocational training program
        under provision of Public Laws, employment referral
        service, community orientation.

Urban League
        The Urban League, formed more than forty-four years
        ago, was responsible for many breakthroughs where laws
        did not exist. This organization is supported by United
        Way, corporate contributions, and contributions from
        private citizens. Its primary efforts are directed toward
        encouraging industry to hire Negroes. It is also vitally
        concerned with the social welfare of the minority com-
        munity, with job development and employment, education
        and youth incentives, fair housing, and public welfare.

Variety International Boys Club
        This is a nonsectarian, educational and guidance agency
        with a recreational program for the social, educational
        and character development of boys between the ages 7
        and 19. Building facility is complete with library, games
        room, gym, locker room, arts and crafts department,
        photography laboratory, club room, and speakers forum.

Welfare Association
        Assistance may be obtained through special arrangement
        with the Juvenile Division of Police Department. Twenty-
        four hour emergency welfare assistance is provided to
        local families and transients, not provided for by other
        public or private agencies.

Young Men's Christian Association
        Community service enterprises and recreational centers
        are conducted in cooperation with other groups and
        individuals in order to render such services to the com-
        munity as well as to secure better economic, social, and
        moral conditions of youth and adults.

Young Women's Christian Association
>Individual and group activities to meet religious, social,
and educational, vocational and recreational needs of girls
and young women.

Youth Opportunities Board
>A "joint powers" agency which provides coordination,
program development assistance, and monitoring functions
in an attempt to find solutions to community-wide problems
such as juvenile delinquency, unemployment and school
dropouts. Its work includes anti-poverty programs and
problems.

Youth Opportunity Center
>Intensive vocational counseling and placement services for
youth 16 through 21, including individual and group counseling; referral to Job Corps; and Neighborhood Youth Corps;
referral to all types of retraining; training in job findings;
motivational services and referral to other agencies.   The
ultimate goal is job placement at the youth's highest
potential.

Appendix F

A statement of the purpose and a description of the
Los Angeles Police Department Community Relations Program of
1968.

Purpose of the Community Relations Program

Safe streets, a secure home, a personal sense of security,
are everyone's business. They are not only shared goals
but a joint responsibility. The creation of a professional
police service does not divest the individual citizen of a
personal responsibility for his own orderly behavior and
a general responsibility for an orderly community.

The achievement of "social order" by both legal process
and by well ordered personal conduct can only exist if
there is a partnership between citizens of the community
and the police. The purpose of a police community
relations program is to establish such a partnership.

Ingredients Of A Police Community Relations Program

The essence of a community relations program is to
establish an effective working relationship between the
members of the community and their police. Consequently,
the program must consist of those activities which make
for:

a) A clearer understanding of the function of "public order"
   in our society and the role of the community and the
   police in establishing and maintaining it.

b) An atmosphere which encourages a partnership between
   the community and the police in establishing and
   maintaining "public order."

c) A cooperative effort to identify areas of common interest, barriers to communication and understanding,
   sources of tension, hostility, and conflict.

d) Opportunities to mutually develop plans and to work
   together in their implementation.

e) Communication of those things necessary to an
   understanding of the others' point of view.

f) Development of mutual trust and respect.

g) A cooperative effort to develop solutions to problems.

Responsibilities of the Director of Community Relations

> The stimulation, development, coordination, and functional supervision of the Department's Community Relations Program.
>
> The implementation of community relations policies, objectives, and programs as directed by the Chief of Police.
>
> Liaison at the appropriate level with other agencies, and community-wide organizations, both governmental and community.
>
> Development and coordination of "model" community relations program, Department community relations training activities such as conferences, seminars, community-wide workshops.
>
> Provide staff assistance to other Bureaus in community relations matters.

Los Angeles Police Department Community Relations Program

> The Los Angeles Police Department Community Relations Program as now constituted provides methods for improvement of police-community relations in the following areas:
>
> Youth
>
> Schools (Students and Administrators)
>
> Colleges and Universities
>
> Minority Communities
>
> Militant and Revolutionist Groups
>
> Disadvantaged Communities
>
> Affluent Communities
>
> Religious Groups
>
> News, Motion Picture, Radio, and Television Media
>
> Police Department

The following report is an organizational breakdown of
the Community Relations structure showing the programs
and activities conducted by each segment.

Communication With General Community

Although the initial efforts of the Community Relations
Program were directed toward the most troubled areas
of the City, the current program includes a broad spec-
trum of activities and programs for the entire community.
Those listed below are embraced in our concept of "Total
Community Involvement."

1) The Crime Prevention Program began with a very
   successful "Lock Your Car" campaign designed to
   deter opportunists who might become automobile
   thieves or car burglars. The next campaign will deal
   with residential and business burglaries, encouraging
   increased security and cooperation with police in
   preventing those crimes.

   The Department is participating in the "Mayor's
   Consumer Protection Committee for Senior Citizens,"
   an effort to protect elderly persons from frauds and
   bunco schemes.

   The Crime Prevention Program promises to be one
   of the most effective relationships between the police
   and the community.

   The Radio Watch Program begins in February, 1968.
   Firms have been organized to use company mobile
   two-way radios as additional eyes and ears for the
   police. These several hundred radio operators should
   prove very effective in reporting crime and disasters
   to the police. The material for this program is
   supplied as a public service by the originator, Motorola
   Corp. The Department will instruct the participating
   firms' dispatchers in our reporting procedures and
   policies. These men will, in turn, train the individual
   drivers. Periodic visits to these firms by Department
   personnel, hopefully, will ensure active participation
   and identify any problem area. An appropriate awards
   program will honor noteworthy acts of assistance.

2) Several Ministerial Associations meet with Community
   Relations personnel and occasionally with the Chief of
   Police personally, to gain insight into crime, juvenile
   delinquency, and community unrest in order to dis-
   seminate accurate information to their congregations.
   The ministers also reflect community attitudes to the

Police Department. Relationships are now being
formalized to establish continuing communication.
Ministerial advisory groups exist at divisional level.

3) Neighborhood Police Forum is a program whose
purpose is to bring together street people and radio
car policemen in a gathering within the concerned
community.

4) The Speakers Unit evaluates, processes and channels
official speech requests emanating from various segments of the community. Speech outlines, research
files, and visual aids are maintained for the utilization
of Department speakers.

Each patrol division maintains a "Speakers Club"
comprised of select personnel qualified to represent
the Department on speaking assignments. Speech
requests on all police subjects are handled by
personnel of the division involved, providing an opportunity for members of the community to identify
with police personnel assigned to their area. Specialists in certain subject areas are provided on request.

5) Eighteen Educational Brochures are now being
distributed dealing with matters of police-community
concern. Three more are being developed. These
brochures are in great demand and reach all segments
of the community.

6) The Chief's Monthly Breakfast, hosted by the Chief of
Police, allows him to converse with selected groups
regarding matters of mutual interest. Selected
programs are offered for those members who make
requests, i.e. tours, meetings, demonstrations, etc.

7) Numerous Police Community Workshops are conducted
as the need or opportunity becomes evident. Among
the most significant is the Community Workshop
sponsored by the University of California at Los
Angeles and funded by the Ford Foundation, which
placed policemen, social workers, educators, businessmen, residents, and militants in an atmosphere of
intimate discussion of mutual problems. Each of the
eight groups met twice at U.C.L.A. and six times
in homes or public buildings within the geographic
area served by the participants in their daily lives.
There are plans to continue this extremely productive
activity.

Many police-community workshops throughout the city
involved participants from various levels of government and society, including those mentioned under
"Schools." Some have been limited to geographic
areas, age groups, or organizations. Others were
"open" meetings and attracted militants and radicals
along with members of the affluent community and
those within the poverty areas. Without exception,
there was benefit realized by the police participants.

8) Annual Open House Of Police Facilities is conducted
   monthly in conjunction with the Junior Chamber of
   Commerce.

9) Personal Appearances by the Chief of Police and his
   staff to all segments of the community, as well as
   radio, television, and various organizations, create
   better understanding of the role of law enforcement
   and the policies and practices of the Police Department. This practice has resulted in innumerable
   favorable reactions from the community who now understand that their top police officials are available to
   them.

10) Citizen Citations are presented by the Police Com-
    mission for meritorious acts brought to the attention
    of Public Affairs Division, in the form of "a letter
    of appreciation from the Chief of Police" or "A
    Police Commission Citation." The formal presentation
    includes full news coverage.

11) The Senior Band's schedule includes junior and senior
    high school appearances, large parades, civic events,
    Academy graduations and Department functions. The
    Band coordinator is the only full-time assigned officer.
    The other members when not performing are deployed
    in their divisions of assignment.

12) Comprehensive Tours are conducted, which aid in
    developing an understanding of our Department for
    visiting police personnel and dignitaries, community
    groups, individuals and other important persons.

When requested, Public Affairs Division coordinates
the activities of visiting government officials, police
personnel and other V.I.P.'s. Appointments for
desired interviews, visits to recreational facilities,
arrangements for hotel or motel accommodations and
transportation are among the services rendered.

13) The Annual Report is published to inform the public
    of the Department's problems and progress. The
    1967 Report will be a true public relations tool,
    rather than a statistical review as it has been in the
    past.

14) Special Requests for information are answered by
    Public Affairs Division. Numerous written requests
    for information are answered in detail. The volume
    has increased to the point where use of automatic
    aids is needed in some instances, but no request goes
    unanswered.

    Interviews are conducted for those who appear person-
    ally seeking information. Files of reference material
    are maintained, supplemented by information provided
    by Department experts in various fields.

15) Community Advisory Councils exist in approximately
    half of the geographical divisions and are being
    established in the others. They are composed of
    community leaders who work with the divisional Com-
    munity Relations Officer in the development of
    programs and the two-way transmittal of information
    between the police and the public. The Councils are
    particularly valuable during times of community un-
    rest when immediate dissemination of accurate infor-
    mation by way of the Councils tends to counteract the
    forces of agitation. This is one of our broadest and
    most effective involvements with the entire city com-
    munity. Among many activities performed by these
    Councils are workshops, dinners, anti-crime campaigns,
    motorcades and parades in support of law enforcement.

Youth

The Youth Programs afford opportunities for police officers
and young people to engage in non-punitive relationships
while working and competing in sports, and numerous other
positive educational character building activities.

1) The Law Enforcement Explorer Program is intended to
   interest young men in a career in law enforcement and
   develop an awareness of civic responsibility. The
   motto is "Learning to protect and to serve." Members
   are selected through a process similar to that
   employed in the selection of regular police officers.
   Training in basic law enforcement procedures, too,
   prepares them for participation in various police-
   related activities. Although chartered by the Boy
   Scouts of America, the program is law enforcement
   oriented and emphasizes good citizenship and character

development. After completion of training at the Los
Angeles Police Academy, explorers participate in the
following activities:

>   Advanced training
>   Inter-post sports
>   Parade duty
>   Divisional service projects
>   Bicycle licensing
>   Department displays at public functions
>   Boy Scout events
>   Tours of local law enforcement agencies
>   Extended trips to law enforcement agencies
>   throughout the nation
>   Overnight trips
>   Annual ten day outings

2) The Los Angeles Police Department Junior Band gives
boys, 12 to 20 years old, who are musically inclined
a meaningful, character-building experience in a quality
marching and concert band. They are taught concert
and marching music, and marching techniques, and
participate in community and state-wide festivities,
concerts, parades, and State and National Junior
Band Contests. The band also travels to other states
for various festivities.

3) Summer Camping consists of four one-week sessions,
Monday through Friday, including swimming, archery,
canoeing and fishing. Instruction in handicrafts
includes woodwork, leatherwork, and wood burning.
Additionally, campfire activities, singing and skits,
movie nights, horseback riding, nature hiking and night
pistol team demonstrations are provided. Athletics
include volleyball, horseshoes, basketball and track
meets. Discussions of problems which involve youth
and the community are part of "talk sessions."

4) The Athletic Unit establishes and coordinates athletic
leagues and events through the Youth Services Officers
of the sixteen geographical patrol divisions. A govern-
ment-funded youth employment project is coordinated
by the athletic unit and administered on the divisional
level. Police officers and youth aides form teams
which are entered in local recreation leagues with
tournaments scheduled between different police-
sponsored teams. A league is also established between
the law enforcement explorer posts in the current
sport. Athletic events are often held at the Police
Academy to facilitate the youths' identification with
the Police Department. The athletic unit coordinates

and supervises the athletic program in the various
Police summer camps.

5) The Special Events Unit coordinates city-wide activities
    for youth, the geographical patrol division assisting
    them in carrying out their youth programs. Tickets
    for the following events are obtained by the special
    events coordinator and made available to the Divisional
    Youth Services Officer: Professional and college foot-
    ball, basketball, soccer, ice hockey, wrestling, and
    boxing. Tours of Parker Center are scheduled along
    with plane trips, tours of naval vessels, and govern-
    ment installations.

6) The Annual Student Leadership Symposium On Law
    and Order sponsored by the Los Angeles City Junior
    Chamber of Commerce in coordination with the Police
    Department involves approximately two hundred fifty
    student leaders from various schools. A presentation,
    discussion groups, and social hour are staffed almost
    entirely by police personnel.

7) The Annual Boys' Day In Government gives students
    throughout the City an opportunity to occupy various
    positions in government including the Police Department
    for one day. This positive program is not only
    informative but allows a very favorable relationship
    between youth and the police.

8) The Annual Boys' Day in Safety program sponsored
    by the Automobile Club of Southern California, in
    cooperation with the Los Angeles Police Department,
    gives selected students an opportunity to spend a day
    with police officers. The program consists of a film
    on traffic safety in the Parker Center auditorium
    and a subsequent tour of the Center and facilities. The
    boys then participate in a program at the Police Aca-
    demy which includes an exhibition of police equipment.
    Each boy is hosted at lunch and presented with a
    citation for meritorious service in safety.

9) The Teen Post Youth Police Program brings into
    contact, in a routine work situation, approximately
    fifty pre-screened ghetto youths between the ages of
    16 and 21 and the Los Angeles Police Department.

Schools

The School Program establishes contact between the police
and students at all grade levels. The humanism and
friendliness of the police officers are imparted to
approximately 8,000 students per week. Police and school

officials agree that this program, presented in an atmosphere of learning, is invaluable in creating a sense of
concern for orderly behavior and responsibility for the
maintenance of law and order. Periodic workshops are
held with top School Board administrators to formulate
curriculum and develop in-service education for teachers.

Since September 1, 1965, the Los Angeles Police Department has moved from a minimal effort of communications
in the city schools to the present-day program of five
schools being visited per day. This is done through
"Policeman Bill" (first, second, and third grades); "Let's
Get Acquainted" (sixth grade); "Stop on a Dime" (All
elementary grades); "You and the Police Officer" (Junior
high); "Driver Education" (tenth grade); and presentations
by selected officers in twelfth grade classes. The program
is augmented by divisional officers' visitations to local
schools and participation in many specially scheduled
programs.

1)   "Policeman Bill" involves discussions of the history of
      police and the role of police in our current society.
      Photographs and other visual aids provide clarity to
      the presentation. One student is designated "Police-
      man's Helper" and wears a large replica of the
      L.A.P.D. badge. The "talking police car" is
      demonstrated with detailed explanation of equipment.
      Other points stressed are "Traffic Safety" and "Danger-
      ous Strangers."

2)   "Let's Get Acquainted" allows discussion of questions
      from the class along with display of the uniform and
      equipment, drug charts, and other visual aids. "The
      Role of the Police," "Good Citizenship," "Rights of
      Students," and "Traffic Safety" are also discussed.

3)   "Stop On A Dime" is a program presented jointly by
      Los Angeles Board of Education safety specialists and
      police officers. Demonstrations show that pedestrians
      bicycles, and vehicles cannot "Stop on a Dime,"
      Students assist and are vividly impressed with the need
      for safety in traffic. Parents are also invited to attend
      the demonstrations.

4)   "You And The Police" permits discussion of "Good
      Citizenship," "Police Brutality," "Traffic Laws,"
      "Narcotics," "Curfew," and "Sex Laws." The students
      suggest the topic by questioning the officer in these
      areas. This program is presented to A8 Social Studies
      Classes by an officer in a business suit.

5) Scheduled <u>Teacher Institutes</u> (four annually) involve 100 Los Angeles teachers in four half-day sessions for exposure to topics of current Police-Board of Education concern, including "Juvenile Procedures," "Narcotics," "Laws Which Apply On and Off Campus," "Police Procedures," "Law Enforcement and Social Change" and others. This program assists in curriculum development and furnishes teachers with accurate current information in handling school matters and classes.

6) <u>Parker Center Tours</u> are provided for schools and other student organizations including displays of police equipment, Wednesday and Saturday evenings. An average of 300 students per month enjoy a film, "2A26," explanation of laboratory facilities, records, property procedures, and a display of the freeway cruiser.

Minority Community Liaison

Although the Community Relations Program is designed for the entire community, some problems are unique to minority groups and must receive special attention. Such problems as a language barrier or cultural misunderstanding often inhibit a satisfactory police contact. Consequently, the Latin-American Affairs Unit consists of Latin-American officers who speak Spanish. A special class in conversational Spanish is being conducted for Los Angeles policemen at a police facility. Negro officers are utilized in Community Relations in the predominantly Negro areas. A Jewish officer is assigned to communicate with the Jewish community members.

1) An Economic and Youth Opportunities Agency-funded <u>Mexican-American Conference</u>, in April, 1967, resulted in the formation of a steering committee of police personnel and Mexican-American community leaders to review programs of action on conference recommendations designed to ease tension and improve conditions within the Mexican-American community. This steering committee has offered its services as an advisory group to the Chief of Police regarding conditions in the Mexican-American community. It is significant that some of the participants were definitely anti-police prior to involvement in the conference. It cannot be stated that all are now pro-police, but much misinformation which had contributed to their negativeness was corrected by virtue of contact with Department Community Relations representatives.

2) The Department sponsors two One-Day Workshops, one for the Mexican-American community and one for the Negro community. The programs are designed to expose the overall community to persons and personalities who govern the Department. Conversely it allows Department personnel the opportunity to become acquainted with minority groups representative of the community.

3) Community-Police Service Corps emerged from within one of the most tense areas of Los Angeles. A group of responsible Negro people who in spite of previously negative feelings about the police formed an association who named themselves the "Community-Police Service Corps." This Police Department-sponsored organization which presently consists of approximately sixty-five young people, aged ten to eighteen years, are supervised by adults and advised by police representatives. Their purpose is to involve youth in positive relationships with the police through recreation or service projects to dispel negative feelings. This type of response from this segment of Los Angeles attests to the effectiveness of the Police Community Relations effort.

4) The Ministerial Alliance was originated within the Negro community to reach the most troubled elements initially. Now it has been expanded to include religious leaders throughout the Los Angeles area. The second conference is scheduled in February. These influential "multipliers of influence" serve to enlighten the Police Department and their congregations regarding matters of mutual concern, e.g., crime, delinquency and disorder.

Other activities include: Liaison with Minority press, Radio and television, Community groups; Conferences and Workshops; Community Relations Presentations; Tours of Parker Center.

Radio, News, and Television

The Radio and Television Unit arranges or produces:

1) Numerous single appearances on radio and television during which various Department representatives describe the functions of the Department or discuss problems facing the Department and community.

2) Regular appearances, e.g., a weekly "Youth and the Police" program places the Chief of Police on a panel with young people before the television screen to discuss matters relating to youth. Another such regular program is "F.Y.I." (For Your Information) which involves various police officers in television discussions.

3) Short traffic safety messages and "Sig-a-lert" emergency broadcasts which advise the motoring public of traffic mishaps and congestion are broadcast regularly over several radio stations.

4) Several "specials" have been produced by radio and television companies, including "Battle of the Badge," "Unit 2A26," and "Adam 12," which depict the activities of the Police Department and the lives of policemen on and off duty.

5) A new concept in television recruitment "shorts" has emerged which identifies to the viewer the human side of police officers by showing them involved in hobbies, home life, and other off-duty activities. These are proving an effective community relations feature as well as a successful recruitment device.

Other News Media Unit responsibilities include:

a. Issuance of press passes to qualified members of the news media.

b. News releases to all newspapers, radio, and television stations to alert them to a forthcoming newsworthy event.

c. Attendance at unusual occurrences, either planned or unplanned, to provide assistance to news media personnel.

d. Presentation of the annual Medal of Valor luncheon sponsored by the Los Angeles Chamber of Commerce to honor police recipients of the Department's highest award.

e. Presentation of traffic safety radio and television meassages and regular daily and weekly shows.

f. Provision of technical advice and assistance for motion picture and television productions.

g. Informative tours of Parker Center for visiting
   police and news agency representatives.

h. Coordination of Department television and radio
   appearances.

Internal Program
          In the belief that a meaningful Police Community Relations
          Program is a two-way process, the Department has
          attempted to implement programs which would improve
          the ability of officers to more successfully communicate
          with persons in the various segments of the community.
          It is hoped that both the community and the police can
          each see themselves as seen by the other. The follow-
          ing programs are directed internally to accomplish this
          objective.

1) Periodic seminars involving top Los Angeles Police
   Department administrators and held away from police
   facilities assist in the development of new ideas and
   assure consistency throughout the Department in
   the administration of the Community Relations
   Program as established by the Chief of Police.

2) Other periodic seminars involve Division Commanders,
   Community Relations personnel, and outside authorities
   in community relations.

3) Los Angeles Police recruits receive training in the
   following subjects: police sociological problems, race
   relations, ethics, internal discipline, disciplinary
   procedures, field assignment orientation, traffic orientation, officer-violator contact, special events handling,
   and police and press relations.

4) Experienced officers periodically receive in-service
   training which includes refresher courses or more
   advanced training in some of the above-mentioned
   subjects.

5) Roll call periods held daily for all field officers
   include a fifteen-to twenty-minute training period.
   At regular intervals, supervisors in each division
   present subjects in human relations and field tactics
   during roll call training. The frequency is determined
   by the staff or the division commander.

6) Lieutenants assigned as patrol division Community
   Relations Officers periodically attend roll calls for
   field officers to inform them of current community
   attitudes and to refresh the officers regarding the

Department's role in the community.

7) Various activities in the Youth Program and other Community Relations programs require the voluntary service of policemen. The response has been gratifying. Such unofficial contacts serve to dispel unhealthy attitudes and stereotypes harbored by both the citizens and the police officers.

8) Regularly scheduled Community Relations Officers' meetings bring Community Relations Officers, Detective Traffic, and Patrol representatives and the Director of Community Relations into a casual conference atmosphere for problem solutions, policy discussions, exchange of information, and to assure consistency and effectiveness in the Community Relations program.

9) The previously described U.C.L.A. Police-Community Workshops and other workshops provide officers with an opportunity to communicate with people on a non-punitive basis and benefit from a deeper understanding of the citizenry.

10) A Community Relations Newsletter designed to inform officers of the progress of the program and community response to our efforts began in 1968. A similar newsletter for external distribution will also be published.

11) Training Division publishes training bulletins dealing with various subjects including community relations which are disseminated to all policemen.

12) A class in conversational Spanish is being conducted for officers who work in the predominantly Mexican-American division to assist the police in overcoming the language barrier in those communities.

13) A Community Relations Travel Study financed by a federal grant is proposed. It is hoped that key personnel will visit major cities throughout the United States to investigate other Community Relations Programs and communities served in order to improve the Los Angeles Police Department program.

14) The National Institute on Police Community Relations is held annually under the auspices of the National Conference of Christians and Jews. This program is designed to assist the police in understanding the complex nature of problems in Police-Community

Relations. The Los Angeles Police Department plans
to send ten representatives this year.

15) Qualified professional psychological assistance has
been obtained to assist Department training officers
in presenting a course in Interpersonal Communications
to recruit-level policemen. A follow-up session will
instruct the same officers after one or two years of
police service. Officers will receive a total 40 hours
of this training by professional during their first year.

16) A psychiatric advisory board has been formed which
meets regularly to advise the Chief of Police and other
top Department staff members.

Programs Under Development

1) Automotive Task Force is a training program in basic
automobile mechanics established for the hard-core
unemployed. The Los Angeles Police Department
assists in locating and placing of trainees.

2) The purpose of the Auxiliary Crossing Guard Project
is to determine alternative methods of providing
crossing guard protection at areas not qualified for
regular guards. Community involvement concepts
utilizing federal funding are being considered.

3) The Summer Training-Work Camp Project is a
program to provide through federal funding a 10-week
summer camping program for boys 15 to 18 as an
extension of their school year.

The project is aimed at the removal of the potential
rioter from the streets during the summer and provides
for him a healthy, stimulating environment where he
will earn, learn, acquire motivation and self discipline.

4) The Concentrated Employment Program has allotted
the Los Angeles Police Department 50 community
relations-oriented job slots for development. These
jobs are part of the C. E. P. effort to provide work
experience, training, and remedial education for unemployed and under-employed persons in designated
areas of Los Angeles County (East Los Angeles and
South Los Angeles). The major objective is to create
New Career jobs in civil service or in private nonprofit agencies. A center will be established in each
target area to provide counseling and remedial education
classes.

Nine other agencies are also engaged in the C. E. P.
Other city departments involved are Building and Safety
and the Traffic Department.

ORGANIZATION OF YOUTH SERVICES SECTION

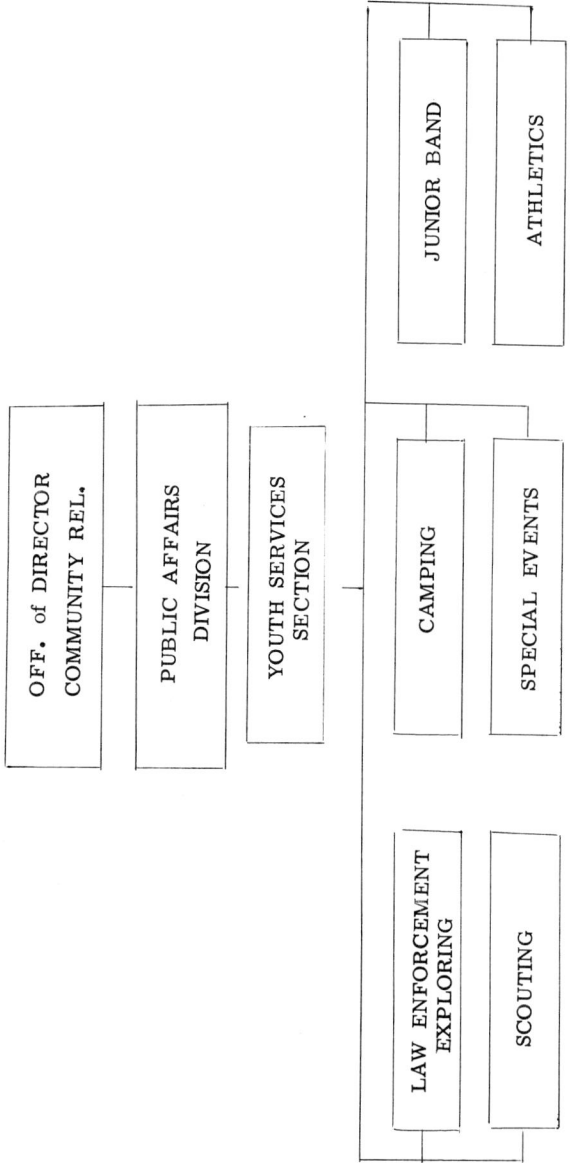

OFF. of DIRECTOR
COMMUNITY REL.

PUBLIC AFFAIRS
DIVISION

YOUTH SERVICES
SECTION

LAW ENFORCEMENT
EXPLORING

SCOUTING

CAMPING

SPECIAL EVENTS

JUNIOR BAND

ATHLETICS

ORGANIZATION OF
SCHOOL PROGRAMS SECTION

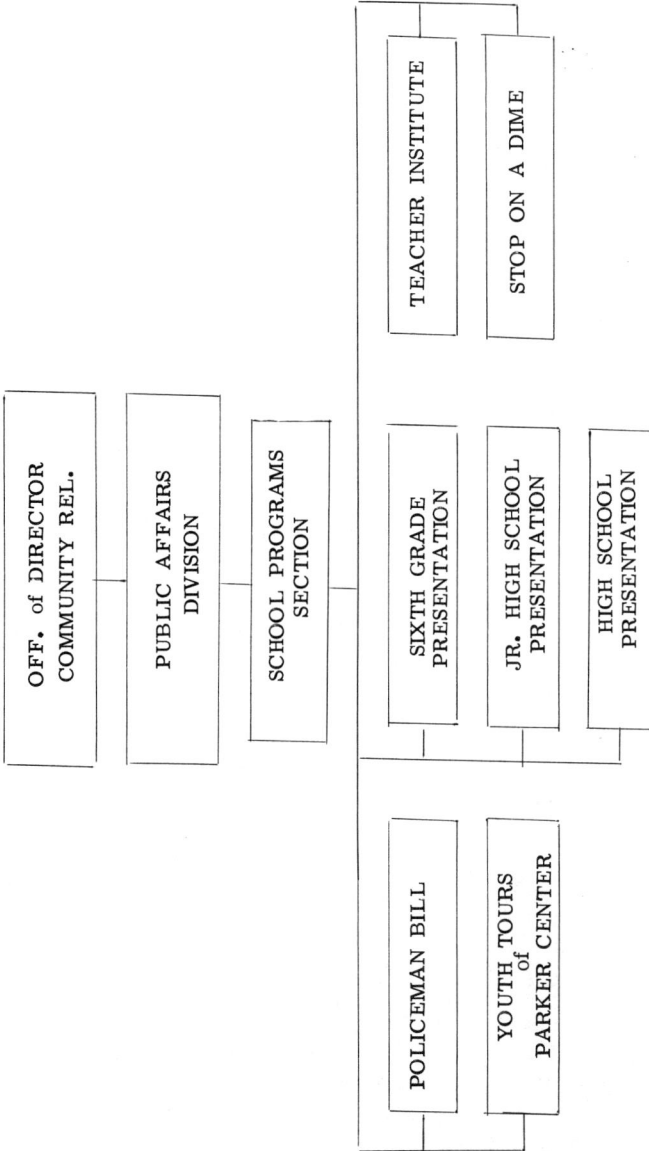

OFF. of DIRECTOR COMMUNITY REL.

PUBLIC AFFAIRS DIVISION

SCHOOL PROGRAMS SECTION

SIXTH GRADE PRESENTATION

JR. HIGH SCHOOL PRESENTATION

HIGH SCHOOL PRESENTATION

TEACHER INSTITUTE

STOP ON A DIME

POLICEMAN BILL

YOUTH TOURS of PARKER CENTER

ORGANIZATION
of
PUBLIC AFFAIRS DIVISION

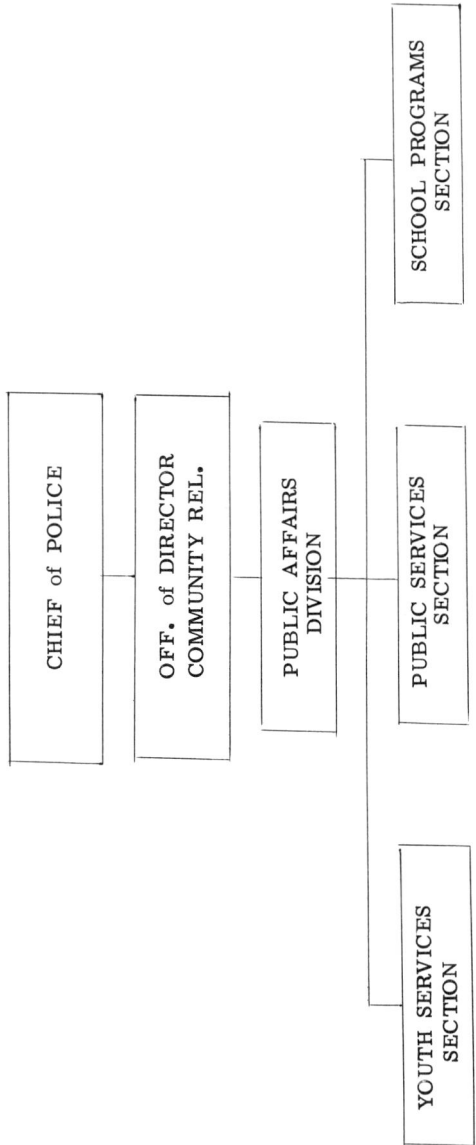

```
┌─────────────────┐
│ CHIEF of POLICE │
└─────────────────┘
         │
┌──────────────────────┐
│ OFF. of DIRECTOR     │
│ COMMUNITY REL.       │
└──────────────────────┘
         │
┌──────────────────────┐
│ PUBLIC AFFAIRS       │
│ DIVISION             │
└──────────────────────┘
         │
   ┌─────┼─────────────────────┐
   │     │                     │
┌──────────┐  ┌──────────────┐  ┌──────────────────┐
│ YOUTH    │  │ PUBLIC       │  │ SCHOOL PROGRAMS  │
│ SERVICES │  │ SERVICES     │  │ SECTION          │
│ SECTION  │  │ SECTION      │  │                  │
└──────────┘  └──────────────┘  └──────────────────┘
```

323

ORGANIZATION of
COMMUNITY PROGRAMS & LIAISON SECTION

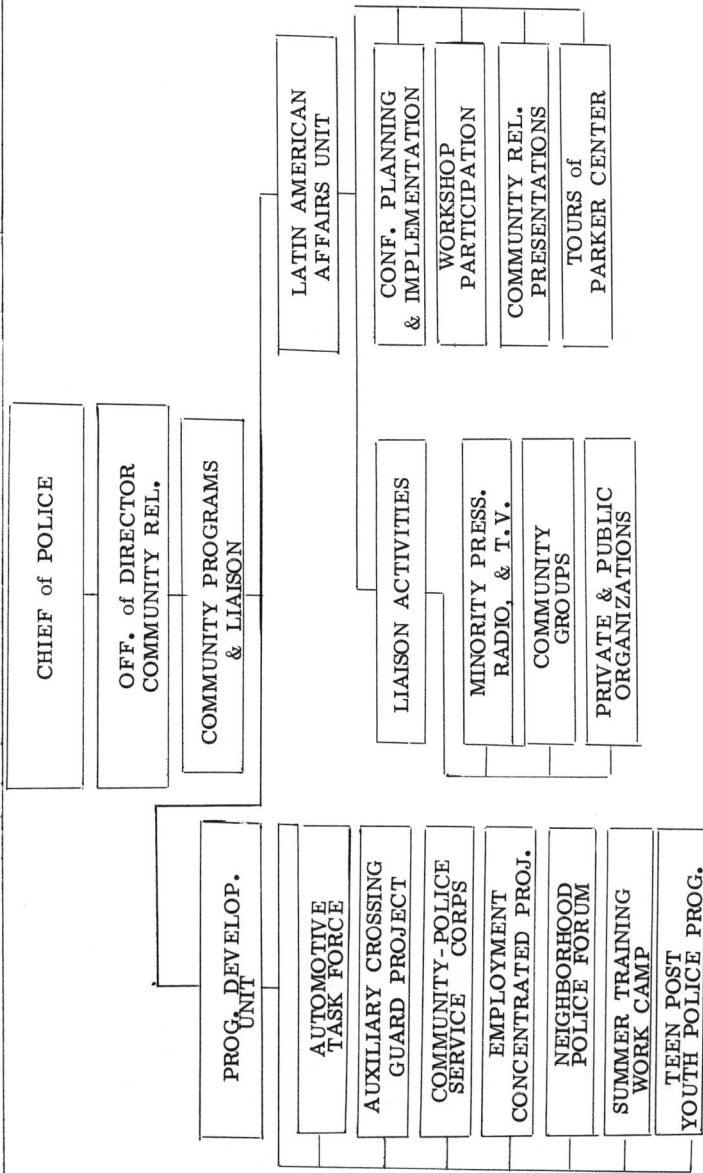

CHIEF of POLICE

OFF. of DIRECTOR
COMMUNITY REL.

COMMUNITY PROGRAMS
& LIAISON

LATIN AMERICAN
AFFAIRS UNIT

CONF. PLANNING
& IMPLEMENTATION

WORKSHOP
PARTICIPATION

COMMUNITY REL.
PRESENTATIONS

TOURS of
PARKER CENTER

LIAISON ACTIVITIES

MINORITY PRESS.
RADIO, & T.V.

COMMUNITY
GROUPS

PRIVATE & PUBLIC
ORGANIZATIONS

PROG. DEVELOP.
UNIT

AUTOMOTIVE
TASK FORCE

AUXILIARY CROSSING
GUARD PROJECT

COMMUNITY-POLICE
SERVICE CORPS

EMPLOYMENT
CONCENTRATED PROJ.

NEIGHBORHOOD
POLICE FORUM

SUMMER TRAINING
WORK CAMP

TEEN POST
YOUTH POLICE PROG.

Index

Abortion 158-162
exceptions to felony 160
history of law 160
incidence of 161
methods of 161
recommendations for legalization of 161
sources of complaints 162
statistics on 159, 160, 161
therapeutic abortions 160
types 159
Administration, Development of
constitutional-legal approach 38-40
socio-psychological approach 38, 43-45
structural-descriptive 38, 41-43
Administrative Behavior 47
Administrative man 50
African Communities League 284
African Patriotic League 284
Alcoholics Anonymous 284
All Nations Boys Club and Community House 284
All Nations Foundation 284
All Peoples Christian Center 284
American Civil Liberties Union 285
American Council to Improve Our Neighborhoods 285
American Friends Service Committee 285
American Jewish Committee 285
American Missionary Association 285
American Youth Hotels 285
Anti-Defamation League 285
Appointments
types of 93
Aquinas, Thomas 60
Assistance League 286
Association for Health and Welfare 286

Attendance Service 286

Baldwin amendment 201
Banfield, Edward C. 51, 52
Behavioral approach 44
Bentham, Jeremy 60
Bibliographic sources for research 282-283
Big Brothers, Inc. 287
Big Sister League 287
Black Anti-Draft Union 287
Black Muslims 206, 287
Black Panther Political Party 287
Board of Police Commissioners 287
Boy Scouts of America 288
Boys Club 288
Bureaucracy 68
rationality of 69
Bureaucratic organizations 68-69

Career executive
definition of term 84
Career service
definition 84
Career system 86
compared with foreign service 88
compared with the military 88
criticism of 87
Catholic Big Brothers, Inc. 288
Catholic Conference for Interracial Justice 288
Catholic-Courts Community Development Project 288
Catholic Welfare Bureau 288
Centralized services 268
Centro Hispano 289
Challenge of Crime in a Free Society 16
Civil Defense and disaster planning
acts for civil defense 193
agencies involved in 196

325

basic policies 192
California laws pertaining
to 195, 196
disaster relief 194
functions of civil defense
192-193
funding 191
reason for 191
police responsibilities in
193-194
warning systems 194
Civil Rights Act 241-242
Civil Service Commission
85, 87
Civil Service System 86
changes in 90
criticism of 89, 90
Cleland House of Neighborly
Service 289
Closed personnel system
83, 84, 88, 89
advantages of 83
characteristic rules of 91-94
opposed to open system
91, 112-133
Code of Ethics 23
California 269
Cogan, Morris L. 18, 155
Commission on Human Relations
289
Committee on Un-American
Activities 204
Communist Control Act
202, 203
Communist Party U.S.A. 205
Community Alert Patrol 289
Community Church 289
Community Coordinating Councils
289
Community organizations
284-303
Community Planning Council
290
Community relations 25, 26,
117-122, 244
improvement of 118
lack of logical approach to 16
training in 118
vs. public relations 117
See also: Present Status of
Municipal Police Agencies
71-73
Community Relations Conference
290

Community Relations Program
(Los Angeles) 304-319
communication with
community 306-309
description of 305-306
ingredients of 304
internal program 316-318
minority community laison
313-314
organization charts: community programs 323; public
affairs 322; school programs
321; youth services
320
programs under development
318-319
purpose of 304
responsibilities of the director
305
school program 311-313
use of radio, news, and T.V.
314-316
youth program 309-311
Community Services Department
290
Community Volunteer Office
290
Community Welfare and Family
Service, Inc. 290
Community Welfare Council
290
Concepts and Issues in Administrative Behavior 60
Congress of Racial Equality
(CORE) 291
Constitutional-legal approach
(philosophy) 38-41, 46, 63
Cooke, Morris L. 41
Correctional Guidance Service
291
Corrections
adult (model) 137, 138;
comparison with juvenile model
137-138
change related to 147-149;
149-150
characteristics of 144
cost of 143
juvenile 133-137
aftercare 136
detention 133
institutions 135
model 134
probation 135
326

objective of 132
statement of the problem
145-147
Council of Churches 291
Council of Integrated Neighbor-
hoods (COIN) 291
Council of Jewish Women 291
Council of Social Agencies 291
Council on Mexican-American
Affairs 291
The Criminal Imbecile 220
Criminal syndicates 210, 212
Critique of Pure Reason 61

Delinquency and Crime
Commission 292
Departmental policy 31, 32
Departmental Reserve Officers
212-217
advantages of 217
citizens night patrol (Michigan)
216
definition 212
disadvantages 216
Hays (Kansas) Reserve 215
Long Beach (Calif.) Reserve
215
operational structure 216
types 213
use of civilian manpower 214
Department of Industrial Relations
292
Department of Justice: F.B.I.
205
Dewey, John 54, 56
District Attorney 292
Dynamic Administration 44
Economic and Youth Opportunities
Agency 292
Economic Development Agency
292
Economic man 50
Economic Negro Union 293
Economic Opportunity Act
Implementation 293
Eisenstadt, S.N. 68
Encyclopedia of the Philosophical
Science 61
Enforcement practices and the
law 32, 33
Epictetus 61
Epicurus 60
Episcopal Church Home for
Children 293

Eros 175
Exchange Club 293
Executive
definition of term 84

Fair Employment Practice
Commission 293
Family Service Department
293
Fayol, Henri 41, 42
Federal Civil Defense
Administration 191
The Federalists 42
Federation of Community
Coordination Councils 293
Felony institutions 140
Felony probation 140
Five Acres 294
Fraternal Order of Police 157
Freedom Now Party 294

Gambling laws (New York) 271
Ginzberg, Eli 87
Ginzburg, Ralph 175
Goldberg, Deputy Chief Inspector:
Case of 270
Goodnow, F.J. 39, 40
Goodwill Industries 294
Gulick, Luther 41, 42

Hard of Hearing Society 294
Hatch Act 203
Hawthorne study 38, 42
Head Start 294
Health Department 295
Hegel, Georg Wilhelm 61
Hobbs, Thomas 61
Homans, George 125, 126,
127, 128, 142, 143, 145,
147, 151; model 129
application of model to
corrections 142
Home 295
Home for Children 295
Homosexuality 171
definition 172
laws in: Britain 173;
California 171, 173-174;
Illinois 172; New York 172
problems associated with 171
theories of causes 172
Human Relations Bureau 295
Human Relations Commission
295

Image making 33
Indian Center Inc. 296
Indian Welcome Center 296
Industrial and General Administration 41
Inspection 200-201
  Baldwin amendment 201
  definition 200
  records and reports on 200, 201
Internal organization 27
Internal Security Act 201
International City Managers' Association 91, 98, 100
International Institute 296
Intoxication 31
Introduction to the Study of Public Administration 41
Irrational Man 46

The Jacksonians 42
Jails, Adult 139-140
Japanese-American Citizens League 296
The Jeffersonians 42
Jewish Community Relations Committee 296

Kahn, Robert L. 120, 149
Kant, Immanuel 61
Katz, Daniel 120, 149
Kendall, Henry P. 41
Ku Klux Klan 206

Labor vs. Management
  history of organized labor 162-164
  largest union 164
  longest strike 164
  Penal Code (Calif.) pertaining to 167
  picketing 166, 170
  police duty in strikes 166
  police impartiality 165
  work stoppages 165
  vocabulary and definition 169-171
Law enforcement
  characteristics of 35
  role of 26, 27
Lawyer Reference Service 296
League of Women Voters 296
Lewin, Kurt 120

Licensing 196-200
  definition of license 197
  duties of police 196
  of beverages 198, 199
  of firearms 199
  of narcotics 199
  of vehicles 197
  reasons for 196
  Volstead Act (Prohibition) 199
Life of Reason 61
Lippitt, Ronald 120
Los Angeles County 29
  Sheriff's Dept. 34
  Police Dept. 103-113
Loyalty 29, 30

McCarran Act 203
Mafia (La Cosa Nostra) 208
  Code of 209
  history of 209
  meetings 210
  structure of 208-209
Malpractice Boards 206
Marsh, Stewart H. 101
Marx, Karl 61
"The Meaning of Principles of Public Administration" 42
Means-end hierarchy 55
Mental illness and the mentally ill 217-229
  amnesia 219
  apprehension of mentally ill 225, 228
  conduct disorders 224-225
  definitions 222, 223
  deviant sexual behavior 228
  Ganser syndrome 222
  hospitalization of 218
  incidence of 217
  insanity 220, 221, 222
  and crime 223
  loss of privileges 220
  McNaughton test 221
  medical correctional institution 220
  mental retardation 221
  punishment of 218
  statistics on 218, 219, 220, 226, 227
Merton, Robert K. 69
The Messengers 297
Mexican-American Community Development (MACD) 297

Mexican-American Opportunity
  Foundation 297
Mexican-American Political
  Association 297
Midnight Mission 297
Mill, John Stewart 60
Minority Group Relations
  237-246
  categories of groups 238
  Civil Rights Act 241-242
  description of 237, 239
  efforts on behalf of 239,
    241
  general principles in relations
    238
  indications of tension 244
  police dealing with 243, 244,
    245, 246
  statistics on 238, 242
  terms pertaining to 240
Misdemeanent probation 137
  organization 139
  types 139
Modern technology 264
  color photography 265
  computers 264, 266
  machines to measure
    intoxication 264
  radios 264
  television 264
  voice prints 264
Moonlighting 21
Moses, Robert 212
Mosher, Frederick G. 85
Mutual Aid 11

National Association for the
  Advancement of Colored
  People 297
National Conference of Christians
  and Jews 297
National Safety Council 298
Neighborhood Adult Participation
  Program (NAPP) 298
Neighborhood Council 298
Neighborhood Legal Service
  Centers 298
Neighborhood Legal Services
  Society 298
Neighborhood Youth Association
  298
Neighborhood Youth Corps 298
Neumeyer Foundation 299

Neumeyer, Martin H. 137
Nicolaidis, Nicholas G. 51,
  52, 54, 55, 62

Open personnel system 83, 84
Operation Bootstrap 299
Operation Escape 299
Opportunities Industrialization
  Center 299
Organization Charts (Police
  Departments)
  Baltimore 280; Cleveland 280;
  Los Angeles 278; Minneapolis
  277; San Francisco 281;
  St. Louis 276.
Organization for Community
  Action 299
Organizational Analysis
  as an external system 126
  as a social system 126
  related to corrections 130
Organized crime 207-212
  description of 207
  criminal syndicates 210, 212
  Kefauver Committee 211
  Mafia 208
  types of 207-208, 209
  U.S. Atty. General's special
    group on 210

Papers on the Science of
  Administration 41, 42
Parent Teacher Association 299
Parole, adult
  definition 141
  methods 141
  objectives 141
P.C.R. (Police Community
  Relations) 34
Personnel 11-14, 78, 246-252
  auxiliary functions 14
  certification (Calif.) 247
  Crime Commission recommend-
    ations on 247, 248
  concepts of effective program
    250-251
  detective work 12
  distribution 11, 12
  functions 12
  Internal Affairs Division 250
  line activities 13, 14
  median annual pay 248
  specific areas of concern 102

staff functions 13, 14
training 247, 249
turnover 96, 97, 103
  formula for 98
Personnel--Promotion 82-83,
  251-252
Personnel--Selection 82
  lateral entry 94, 95, 96
  qualifications 99, 100
  standards for recruitment
    (Calif.) 249
Personnel standards 266
Personnel system
  definition 84
Pfiffner, John M. 47, 50, 102
Philosophical systems 38-45
Planning, research and budgeting
  (PRB) 13
Plato 61
Police Administration 73-80
  concepts of 75, 76, 77
  innovations needed 77, 78, 79
Police and Fire services
  IACP 189
  IAFC 189
  IAFF 188
  integration: advantages for
    187, factors for successful
    integration 190; problems of
    190; reasons for 187; types
    of 185-187
  public safety officer 186, 187
"Police Community Relations"
  34
Police Malpractice Center 299
Police Malpractice Complaint
  Center 299
Policeman and Public 16
Police organizations 22, 23
Policy-Decision and Organization
  Theory 51
Politics and Administration 39
Pornography
  and the Post Office Dept. 176
  definitions of 174, 175, 176
  general state laws 177
  incidence of 174
  legitimate purposes 178
  methods of law enforcement
    174, 175
  movie code 176
POSDCORB 42, 45, 63, 142

P.O.S.T. (Police Officers
  Standards and Training) 22
The Poverty of Philosophy 61
P.R.B. (Planning, research and
  budgeting) 13
President's Commission on Law
  Enforcement 22, 34
President's Committee Report
  43
President's Crime Commission
  240, 241
Presthus, Robert V. 70
Principles of Public Adminis-
  tration 40
Principles of Scientific Manage-
  ment 41
Professionalization 17, 18, 19,
  20, 155-158
Project Action 300
Project Tutor 300
Promotion 15, 92-96
  chances for 100
  characteristics of 101
  examinations 92
  without examination 92
Public Administrative Review 45
Public Defender 300
Public Image 72, 73
Public relations 33, 34, 229-237
  approach to 229, 230
  attitudes about 233
  basic principles of 232
  definition of 230
  essential elements in 229
  formula for 229
  goals of 233
  job of public relations officer
    234, 235
  police officers responsibility
    in 231-232
  public relations programs
    235, 236, 237

Racial disturbances 244
Rationality 46-51, 63, 64
  definitions of 46, 47
  limits of 48, 64
Rationality and decision-making
  processes 51-54, 64
  theories of 54-59, 64
    behavioral model 58, 59
    classical model 57, 59
    normative model 58, 59

values in theories 59-62,
63, 65
Rational Man 46
Recruitment 16, 77
and training standards 267
Selection and Training 28,
29, 30, 31
"Relationship and Organization"
41
The Republican Era 42
Responsibilities of Police Agency
(Calif.) 98
Riot
definition of terms 178
classification of 179
control of 246
army methods 181; new
methods 184-185; police
methods 178-180
prevention of 180-181
Roth test of obscenity 175
Royce, Josiah 61

Salvation Army 300
Santayana, George 61
Scientific management 41, 42
Self-Leadership for all Nation-
alities Today (SLANT) 300
Sexual promiscuity 31
Shop Management 41
Simon, Herbert A. 40, 43, 44,
47, 48, 50, 53, 54, 55, 56,
57, 64
Smith Act 202
Social-dynamic approach 44-45
Social organization 26
Socio-psychological approach
43-45, 63
Special Service for Groups Inc.
300
Spinoza 61
State Industrial Relations Depart-
ment: Fair Employment
Practices Division 300
Status of police agencies 71
Structural-descriptive approach
(philosophy) 41-43, 63
Subversive Activities Control
Board 201, 203
Subversives 201-206
Committee on Un-American
Activities 204
Communist Control Act 202,
203

Communist Party USA 205
Department of Justice: F.B.I.
205
Hatch Act 203
Internal Security Act 201
investigating committee
(Calif.) 205
Ku Klux Klan 206
McCarran Act 203
methods of subversion
205, 206
Smith Act 202
Subversive Activities Control
Board 201, 203
subversive organizations 204
treason against the state
202, 203, 204
Suicide Prevention Center 301

Tappan, Paul W. 125, 132
Task Force Report: Corrections
145
"Task Force Report on the
Police" 34
Taylor, Frederick W. 74
Team policing 266
Teen Post Program 301
Temporary Alliance of Local
Organizations 301
Training 14, 15, 21-22
selection and 28, 29,
30, 31
Travelers Aid Society 301

Udy, Stanley H. 69
United States Bureau of Family
Services 302
United States Commission on
Civil Rights 302
United States Government,
Interior Department, Indian
Affairs Bureau 302
Urban League 302
Urwick, Lyndall 41, 42

Variety International Boys Club
302
Visibility contact 12
visual-physical presence 27
Vollmer, August 98
Vollmer system 246
Volstead Act 199

331

Waldo, Dwight 41
Warner, W. Lloyd 87, 94, 95
Weber, Max 57, 68, 69, 70, 74
Welfare Association 302
West's California Codes 197, 198, 204
Willoughby, W. F. 39, 40
Wilson, Woodrow 38, 39, 40
Woods, Arthur 16, 33

Young Men's Christian Association 302
Young Women's Christian Association 303
Youth Opportunities Board 303
Youth Opportunity Center 303